PROVERBS

A Bible Commentary in the Wesleyan Tradition

STEPHEN J. LENNOX

General Publisher: Nathan Birky
General Editor: Ray E. Barnwell
Senior Editor: David Higle
Managing Editor: Russell Gunsalus
Editor: Kelly Trennepohl

CONTENTS

Proverbs

EDITOR'S PREFACE

This book is part of a series of commentaries seeking to interpret the books of the Bible from a Wesleyan perspective. It is designed primarily for laypeople, especially teachers of Sunday school and leaders of Bible studies. Pastors will also find this series very helpful. In addition, this series is for people who want to read and study on their own for spiritual edification.

Each book of the Bible will be explained paragraph by paragraph. This "wide-angle lens" approach helps the reader to follow the primary flow of thought in each passage. This, in turn, will help the reader to avoid "missing the forest because of the trees," a problem many people encounter when reading commentaries.

At the same time, the authors slow down often to examine particular details and concepts that are important for understanding the bigger picture. Where there are alternative understandings of key passages, the authors acknowledge these so the reader will experience a broader knowledge of the various theological traditions and how the Wesleyan perspective relates to them.

These commentaries follow the New International Version and are intended to be read with your Bible open. With this in mind, the biblical text is not reproduced in full, but appears in bold type throughout the discussion of each passage. Greater insight will be gained by reading along in your Bible as you read the commentaries.

These volumes do not replace the valuable technical commentaries that offer in-depth grammatical and textual analysis. What they do offer is an interpretation of the Bible that we hope will lead to a greater understanding of what the Bible says, its significance for our lives today, and further transformation into the image of Christ.

David A. Higle
Senior Editor

AUTHOR'S PREFACE

The book of Proverbs has the reputation for being practical and straightforward. Indeed, as I explain in the introduction, God used the practicality of this book to spark my passion for the Bible. After having completed this commentary, however, I have discovered that Proverbs, while practical, is anything but simple. It raises questions not easily answered, pictures God in striking colors, and provides perspectives which sometimes differ from other biblical passages. It is my prayer and hope that this book will assist local church educators to better understand the complexities of Proverbs so that these practical truths can make a powerful impact on their students.

Whatever I have accomplished is due, largely, to the help of others. In particular, I must thank my wife, Eileen, and our children, Abigail and Ethan, for their encouragement and patience. Thanks to Dave Higle for inviting me to participate, and to the leadership of The Wesleyan Church which has embraced the goal of biblical education. I am grateful to Dr. Bud Bence and Indiana Wesleyan University for encouraging my writing and to my Sunday school class at College Wesleyan Church for their challenging questions and perceptive insights during our discussions on Proverbs. Studying and writing on this book of the Bible has made me especially grateful to my parents, Ian and Charmaine Lennox, who taught me the wisdom of Proverbs by their words and lives. It is to them that this commentary is dedicated.

Stephen J. Lennox
Marion, Indiana
August 1998

INTRODUCTION

amily devotions were a regular part of my upbringing in a godly, Christian home. Every night, after dinner, Dad would take the Bible, read a passage, and lead us in a brief discussion followed by prayer. I confess to having little interest in what was read or said until, one day, my father read from the Living Bible version of Proverbs. I was mesmerized. Finally, I heard something I understood, something that made sense, something I could put into practice. My love for God's Word can be traced back to those moments at the dining room table. I did not understand anything of the complexities of the book: its organized randomness, how its clear-cut moral imperatives fit the complexities of the real world, why it says so little of the Law.[1] But I knew it made sense and, somehow, that it was God's voice speaking to me.

This would probably not have happened without parents who wanted to bring up their children God's way and with a knowledge of God's Word. This is what Proverbs is all about: God's words and God's ways coming alive in God's children through godly parental guidance.

AUTHORSHIP AND DATE

The book of Proverbs is closely identified with Solomon, David's son, who ruled Israel in the tenth century B.C. Its opening verse credits him with what follows. He is mentioned in 10:1 as the source for the proverbs in that section, which concludes in 22:16, and Hezekiah's scribes provide us with "more proverbs of Solomon," according to 25:1. The association of Solomon with Proverbs is not surprising, given the king's world-famous, even world-surpassing, wisdom. He taught about plants, animals, birds, reptiles, and fish, wrote more than a thousand songs, and "spoke three thousand proverbs" (1 Kings 4:29-34). "Spoke" suggests that at least some of these proverbs were collected by, but did not originate with, Solomon. This was, in fact, the nature of wisdom in the ancient Near East. What was wisdom in one culture was assumed to be wisdom in any other, so wisdom material circulated widely, and scholars traveled from country to country to learn and collect (see 1 Kings 4:34).

A closer look at Proverbs reveals that not all of Solomon's three thousand proverbs are included, and that Solomon is not responsible for everything contained within these 31 chapters. Anonymous wise men are credited with 22:17 through 24:34, Agur wrote all or part of 30, and King Lemuel gave us 31:1-9 from the mouth of his mother. Nor was Solomon the person who compiled the book into its final form. According to 25:1, the book could not have been arranged until the time of Hezekiah (715–686 B.C.) and may have even changed shape from that time until it reached its present form in about 100 B.C. We would do better to see Solomon as the patron of Proverbs, rather than as its author. He wrote, collected, and inspired this book, which was then credited to him in tribute.

PROVERBS AS LITERATURE

Since Proverbs is a form of Hebrew poetry, it relies heavily on parallelism, the Hebrew poet's most fundamental tool. In parallelism, the meaning of one line is repeated in similar but often more intense or specific form in the second line. Much of English poetry involves rhyming words; parallelism involves rhyming thoughts. Most poetry of the ancient Near East employed this technique, which aided in memorization. The simplest form is "synonymous" parallelism, a good example of which can be found in 1:28:

Then they will call to me but I will not answer;
they will look for me but will not find me.

Notice how "Then they will call" is echoed in meaning by "they will look for me," and how "but I will not answer" is paralleled by "but [they] will not find me." This basic pattern is modified in many different ways.

One of the most common variations on synonymous parallelism in Proverbs is "antithetic" parallelism where the second line states the opposite of the first, with a single meaning produced:

Misfortune pursues the sinner,
but prosperity is the reward of the righteous (13:21).

"Misfortune" and "prosperity" are meant as opposites, as are "pursues" and "rewards," and "sinner" and "righteous." Together these opposites combine to teach how our actions—wrong or right—will produce corresponding consequences.

Often in Proverbs, the lines compare one attitude or action to another:

> Better is open rebuke
> than hidden love (27:5).

Or else the comparison is to a well-known phenomenon of nature or everyday life:

> Like clouds and wind without rain
> is a man who boasts of gifts he does not give (25:14).

Such comparisons can usually be recognized by the addition of *like* or *as* (although these words are not always present in the original Hebrew). Another fairly common variation is when an element is included in one line but no parallel element is given in the other:

> Let another praise you, and not your own mouth;
> someone else, and not your own lips (27:2).

The second line must borrow its verb "praise" from the first.

For the sake of variety, the order of the elements in one line is often reversed in the next. This is known as a "chiasm" (pronounced ky'-asm), named after the Greek letter *Chi*, which is shaped like an *X*, representing the reversal of order in the lines. This reversal is often lost in translation, such as in 27:26, which literally reads,

> Lambs for your clothing,
> and the price of a field, goats.

Notice how "lambs" begins the first line, while "goats," a counterpart to lambs, concludes the second line. "Clothing" at the end of the first line contrasts with "the price of a field," which begins the second line. Proverbs 28:1 also displays a chiasm by its literal reading:

> They flee when no one is pursuing, the wicked
> but the righteous, like a lion, are bold.

"They flee when no one is pursuing" is the opposite of "bold," while "the wicked" finds its counterpart in "the righteous." Chiasmic variations add interest to the proverb.

The book of Proverbs takes its name from the word *mashal* (plural: *mashalim*), a very broad term which can also describe a parable (Ezekiel 17:2), a prophetic message (Numbers 23:7, 18), or the taunting words of one enemy to another (Isaiah 14:4). At its heart, a *mashal* is a comparison. In Proverbs it most often takes shape as a pithy, two-line saying or epigram packed full of a time-honored truth about humanity. The two-line format, characteristic of parallelism, fosters reflection by encouraging comparison between the first and second lines.[2]

As with other examples of ancient Near Eastern wisdom, the proverbs are arranged as an anthology, a format that fosters learning. The teacher's point "needs to be driven home again precisely because it has been heard, and ignored, so often in the past."[3] The nature of wisdom is too vast for any thorough and systematic treatment. The wise person, "mastering a thousand discrete insights handed down from here and there, can nevertheless assemble them into a single book and so pass on to future generations something of the great divine order by which the world is run."[4]

Proverbs employs other literary devices besides epigrams. Many of the passages are framed as parental advice (see chapters 1–7). Wisdom is personified in Proverbs 1 through 9, especially in chapters 8 and 9. Lists of things are often given as "three things—no, four" or "six things—no, seven" (see 6:16; 30:15, 18, 21, 29), which seems to suggest that the lists were open-ended and could be added to. Rhetorical questions are asked (see 23:29-30; 30:4), and the book concludes with an alphabet acrostic poem (31:10-31).

Both in form and content, the book of Proverbs is similar to other ancient Near Eastern wisdom, especially to that of Egypt.[5] Both are presented as parental advice, and both may have been used in the king's court to train the next generation of public servants. The shared nature of ancient wisdom and the similarities in content and form suggest that Israel borrowed some of its wisdom from its neighbors.

Even where the content was closest, Israel filtered the borrowed material through its own distinctive theology and world view. The nature of Israel's wisdom was different than that of her neighbors. Ancient Near Eastern wisdom spoke of wise behavior or teachings. Israel, on the contrary, had something greater for its goal than these: wisdom itself.[6] Israel's motivation for being wise also differed from that of her neighbors, who saw wisdom as the path to success; Israel, however, was concerned primarily about how she could please God. The motto of Israel's wisdom—"The fear of the LORD is the beginning of knowledge" (1:7a)—had no counterpart in the wisdom of her neighbors.[7]

WHAT IS WISDOM?

Proverbs defines wisdom differently than the way we use the term today. We often think of it as the result of intelligence or education, as synonymous with experience ("School of Hard Knocks"), or as the inevitable by-product of old age. Although not critical of any of these, Proverbs understands wisdom as something greater, including but surpassing each of them.

A survey of the main Hebrew term for wisdom, *chokmah,* reveals a wide range of meaning. It describes the skill of working with one's hands (Exodus 28:3; 35:35) or as a body of knowledge acquired through study (1 Kings 10:4; Daniel 1:4, 17, 20). The wise person possesses discernment (2 Samuel 14:20; 20:22; Exodus 1:10) and the ability to accomplish great things in and through others (Deuteronomy 34:9), including diplomacy (1 Kings 5:12), harmony (Deuteronomy 4:6), and prosperity (1 Kings 10:4-9). Throughout the Old Testament, wisdom was regarded as having great value (Proverbs 7:4; Ecclesiastes 7:11, 19; 9:18; Job 28:18). Wisdom could be gained from one's parents (Proverbs 4:5, 11; 5:1; 31:26) and from the government (Psalm 105:20-22), and was known to come through discipline (Proverbs 29:15). One could also acquire it through observation (Proverbs 6:6), experience, and age (Job 12:12; 32:7); in fact, one was obligated to pursue it (Proverbs 2:2; 4:5, 7; 23:23). But however it was received, one must never imagine it came from any other source but God (Job 28:12; Proverbs 30:3; 1:20; 8:1, 33; 9:1).

Wisdom is an essential element in the created order. God made both wisdom and the creation (Psalm 104:24; Proverbs 2:6; 3:19; Jeremiah 10:12; 51:15; Job 11:5-6; 12:13; 15:8; Psalm 51:6; 90:12; 111:10; Ecclesiastes 2:26). This is why skilled artisans are considered wise. Their ability to produce beauty from the created order reveals their understanding of the natural world and illustrates the creative activity of God. Further, the study of creation, including the natural world and the realm of human interaction, reveals wisdom, "the great set of master plans" by which "God had created and continued to run the world."[8] Those who discover "the grammar of life,"[9] gain the power to live successfully, achieving harmonious relationships with God and humanity, as well as material prosperity. An essential component of this success is a righteous life. Although never synonyms, wisdom and righteousness travel hand in hand through these pages (see Proverbs 4:10-19; 11:30; 13:10; 23:24; 29:7). Israel's wisdom is concerned not simply with how to get what humankind wants, but with what is right. "To be sure," one commentator has written, "Proverbs is concerned to point out that what is right and what pays may travel long distances together; but it leaves us in no doubt which we are to follow when their paths diverge."[10]

Like creation, wisdom is universal. Something could not be true unless it were true for all cultures. This is one reason why the book of Proverbs says so little that is specifically Israelite; "references to biblical Israel or to individual figures or events in its history surely must have seemed to violate the international, eternally valid character of wisdom."[11] This is also why ancient cultures, including Israel, borrowed wisdom so extensively.

Do not, however, make the mistake of calling this wisdom secular. Although beginning with the natural world, the Old Testament contends that a search for wisdom ultimately brought one to the Wise Creator himself (see 9:10). God is the source of this search, as well as its goal: "the fear of the LORD is the beginning of knowledge" (1:7a). God, not wisdom, must remain the motivation for our search (see 21:30; Isaiah 29:14). Those who pursue wisdom as their goal end up as disillusioned as the writer of Ecclesiastes (see Ecclesiastes 1:12-18). Wisdom "realises that the ultimate precept and the ultimate grip on humanity are not possible in this reality"[12] (see Proverbs 25:2); the wise person grants knowledge of the ultimate to God alone.

Nor should we assume that because some of this wisdom was borrowed from uninspired sources, Proverbs is any less inspired. That others grasped important truths about the universe only served to advance Yahweh (Israel's name for God), the Creator of all people. "Nobody has the franchise on truth but God," wrote C. Hassell Bullock. "If one culture has come by means of natural revelation to share certain basic ideas and ethical principles with the biblical faith (see Romans 1:18-20), we are free to recognize that without diminishing the value of and need for special revelation."[13] The gold, silver, bronze, and jewels that beautified the Tabernacle in the wilderness once belonged to Egyptian men and women. God allowed the Israelites, once again, to plunder the Egyptians (see Exodus 12:36), this time of their wisdom.

When I asked my Sunday school class why wisdom is often personified in Proverbs as a woman, one man responded, "If you have to ask, you wouldn't understand." There are many reasons to call wisdom a woman. Women do have a way of understanding that differs from men; some call it intuition. Wisdom, like most women, is not aggressive but persuades by quieter, gentler means. As women bring forth and nurture life, so does wisdom. Wisdom's beauty and grace deserves comparison to something equally beautiful and gracious.[14] Personify wisdom as a woman, and you have the attention of the young man to whom these words are addressed. You have also connected, in his mind, wisdom and marriage, the goal toward which all young people strove in ancient Israel. Certainly not the least important reason to personify wisdom as a woman is a grammatical one. Unlike English, all Hebrew nouns have a gender, either masculine or feminine. Although the gender is not always related to the meaning, the gender of the Hebrew noun for wisdom *(chokmah)* is feminine.

PURPOSE FOR PROVERBS

The primary purpose for the anthology of *mashalim,* which we know as Proverbs (see "Proverbs As Literature" above), was to make people wise by encouraging them to fear the Lord. The phrase, "the fear of the LORD," occurs more times in Proverbs than anywhere else in the Old Testament.[15] Its placement at the beginning of the book (1:7), at the conclusion of Part One (9:10; see below, "Overview of Proverbs"), and at the very end of the book (31:30) "testifies to the centrality of the idea in the book as a whole."[16]

"Fear" describes not terror, but a reverence for God that determines how one lives. Awe that does not alter behavior is not "godly fear." The other part of this important phrase, "of the LORD," describes the object of our fear—the Lord (Yahweh[17]). That we are instructed to fear the Lord is significant, for this is the name by which God made himself known to the Israelites. To fear the Lord meant showing reverence to this God with whom they had a relationship. A proper understanding of "the fear of the LORD" requires this combination of both reverence and relationship. Without reverence, one loses the proper motivation for obedience. Without relationship, one is too frightened to come to God. When we revere the One whom we know, we begin to become wise (see 1:7).

While one can learn a great deal about human nature from Proverbs, observations are rarely, if ever, offered to provide information alone. Instead, they are intended to produce a wise response. For example, while it is true that

The poor are shunned even by their neighbors,
but the rich have many friends (14:20),

this verse is not meant either to condone such behavior or to merely state a fact. The verse sets the stage for a righteous and charitable reaction in line with 14:21. The primary purpose of Proverbs is to make people wiser through the fear of the Lord, not just smarter.

Proverbs has several secondary purposes as well. Since a large number of verses concern human relationships, it would appear that this book seeks to foster an orderly, tranquil society. One could even speak of Proverbs as a conservative effort to preserve the status quo in a hierarchical and patriarchal society. It must also be kept in mind, however, that there is something radical and unsettling about a book which puts rich and poor on equal footing before God (see 22:2) and has Lady Wisdom publicly and aggressively seeking followers.

Proverbs may also be a reaction against the pessimism and cynicism found in other biblical Wisdom works[18] which point out the randomness and irrationality of life. Proverbs, on a much more optimistic note, counters that life is orderly and reasonable. One might even consider Proverbs a form of praise to God. Unlike the Psalms, which are generally directed to *God* and which take Him as their subject, these proverbs are directed to *God's people* and make only scattered reference to God by name. Yet they contain God's praise. They celebrate His world, which is characterized by His wisdom, and provide direction for how to live here to His glory.

Can we be more specific about the purpose for which this anthology of proverbs was prepared? Many interpret the domestic references literally and see Proverbs as parental instruction for a son. Others take those references figuratively and note the more than thirty references in Proverbs to the king. They take this book as a resource used to train future public servants in the king's court.[19] However, these royal proverbs teach what is applicable on several levels, from the king to the commoner, and they represent only a small percent of the total number. It is best to take the proverbs' domestic language figuratively, as a way of setting an instructive tone, but also to understand the proposed audience as broader than home or court.

OVERVIEW OF PROVERBS

The book of Proverbs is composed of eight sections arranged in two unequal parts. Part 1 contains the introduction to the book, extending from chapter 1 through chapter 9. Part 2 (10:1–31:31) begins with a collection of Solomon's proverbs (10:1–22:16) and is followed by two small collections of sayings from anonymous wise men (22:17–24:22; 24:23–34). Additional proverbs from Solomon follow as the fifth section (25:1–29:27), which was added in the days of Hezekiah, king of Judah from 715 to 686 B.C. The sixth section (30:1-33) represents the last words of Agur, son of Jakeh. The seventh section, maternal advice on being a good king (31:1-9), is followed by an acrostic poem on the noble wife in the eighth section (31:10-31).

The apparent randomness of the proverbs in 10:1 through 22:16 troubles many readers.[20] Some commentators have thrown up their hands in despair and contented themselves with rearranging the order along similar themes. The appearance of randomness ought not obscure the links that do exist. Thematic linkings, although brief, are present (see, for example, 26:1-12, 13-16, 17-28) as are verbal linkings (see 25:11-12, 13-14). This kind of arrangement where a verse or clusters of verses are strung together may represent an early form of "pearl-stringing," one teaching method of later rabbis.

This apparent randomness is deliberate and serves the purposes of both method and message. Much of what we learn, we learn haphazardly. Information I need to know intersects my life continually, but I do not learn it until I need to know it. Teachable moments cannot be programmed; "eureka" experiences come at the most surprising times. "That is why inculcating—pounding, grinding the ideas in—is what he [the writer of Proverbs] is all about: his point needs to be driven home again precisely because it has been heard, and ignored, so often in the past."[21]

Randomness also serves the message of Proverbs. If I want to know how to succeed at life, I need a book which shows me what life is really like, and most of life is fairly random (from a human point of view). Life does not come to us wrapped and neatly labeled. It is always hooked on to something else, like trying to get a hanger from the closet. How I interpret a particular piece of information or event depends on when and where I hear it, whether or not I have eaten lunch, how much sleep I got the night before, who else is talking, whether it is sunny or raining, what else I am thinking about, and a host of other random details. When the proverbs are placed together in apparently random order, the new arrangement creates new meaning, greater than the sum of the parts. Take, for example, 13:24, which instructs parents on how to discipline their children. Standing alone, that verse would be clear enough, but placed in the context of chapter 13, which talks about the blessings of righteousness, the need for discipline becomes all the greater.

THE THEOLOGY OF PROVERBS

Much of Proverbs promises retribution, the dispensing of reward or punishment based on one's actions. This theme, common to other parts of the Old Testament such as Deuteronomy and the Historical Books, is found in as many as one-fourth of all Proverbs.[22] A clear statement of retribution can be found in 11:21:

> Be sure of this: The wicked will not go unpunished,
> but those who are righteous will go free.

The punishment was anticipated in this life, not the next; the ancient Israelite did not yet understand the concept of eternal reward or punishment as it is understood in the New Testament.

The view that the wicked will be punished and the righteous rewarded in this life is routinely criticized as naive. Mature faith, many argue, has moved beyond this level. According to a recent study of the different levels of spiritual maturity, however, Proverbs, with its view of retribution, may well reflect not an immature, but an advanced stage of faith.[23]

Several other factors concerning the doctrine of retribution deserve consideration. Such statements were intended as generalizations based on observation, not absolutes based on revelation. If I say, "It never rains in southern California," I do not mean that rain is impossible there, but that sunshine is more likely. Actually, promises of retribution are based on observation plus something more: the character of God. Even though the writer knew that sometimes the wicked were allowed to flourish, he also knew that God's righteousness demanded a day of reckoning. Without a concept of eternity, he could only envision that day during this life; the very nature of God depended upon it.

These promises of retribution were ultimately more concerned with the way things ought to be rather than with the way they actually were. Those of us with a clearer understanding of eternal life and eternal punishment can confirm the accuracy of the writer's conclusions, even if we now see them as shortsighted. Remember, too, that these idealistic promises of retribution are found in parental advice to a young man at the crossroads of life. This is not the time for subtlety or mixed messages. A young person needs clear guidance; too much hangs in the balance.

While the promise of retribution is strong in Proverbs, it is not the only note that is heard. Throughout there is a clear countermelody reminding us that things are not as simple as they appear. Many proverbs carry the implied message to the righteous, "Wait" (see 20:22). Agur's prayer in 30:1-9 also balances the act-consequence sequence found in the rest of Proverbs. These verses recognize that everything comes from God and that life's outcome does not depend entirely on us. Not just this prayer but all of chapter 30 takes, as its theme, the humility which prevents us from becoming arrogant at what our righteousness has achieved. Proverbs also recognizes the mysteries of life, how some things do not fit the pattern:

In his heart a man plans his course,
but the LORD determines his steps (16:9).

In the words of one writer, "the greatest limitation on Wisdom was the Lord himself. . . . An appreciation of the divine mystery, God's being beyond wisdom, underlies the entire enterprise."[24]

While retribution is frequently mentioned in Proverbs, we hear very little of the Law[25] and almost nothing of the sacrificial system. What are we to make of this silence? As noted above, wisdom is universal. Those elements unique to a particular culture, such as the Mosaic law, were not appropriate to such a discussion. If I fail to mention my wife and children in a discussion you and I are having about the weather, do not assume they are unimportant to me, only that the subject never came up.

Actually, to say that Proverbs is silent on the Law is not correct. Behind this book is what we might call a covenant context.[26] God's special relationship with Israel, including the Mosaic law, is assumed. Proverbs then proceeds to show how Israel is to live as God's people. This can be seen in the prominence of the phrase, "the fear of the LORD" (see, for example, 1:7), which is lacking in the wisdom literature of Israel's neighbors. Yahweh's name[27] and explicit mention of the Law, though not frequent, are never far away. An important element of God's covenant with Israel, the giving of the Promised Land, is assumed (see 2:22). God stands behind this book as the Creator of all (8:22-31), including humanity (22:2), as the revealer of wisdom (2:6), and as wisdom's supervisor (22:12). The Law contains a vertical dimension—humanity's relationship with God—and a horizontal dimension—humanity's relationship with each other. Proverbs assumes the first, but pays more attention to the second. The book probes how we "love our neighbors as ourselves" (see Matthew 19:19). As commentator Derek Kidner has written, the proverbs' "function in Scripture is to put godliness in working clothes; to name business and society as spheres in which we are to acquit ourselves with credit to our Lord, and in which we are to look for His training."[28]

GUIDELINES FOR INTERPRETING PROVERBS

Interpreting Proverbs is not difficult, but certain ground rules must be kept in mind.

The first guideline is this: These proverbs were written as principles, not promises. A promise is a contract, full of words that clarify details, plug loopholes, and attempt to eliminate all possibility of misunderstanding. That is not what we have in a proverb. It is more like a bumper sticker. Words are kept to the bare minimum and are chosen for their impact. The proverb is written to be remembered, not to say all there is to say on a given topic. A proverb is meant to express a reality that is generally true, not to pronounce a reality that God guarantees to be true. Many proverbs predict an early end for the wicked and blessing for the righteous, but God has not broken His promise when the wicked prosper and the righteous suffer. The verse which, more than any other, has been misinterpreted as a promise is 22:6:

Train a child in the way he should go,
and when he is old he will not turn from it.

Raising your child in the proper way does not guarantee success, only your best chance at success. Common sense and the rest of the Bible (see below) make it clear that your child retains the freedom to choose to accept or reject God. This was written as a principle, not a promise.

A second guideline for interpretation involves an important principle of biblical interpretation: Always interpret a passage in its context. This is especially important because the proverbs appear to have no context. They appear to stand apart from one another and speak a universal message.

The proverbs do, however, have a context. In fact, they have several contexts. There is the *immediate context,* the surrounding verses in which a proverb is found. As was proposed above (see "Overview of Proverbs"), the arrangement of the proverbs is not random, but deliberate. Connections should not be forced, but should be allowed to surface with the help of common sense. At times the connections are unmistakable. Proverbs 26:4-5 is a good example of two verses, mutually contradictory, which are deliberately placed side by side and offer a meaning greater than the sum of the parts. The *larger context* of 10:1 through 31:31 is what precedes them in Proverbs 1 through 9. This foundation of wisdom and righteousness guides our reading of the rest of the book. When we read, for example,

> A bribe is a charm to the one who gives it;
> wherever he turns, he succeeds (17:8),

the immediate context (see 17:3-5, 15) and the calls to righteousness in Proverbs 1 through 9 and elsewhere keep us from interpreting this as an encouragement to use bribery. The proverbs must also be interpreted according to their *covenant context* (see "Theology of Proverbs" above). A book based on Israel's relationship with Yahweh, as spelled out in their Law, should be interpreted consistently with that Law. Verses like 10:12 and 16:6 must not be used to contradict the sacrificial system, but to clarify it. Finally, there is the context of the *Bible in its entirety*. While neither the authors of these proverbs nor the editors responsible for their final form could see how they would fit into this context, God certainly could. So, too, could the New Testament writers who used proverbs, and so should we as we interpret it. The proper interpretation of any given proverb will not violate the overall message of the Bible.

A third guideline for interpretation is this: Let common sense guide you. Everyone knows that, in spite of the proverbs' claims, righteousness may actually create more problems for us than it solves. The writer knew that, too, and meant for us to interpret accordingly.

One final guideline is based on the assumption that God has given us the Bible primarily for the purpose of revealing himself. We might—and in Proverbs we certainly do—find it a helpful source of principles for living, but more than any principles, history lessons, or future predictions, God wants us to meet Him in these pages. If this is true, then the most important question we can ask of any proverb is, What does this tell me about God? We can learn about Him from what He says and does and from what others say about Him. He reveals himself to us in what He requires us to say and do. By understanding how He designed this world to operate—both in the realms of nature and human interaction—we learn something about the Designer. As we understand God, we find an unchanging moral compass to guide us through life and yet find another reason to praise Him.

ENDNOTES

[1]Law refers to either the Levitical Code (all God's rules and regulations), the Ten Commandments, or the Pentateuch (the first five books of the Old Testament: Genesis, Exodus, Leviticus, Numbers, and Deuteronomy; also called the Law of Moses or Mosaic law). It is often capitalized when it means the Pentateuch or the Ten Commandments.

[2]Donald K. Berry, *An Introduction to Wisdom and Poetry of the Old Testament* (Nashville: Broadman and Holman, 1995), p. 118.

[3]James Kugel, "Wisdom and the Anthological Temper," *Prooftexts,* vol. 17, no. 1 (1997), pp. 9–32.

[4]Ibid., p. 30.

[5]Many scholars have noted the similarities between Proverbs 22:17–24:22 and the Egyptian "Instruction of Amenomope" (ca. 1200 B.C.).

[6]Michael V. Fox, "Ideas of Wisdom in Proverbs 1–9," *Journal of Biblical Literature,* vol. 116, no. 4, pp. 613–33.

[7]Lindsay Wilson, "The Book of Job and the Fear of God," *Tyndale Bulletin,* vol. 46, no. 1 (1995), pp. 59–79.

[8]Kugel, p. 10.

[9]Philip Nel, "The Voice of Ms. Wisdom: Wisdom as Intertext," *Old Testament Essays,* vol. 9, no. 3 (1996), pp. 423–50.

[10]Derek Kidner, *Proverbs: An Introduction and Commentary,* Tyndale Old Testament Commentaries, ed. D. J. Wiseman (Downers Grove, Illinois: InterVarsity Press, 1964), p. 31.

[11]Kugel, p. 27.

[12]Nel, p. 443.

[13]C. Hassell Bullock, *An Introduction to the Old Testament Poetic Books,* revised and expanded edition (Chicago: Moody Press, 1988), p. 165.

[14]Ben Witherington, "Three Modern Faces of Wisdom," *Ashland Theological Journal,* vol. 25 (1993), pp. 96–121.

[15]Berry, p. 125.

[16]Wilson, p. 62.

[17]The New International Version and other translations render this with LORD in small capital letters following an initial capital *L.*

[18]Wisdom literature includes the books of Job, Proverbs, Ecclesiastes, and Song of Songs (Song of Solomon). These writings are collections of statements of wisdom, often dealing with the great issues of life, such as the problem of suffering, practical ethics and morality, and the meaning of life and love.

[19]Michael Carasik, "Who Were the 'Men of Hezekiah' (Proverbs XXV 1)?, *Vetus Testamentum,* vol. 44, no. 3 (1994), pp. 289–300.

[20]Wilson, p. 61. These proverbs are sometimes referred to as sentence literature because they appear isolated from the surrounding verses.

[21]Kugel, p. 20.

[22]Berry, p. 122.

[23]R. R. Wyse and W. S. Prinsloo, "Faith Development and Proverbial Wisdom," *Old Testament Essays,* vol. 9, no. 1 (1996), pp. 129–43.

[24]Roland E. Murphy, "Wisdom and Creation," *Journal of Biblical Literature,* vol. 104, no. 1 (1985), pp. 3–11.

[25]See endnote 1.

[26]A covenant is a solemn promise made binding by a pledge or vow, which may be either a verbal formula or a symbolic action. Covenant often referred to a legal obligation in ancient times. In Old Testament terms, the word was often used in describing the relationship between God and His chosen people, in which their sacrifices of blood afforded them His atonement for sin, and in which their fulfillment of a promise to live in obedience to God was rewarded by His blessings. In New Testament terms, this relationship (the new covenant) was now made possible on a personal basis through Jesus Christ and His sacrifice of His own blood.

[27]See endnote 17.

[28]Kidner, p. 35.

PROVERBS OUTLINE

I. **WISDOM AND GODLINESS** **(1:1–9:18)**
   A. **Proverbs 1 (1:1-33)**
      1. 1:1-7   Wisdom's Summons
      2. 1:8-33   Encouragement to Pursue Wisdom
         a. 1:8-19   Parental Advice
         b. 1:20-33   Warning Against Rejecting Wisdom
   B. **Proverbs 2 (2:1-22)**
      1. 2:1-11   Knowledge of God
      2. 2:12-15   Protection From Wicked Men
      3. 2:16-19   Protection From Wicked Women
      4. 2:20-22   Conclusion: Be Wise
   C. **Proverbs 3 (3:1-35)**
      1. 3:1-26   Wisdom Brings Blessings
      2. 3:27-32   Series of Prohibitions
      3. 3:33-35   Summary: God Curses the Wicked but Blesses the Righteous
   D. **Proverbs 4 (4:1-27)**
      1. 4:1-4a   A Father's Wisdom
      2. 4:4b-9   Grandfather's Advice
      3. 4:10-19   Two Paths
      4. 4:20-27   Guard Your Heart
   E. **Proverbs 5 (5:1-23)**
      1. 5:1-6   Watch Out for That Woman
      2. 5:7-14   Warning Against Adultery
      3. 5:15-20   Fidelity: The Alternative to Adultery
      4. 5:21-23   God Sees All We Do
   F. **Proverbs 6 (6:1-35)**
      1. 6:1-5   Warning Against Suretyship
      2. 6:6-11   Warning Against Idleness
      3. 6:12-19   Warning Against Interpersonal Discord
      4. 6:20-35   Continued Warning Against Adultery
   G. **Proverbs 7 (7:1-27)**
      1. 7:1-5   Avoiding Adultery
      2. 7:6-23   Scene of Enticement
      3. 7:24-27   Final Warning

C. Proverbs 12 (12:1-28)

1.	12:1	You Have to Love Discipline!
2.	12:2	God Is Watching Our Actions
3.	12:3	The Path to True Stability
4.	12:4	Adornment or Undoing
5.	12:5	How Do You Think About Others?
6.	12:6	What Do You Say About Others?
7.	12:7	Thoughts, Words, Destiny
8.	12:8	The Honor of Wisdom
9.	12:9	You Can't Eat an Image
10.	12:10	Would Your Dog Give You a Good Character Reference?
11.	12:11	You Can't Eat a Fantasy
12.	12:12	Secure Under Siege
13.	12:13	The Power of Words for Evil
14.	12:14	The Power of Words for Good
15.	12:15	The Know-It-All Fool
16.	12:16	The Quick-Tempered Fool
17.	12:17	The Truth, the Whole Truth, and Nothing but the Truth
18.	12:18	Do Your Words Harm or Heal?
19.	12:19	Long-Term Lips
20.	12:20	Motivated by Joy
21.	12:21	Don't Poke a Hole in Your Own Boat
22.	12:22	God Loves Truth
23.	12:23	When Knowledge Should Be Hidden
24.	12:24	Another Benefit of Diligence
25.	12:25	The Power of a Good Word
26.	12:26	Choose Your Friends Carefully
27.	12:27	Treasure Life
28.	12:28	Life or Death

D. Proverbs 13 (13:1-25)

1.	13:1	Father Knows Best
2.	13:2	When Eating Your Words Is a Good Thing
3.	13:3	When Eating Your Words Is a Bad Thing
4.	13:4	Desire Is No Substitute for Diligence
5.	13:5	Do You Hate What Is False?
6.	13:6	The Best Defense Is Righteousness
7.	13:7	Wealth: The Illusion
8.	13:8	Wealth: The Danger

26. 29:26   Seek an Audience With the King
27. 29:27   Mutually Abhorrent Society

U. Proverbs 30 (30:1-33)
1. 30:1-9   An Old Man Speaks
2. 30:10-14   The Slanderous Son
3. 30:15-16   Never Enough
4. 30:17   The Mocking Eye
5. 30:18-19   Four Wonders
6. 30:20   Incredible Impudence
7. 30:21-23   Four Things Too Heavy to Bear
8. 30:24-28   Small, but Mighty
9. 30:29-31   Stately in Their Stride
10. 30:32-33   Churning Up Anger

V. Proverbs 31 (31:1-31)
1. 31:1-9   Maternal Advice
2. 31:10-31   In Praise of a Virtuous Woman

Part One

WISDOM AND GODLINESS

Proverbs 1:1–9:18

T he first section of Proverbs opens with the preamble and motto of the book in 1:1-7 and concludes with a contrast between wisdom and folly (see Proverbs 9). These nine chapters "focus on the formation of a godly character that comes from embracing wisdom, which is then presupposed in the individual proverbial sayings."[1] Beginning and ending this introductory material (see 1:7; 9:10) is the call to **fear the LORD**[2]; the rest of the book assumes the godly character promoted in chapters 1 through 9. Between these calls to **fear the LORD,** the writer tries to convince the reader to pursue wisdom for the protection and blessing she affords. He also warns the reader against pursuing wisdom's alternatives, such as pledging surety, idleness, interpersonal discord and, especially, adultery. This last vice serves not only as a literal and serious danger, but as an analogy for the choice of folly. The section closes with a clear contrast between what wisdom and folly have to offer.

ENDNOTES

[1]Lindsay Wilson, "The Book of Job and the Fear of God," *Tyndale Bulletin,* vol. 46, no. 1 (1995), p. 61.

[2]The New International Version and other translations use LORD in small capitals following an initial capital *L* to denote "Yahweh" in the original Hebrew.

PROVERBS 1

1:1-33

Aflter a brief prologue in which the purpose of the book is revealed (Proverbs 1:1-7), the rest of chapter 1 contains parental advice (1:8-19) and wisdom's call (1:20-33). The strongly negative flavor of the latter two sections reveals the importance of this search for wisdom.

1. WISDOM'S SUMMONS 1:1-7

The first seven verses of Proverbs chart our course for the chapters ahead. We see our purpose: to produce life-transforming wisdom. We are shown how this wisdom is produced: by **the fear of the LORD** (1:7).[1] We even see that all are invited to become wise, young and old, smart and simple. The book contains **proverbs** (1:1), a word whose root meaning suggests comparison. Some proverbs are two-line epigrams (witty, pointed sayings; see 11:22); others are more extended comparison (see 1:20-33). As used in verse 1, **proverbs** might better be translated "wise sayings."[2]

The book of Proverbs seeks to produce wisdom of all kinds. The wise person knows **discipline** (1:2), a word found more often in Proverbs than elsewhere in the Old Testament. This word can refer to the physical correction a parent gives a wayward child (see 23:13) or to wise counsel and direction (see 1:8). "To understand words of understanding" attempts to capture the play on words in the Hebrew phrase translated **understanding words of insight** (1:2).

No one is truly wise, however, until wisdom goes to work. Notice the practical results of the wisdom of 1:2: **a disciplined and prudent life** (1:3) marked by righteousness, justice and fairness. A person who *is* disciplined is one who *has been* disciplined. Prudence or "good conduct" (1:3 NLT) results from one who understands and acts on what is understood. This real-life wisdom is for everyone; even the **simple** can gain **prudence** (1:4). This latter word translates a different Hebrew word than the one rendered **prudent** in 1:3; here it refers to a shrewdness that is morally neutral.[3] In other words, those who are notoriously dim can become clever. The young can also learn and develop their ability to discern. Even the **wise** can become wiser while those who are already **discerning** will receive **guidance** (1:5). The Hebrew word translated **guidance** refers to the ability to successfully navigate life,[4] prompting one translation: "learn the ropes."[5]

According to 1:6, the wise will be able to understand **proverbs and parables, . . . sayings and riddles.** Here **proverbs** may have the more familiar meaning of "epigram." The Hebrew word translated **parables** might better be rendered "satire" (see Habakkuk 2:6) or "obscure sayings" (Prov. 1:6 NJB) requiring interpretation.[6] **Sayings** are the words of **wise** people (Prov. 1:6), while **riddles** is the same word used to describe Samson's "riddle" in Judges 14:12-20 and Ezekiel's "allegory" of eagles (Ezek. 17:2). The New International Version translates this same word "intrigue" in Daniel 8:23.

In what may be the most important statement in Proverbs,[7] the source of such wisdom is revealed: **The fear of the Lord is the beginning of knowledge** (Prov. 1:7a).[8] Here **fear** does not mean terror but a reverence or respect that produces a submissive attitude toward God. Fear of God implies a recognition that He exists, that He knows all about us, and that He will reward or punish based upon His knowledge. Those who truly fear God have put these insights into practice and have made choices that reflect their submission to **the Lord. Lord** translates the special name by which God made himself known to His people—Yahweh. By using this name, the writer calls to mind the special relationship that existed between God and Israel. To **fear . . . the Lord** meant submitting to a God who had already made known His love to them. It means reverence within a relationship.

Beginning is, literally, "head," a word that could have one of several meanings. It could refer to the threshold of wisdom except that the fear of God is not left behind as one proceeds further into wisdom. "Head" here could mean first in importance (see Amos 6:1 where the same word is translated "foremost" in the NIV), suggesting that fearing God is the wisest thing one can do. While this is no doubt true, there seems to be a better way of understanding this term. "Head" here suggests a fountain from which wisdom flows, a posture that enables true wisdom to be obtained. Only with such fear can the thirst for wisdom be satisfied. This is the only lens through which reality can be seen. While many pursue knowledge as an end in itself, this verse suggests that God designed wisdom as a by-product of our relationship with Him. Some, who believe the term is deliberately unclear and has more than one of these meanings, translate "head" ambiguously as "first principle."⁹ **Fools,** those morally disabled, reject **wisdom and discipline,** the crucial elements with which the prologue began (Prov. 1:7; see 1:2). An illustration of such **fools** follows in the next section.

2. ENCOURAGEMENT TO PURSUE WISDOM 1:8-33

a. Parental Advice (1:8-19). Though it may seem strange, at first, the previous "prologue" is followed by two quite negative passages (see Proverbs 1:8-19; 20-33). In fact, these warnings are needed to clear away some of the stumbling blocks that would prevent this young man from becoming wise. The parental advice found in the first passage warns against one such stumbling block, evil that entices. Anyone could give this kind of advice, but no one more effectively than a parent. The first reason for listening and obeying is positive: Wisdom can beautify your life—that is, "improve your character." The **garland to grace your head** could refer to a crown or to a "handsome turban" (TEV), while the **chain** appears to be a necklace, perhaps of some precious metal or valuable beads (1:9).¹⁰

The second reason for obeying is given at greater length and is negative: Disobedience can have disastrous, even deadly consequences (see 1:10-19). The young man may see it as "just some guys who want me to hang out with them," but the parents have sized up things correctly: These are **sinners** out to **entice you** (1:10) with tantalizing lures. Unsuspecting victims (see 1:11) implies easy money at no risk. Boasts of swallowing them **alive . . . and whole** reflect nothing but swaggering braggadocio (1:12), while the glitter of spoils is meant to tempt the greedy (see 1:13). Perhaps the most appealing temptation is the camaraderie implied in 1:14. **Throw in your lot with us** (literally, "your lot shall be cast in our midst") and the promise of **a common purse** imply that there will be honor among these thieves. The loot will be distributed fairly, by lot, so that everyone gets his share.¹¹

According to 1:15-19, father and mother know best: **Do not go along with them, do not set foot on their paths** (note how the second phrase is more intense than the first) or your feet will be like theirs, which **rush into sin** (1:15-16).¹² These sinners are blind to the irony of their actions. They compare themselves to **the grave** and **the pit** (1:12) into which the unsuspecting will fall, when that is their own destination (see 1:18); they are the unsuspecting. Even a bird has enough sense to avoid a trap when it becomes aware of it, but these "birdbrains" run hell-bent into the trap they set with their own hands. They think they **lie in wait** and **waylay** others (1:11), but in fact they **lie in wait for their own blood** and **waylay only themselves** (1:18). No sinner is crafty enough to avoid this end: **All who go after ill-gotten gain** suffer this same fate (1:19). God cares too much about the well-being of His creation to allow the innocent to be harmed, so He designed evil with a short fuse; it harms those who seek to use it against others.

b. Warning Against Rejecting Wisdom (1:20-33). Lady Wisdom here steps, for the first time, onto the proverbs' stage. Why is wisdom presented as a female? When I asked that question of my adult Sunday school class, one pupil answered with a shake of his head, "If you have to ask, you wouldn't understand." Aside from the allusion to a woman's intuition, the connection may be, in part, grammatical. All Hebrew words have a gender, either masculine, feminine or neuter; wisdom is feminine. Another reason to describe wisdom as a woman may have something to do with the author's overall purpose, that of presenting counsel to a young man (see 1:8). Much of this counsel, especially early on, is designed to guide a young man into a healthy marital relationship. Lady Wisdom represents Miss Right, the ideal woman this young man is to seek. The Hebrew word translated **Wisdom** (1:20) is here in the plural to demonstrate her fullness and completeness.

The young (see 1:8) need to realize that "sinners" are not the only ones calling (1:10). Lady Wisdom makes her voice heard with siren-like intensity.[13] Because she wants everyone to hear her message, she takes to the **street** (1:20) where the people are. The **public squares** (1:20) refer to the open spaces in the city where people gather. Her message sounds **at the head of the noisy streets,** the most crowded part (1:21). Some English translations follow the Septuagint[14] and render this phrase "on the tops of the walls," but this change seems unnecessary. At **the gateways of the city** (1:21) people would meet, discuss news, and bring issues for judgment by the elders. The seriousness of her mission—bringing maximum exposure to her message of wisdom—prompts Lady Wisdom to engage in public presentation, a brazen task for a woman.

The young man's parents try to clear aside one stumbling block to the attainment of wisdom: the lure of evil (1:8-19). Lady Wisdom exposes another obstacle: missed opportunities. Perhaps the **simple ones . . . mockers . . . and fools** (1:22) she addresses are the same group of "sinners" warned against in 1:8-19. Like the **simple** (1:22; see 1:4), **mockers** are morally, not mentally, challenged, only more so. The mocker scornfully ridicules what he cannot understand, too wise in his own eyes to see the truth. "Strife . . . quarrels, and insults" follow in his train (22:10) until God brings his mocking to an end (see 3:34).

In spite of the senselessness of her listeners, Lady Wisdom willingly makes herself available. She takes her message to the streets, calling out to all who will hear (the Hebrew word for "behold" is left untranslated in 1:23). What a picture of God's love, willing to make His truth known to all, even to those who will not hear and who have rejected earlier rebukes! If only they had responded, how willingly Wisdom would have **poured out [her] heart** or **thoughts**[15] (literally "spirit;" 1:23). Their folly sprang not from Wisdom's elusiveness, but from their stubborn refusal to accept what she had to offer. They **love** their **simple ways . . . delight in mockery**, and **hate knowledge** (1:22). They paid no attention to what she had to offer (see 1:24), **ignored [her] advice and would not accept [her] rebuke** (1:25). **They hated knowledge and did not choose to fear the LORD** (1:29).

In 1:28, Wisdom turns from the wicked and speaks about them, perhaps to show how she ignores them. They would not listen when she called; she will not listen when they call. When judgment comes, the punishment is as much self-inflicted as administered by God. **The fruit of their ways** and **their schemes . . . will destroy them** (1:31-32). God has provided a way to avoid disaster, however. Those who listen to His Wisdom—that is, those who obey Wisdom—**will live in safety and be at ease, without fear of harm** (1:33). To **be at ease** implies a comfortable and relaxing rest, quite the opposite of the disaster that awaits the foolish (see the same Hebrew word in Job 3:18; Jeremiah 30:10; 48:11). **Without fear of harm** (Prov. 1:33; literally, "from calamity of fear") could also be rendered "from fearful calamity." The calamity that will overtake the foolish (it is the same Hebrew here as in 1:26-27) will not come to those who obey Wisdom.

ENDNOTES

[1] The New International Version and other translations use LORD in small capitals following an initial capital *L* to denote "Yahweh" in the original Hebrew.

[2] R. B. Y. Scott, *Proverbs, Ecclesiastes* in The Anchor Bible, vol. 18, eds. William F. Albright and David Noel Freedman (New York: Doubleday, 1965), p. 36.

[3] R. N. Whybray, *Proverbs,* The New Century Bible Commentary (Grand Rapids, Michigan: Wm. B. Eerdmans Publishing Co., 1994), p. 33.

[4]Ibid., p. 34.

[5]William McKane, *Proverbs,* The Old Testament Library (Philadelphia: Westminster Press, 1970), p. 211.

[6]See the discussion in Whybray, p. 34 and Derek Kidner, *Proverbs: An Introduction and Commentary,* Tyndale Old Testament Commentaries, ed. D. J. Wiseman (Downers Grove, Illinois: InterVarsity Press, 1964), p. 58.

[7]Lindsay Wilson, "The Book of Job and the Fear of God," *Tyndale Bulletin,* vol. 46, no. 1 (1995), p. 62.

[8]This same loyal relationship could be suggested by the alternative, "Fear of God." The context for each should be considered (Wilson, p. 64).

[9]Wilson, p. 61; Scott, p. 33.

[10]Scott, p. 38.

[11]Whybray, p. 40

[12]Verse 16 may not have been in the original Hebrew since it is missing from the best manuscripts of the Septuagint (see endnote 14). It is found in Isaiah 59:7, and some suggest a copyist may have written it here because of the similarities between that context and this. Paul quotes a portion of this verse in Romans 3:15.

[13]Whybray, p. 45.

[14]The Septuagint is the Greek version of the Old Testament, translated from the original Hebrew scrolls, and written in the second and third centuries B.C. It is often indicated by the Roman numerals LXX in accordance with the legend that it was translated by seventy scribes.

[15]Whybray, p. 47.

2

PROVERBS 2

2:1-22

Proverbs 2, one long, very complex "if-then" sentence in the Hebrew, describes what is to be gained by those who walk the path of wisdom. The chapter serves an introductory function since many of these benefits are expanded upon later in Proverbs.

1. KNOWLEDGE OF GOD 2:1-11

The kind of search that brings results is described in the opening verses of Proverbs 2. Wisdom first must be accepted and absorbed. **Store up** (2:1) translates the same Hebrew word rendered "waylay" in 1:11, 18. Perhaps we should see some connection: Instead of hiding with others to do evil, hide these words of wisdom in your heart.

The **ear** and **heart** should also be employed in the pursuit; 2:2 refers back to Wisdom's offer in 1:24 where no one paid attention to her calls. Here, in quite similar terms, the **son** is asked to listen to Wisdom and apply his heart to what he hears. The verb translated **applying** is used elsewhere to describe the process of turning an animal onto a certain road (see Numbers 22:23). Those who would become wise must listen to Wisdom's call and steer their hearts toward it.

The pursuit of wisdom becomes more aggressive with 2:3. Instead of merely receiving what a teacher offers, the pupil must actively search. Verses 1 through 3 form the counterpart to 1:20-33. There Wisdom was clamoring to be heard; here the pupil must clamor.[1] Sometimes Wisdom is clearly seen, at other times she must be summoned and searched for. Nor will a haphazard and halfhearted search succeed. To receive her **commands** (2:1) means to reject competing commands. To incline one's **heart** toward **wisdom** (2:2) is to incline it away from other directions. To **call out** and **cry aloud** (2:3) may disturb others. A search for hidden treasure implies intensity and exclusivity, but it is this kind of exploration that succeeds.

The results of such a search are described in five sections: One gains a **knowledge of God** (2:5-8), which produces guidance (2:9-11); Wisdom saves from both **wicked men** (2:12-15) and wicked women (2:16-19), and produces a long and secure life (2:20-22).

The most significant result of the search for wisdom is mentioned first: One comes to know God. Verse 6 makes it clear that to find God (**LORD** is emphasized in the Hebrew[2]) is to find the source of all wisdom. The two phrases in 2:5—**understand the fear of the LORD** and **find the knowledge of God**—express the mystery and comfort that characterizes what it means to know the Lord. We learn about God only because He has graciously chosen to reveal himself to us (see discussion of **LORD** in 1:7) but learning these truths fills us with awe and wonder.

Those who fear the Lord need fear nothing else (2:7-8), for God **holds victory in store for** them. **Store** translates the same Hebrew word found in 2:1 suggesting that for those who "store up" wisdom, God stores up victory. A God who wants me to be victorious is well worth knowing. The wise are now referred to as **upright** and **blameless** (2:7), another reminder that wisdom comes from reverence for God. They are also called **faithful ones** or saints (2:8); the Hebrew term refers to those who keep God's covenant.[3] How God protects His own is described in 2:9-11. He provides wisdom which allows the discovery of **every good path**— that is, those which are **right and just and fair** (the same three terms are found together in 1:3). Wisdom will bring pleasure (2:10), making the temptation to evil less appealing. Whereas in 2:8 God was described as protecting and guarding, here that task is done by God's gift of wisdom (the same verbs are used here but in reverse order). Two specific ways that God's wisdom protects His people are described in 2:12-22.

2. PROTECTION FROM WICKED MEN 2:12-15

Wicked men (2:12-15) are characterized first by their behavior (**ways;** see 1:8-19) and then by their speech (**whose words are perverse**). In Proverbs, **words** are often seen as windows to the way of life. **Perverse** words produce "dissension" (16:28) through deceitfulness (see 6:14; 16:30; also 23:33 where this word is used as a synonym to hallucinations). The wicked **leave the straight paths** (**straight** is related to the word translated "upright" in 2:7) for **dark ways** where their evil behavior can go unnoticed and unpunished (2:13). Far from being remorseful, they **delight** and **rejoice in** their **crooked and . . . devious ways** (2:14-15).

3. PROTECTION FROM WICKED WOMEN 2:16-19

The same Hebrew phrase begins Proverbs 2:16 as began 2:12: literally, "to save you." Not only will wisdom protect you from the wicked man, it will also protect you from the wicked woman. She is, literally, a foreign woman, a term most commentators take to mean an adulteress. While the context makes clear this is the intended meaning, such a reference suggests more may be in view. Perhaps this serves as a reminder to Israel of the danger of following foreign gods (a danger Solomon did not take seriously enough). Note again the connection between behavior and speech. In this case her words are **seductive** (2:16) or, more literally, slippery (for an example of her seductive speech, read 7:14-20). The related verb refers to the process of smoothing metal, and the related noun describes a river stone smoothed by the passage of water (see Isaiah 57:6). She has breached her commitment to her husband, referred to as the **partner of her youth** to further heighten the seriousness of this violation (2:17). She has also breached her covenant with God (or **before God** as the NIV suggests; see 2:17). The same Hebrew verb used to describe the action of wicked men in 2:13 (there translated "who leave") is used in 2:17 for the wicked woman. They left the paths of the "upright" (2:7) just as she left her **partner.**

This woman should be avoided at all costs for death will result (2:18). A "grammatical difficulty"[4] in this verse raises some question about how it should be translated. Is her house the doorway to death or is the house itself sinking down to death? The end is the same either way. Contrary to the general feeling among the disobedient that "I'll get away with it," no one ever does, according to verse 19.

4. CONCLUSION: BE WISE 2:20-22

The conclusion of this long sentence compares the outcome of the those who follow wisdom (described in Proverbs 2:5-11) with those who do not (see 2:12-19; also Psalm 1:6). As if to reinforce their message, these verses borrow heavily from terms used earlier: **ways** (Prov. 2:20; see 2:8, 12-13); **paths** (2:20; see 2:8, 13, 15, 19); **keep** (2:20; see 2:8, 11); and **upright** (2:21; see 2:7). **Thus you will walk** (expressing the result; 2:20) should be translated "In order that you may walk" (expressing the purpose for what has just been said).[5] That life and security **in the land** await those who are righteous (2:21) were rich promises to Israel whose identity was so closely tied to the Promised Land. By contrast, the warning sounded in verse 22 is all the more ominous.

ENDNOTES

[1]Derek Kidner, *Proverbs: An Introduction and Commentary,* Tyndale Old Testament Commentaries, ed. D. J. Wiseman (Downers Grove, Illinois: InterVarsity Press, 1964), p. 61.

[2]The New International Version and other translations use LORD in small capitals following an initial capital *L* to denote "Yahweh" in the original Hebrew.

[3]Kidner.

A covenant is a solemn promise made binding by a pledge or vow, which may be either a verbal formula or a symbolic action. Covenant often referred to a legal obligation in ancient times. In Old Testament terms, the word was often used in describing the relationship between God and His chosen people, in which their sacrifices of blood afforded them His atonement for sin, and in which their fulfillment of a promise to live in obedience to God was rewarded by His blessings. In New Testament terms, this relationship (the new covenant) was now made possible on a personal basis through Jesus Christ and His sacrifice of His own blood.

[4]Kidner, p. 62.

[5]R. N. Whybray, *Proverbs,* The New Century Bible Commentary (Grand Rapids, Michigan: Wm. B. Eerdmans Publishing Co., 1994), p. 57.

PROVERBS 3

3:1-35

In the second chapter of Proverbs, wisdom was promoted as the protector against moral corruption. This chapter trumpets additional benefits in order to encourage the "young man" to choose the wise way.

1. WISDOM BRINGS BLESSINGS 3:1-26

Proverbs 3:1-10 contains five calls, each followed by a corresponding benefit.

Obedience brings long life and prosperity, according to 3:1-2. The parent's **teaching** has been learned and now must be remembered (3:1). **Teaching** translates the Hebrew word which can describe what Moses received on Mount Sinai (see 28:9; 29:18) or parental instruction (see 1:8), the meaning here. The following verses make it clear that such teaching is not simply to be learned and remembered, but put into practice. Those who do so will find that God has made Wisdom Road pass through very prosperous pastures.

The second call of the writer (3:3-4) is for **love and faithfulness.** The first term translates an important Hebrew word, *chesed,* for which there is no good English equivalent. **Love** is inadequate because of its romantic connotations; this word has more to do with a commitment of the will than a feeling in the heart. Used often in the Old Testament, *chesed* describes God's attitude toward the nation of Israel with whom He had a covenant relationship.[1] Israel's obligation, as God's covenant people, was to show *chesed* toward each other and toward God, to always act in **love and faithfulness.** Such action characterizes the wise person. The difficulty of maintaining this kind of commitment is expressed in the command, **Let love and faithfulness never leave you** (3:3a), or as the New Living Translation states it, "Never let loyalty and kindness get away from you!" To **bind them around your neck . . .** implies that such qualities could and should be worn like a necklace, beautifying one's life (3:3b; see 1:9). If you want this pair to permanently shape your choices, **. . . write them on the tablet of your heart** (3:3b) as God inscribed the Law[2] on tablets of stone. He recognizes and honors such covenant loyalty with **favor** [or grace] **and a good name** (3:4). The latter term translates two Hebrew words used together in Psalm 111:10. What God may be promising is not merely a good reputation but a reputation for good understanding.

In what have become some of the proverbs' most familiar verses, God promises clear direction to those who trust Him entirely (see Proverbs 3:5-6). Wisdom cannot replace trust in God, a truth brought out again in 3:7. While a call for complete trust in God may seem to contradict a call to pursue wisdom, both are true; human beings must value wisdom supremely *and* trust God completely. Only with this balance can we become all God made us to be. Verse 6 tells how to keep your balance in a world that seems to drive a wedge between wisdom and trust: **acknowledge** God. Although usually taken to mean we should recognize God's lordship before we act, another interpretation is possible. Since the underlying Hebrew word can be translated as "know," perhaps we are being told to recognize God's presence with each step. He is there, Lord of every turn and detour, wanting us to acknowledge His presence. To enjoy fellowship with Him will not only enable complete trust but will either **make your paths straight** (3:6) or provide clear direction (see NIV margin note). Translators seem evenly divided between these two options; either reading fits the context and the verb (**make**) fits both. **Straight** or smooth paths are those made easier for travel by removing curves, inclines, and obstacles. By emphasizing the pronoun **he** in the Hebrew (3:6), there is no question that God will honor our trust.

Once again the reader is summoned to wisdom (see 3:7-8), this time to wisdom as evidenced by a righteous life. Reverence for the Lord implies the humility to choose God's way over our own, thereby shunning evil. Such righteousness results in physical health, a connection that has the full support of scientific research and experience. **Body** (3:8) is, literally, "umbilical cord" or navel (see Ezekiel 16:4; Song of Songs 7:2) implying that healing comes to the very center of our existence, to that which represents our very beginning. **Bones** (Prov. 3:8), here representing the body, are nourished and refreshed by righteousness.

Wisdom as expressed through sacrificial offerings is the subject for the final call in these verses (see 3:9-10). When we honor God by showing that He is more important than our wealth (the root idea of **honor**), He shows himself Lord of the harvest and fills our **barns** and **vats** with the very best the land has to offer (3:10).

Perhaps to remove the suggestion that the road to wisdom has no potholes, 3:11-12 counsels patience when God disciplines us. Like a caring father, He must sometimes direct and correct His children. We should not chafe under the chastening rod, for such discipline demonstrates God's love, the best motivation known to humanity. Embrace wisdom, for even at its most difficult moments, this is still the path of greatest blessing.

Verses 13 through 18 contain a beautiful poem in praise of wisdom, highlighting the blessings that accompany its discovery. The poem begins and ends with happiness, a constant theme throughout Proverbs. Wisdom's dividends outperform wealth itself (see 3:14). Wealth is not bad, as the rest of Proverbs 3 makes clear, but wealth alone leaves one poor. Earth's most precious jewels are not a match for wisdom, a truth emphasized when, in this poem, the author turns directly to the reader for the first time. Its surpassing value established, wisdom's benefits glitter: long life, wealth, a good reputation, pleasure, and peace *(shalom)*. A life-giving, living tree, it is the very source of blessings to those who look nowhere else, for this is the tree of God's own planting.

A two-verse poem (see 3:19-20) follows in which wisdom's role in creation is identified and celebrated (a theme developed more fully in later chapters). As wisdom has been elevated to lofty heights in the preceding verses, the God who can use it to fashion this world becomes even more elevated. In view is the order and design of creation as seen in the solid foundation of the earth and the spreading out (see 3:19 NJB) of the heavens. Reference to the **deeps . . . and the clouds** (3:20) implies God's control over all that lies between these extremes. The dividing (or cleaving) of the **deeps** suggests the breaking open of the earth's crust to permit springs and streams to arise. In a beautiful poetic contrast, the mighty gushing of water from below is followed by the fine dusting of dew from above. Both **deeps** and **dew** (3:20) produce moisture for the crops to grow, wonderful gifts in the parched climate of the Middle East. How does such a poem encourage one to become wise? The powerful God who created such diverse water sources wants to also give us the greater gift of wisdom.

Still another blessing provided by wisdom is peace and safety (see 3:21-26). When **sound judgment and discernment** are kept in sight (3:21; the same verb as in 3:1), **life** and beauty follow (3:22; **ornament** translates the Hebrew word sometimes rendered "grace"). **Life** is further explained as peace and **safety** (3:23). Wisdom lets you walk without stumbling because the pathway is uncluttered by the debris of bad decisions. When you stop to rest or lie down, you need not be afraid. It is as if wisdom erects a fence around your sleeping bag and removes all worry, allowing you to sleep sweetly. Some versions translate the first **lie down** in 3:24 as "sit down" (since the progression of walking, sitting, and lying down makes more sense and since this would require the addition of only one letter in the Hebrew). Even **sudden disaster** need not give the wise any cause for alarm, for wisdom's fence is really the LORD himself (3:25-26; LORD is emphasized in the Hebrew[3]). Back on the path in the morning, your journey resumed, you can walk confidently, unafraid of either the ruinous storm or the hidden snare.

2. SERIES OF PROHIBITIONS 3:27-32

In this otherwise positive appeal for wisdom, the author surprises us with four specific prohibitions (see Proverbs 3:27-35), obedience to which proves that wisdom is really present. By presenting the two options of wisdom and folly so clearly, the choice is made clear. These specific prohibitions are chosen, in part, because the behavior they forbid—selfishness, deceit, violence—stands in striking contrast to the way God treats us. Wisdom becomes more appealing when it is understood to be the path that makes us most like God. The prohibitions make it clear that wisdom is more than thinking wise thoughts, but includes how we treat our neighbors.

The wise person will **not withhold good from those who deserve it** (3:27). The phrase rendered **when you now have it with you** (3:28) is stronger when translated more literally, "And there it is with you!" The preceding verses, especially 3:1-10, make clear that God does not withhold His best; how can we treat others this way?

Nor will the truly wise **plot harm against [a] neighbor** (3:29). We can trust in God's protection at our most vulnerable, unsuspecting moments (see 3:23-26); others should also be able to trust us. The wise person will not falsely **accuse** another in court (3:30) or **envy a violent person** (3:31). Unlike the previous prohibitions, 3:31 contains a reason: God hates the **perverse** but honors the **upright** (3:32). The two terms are opposite, like crooked and straight. God **detests a perverse man** and, by implication, chooses to avoid his company entirely. By contrast, the **upright** person is taken **into [God's] confidence.** The Hebrew which lies behind this term **confidence** can also be rendered "council" (as in a group of God's counselors [Genesis 49:6; Job 15:8; Psalm 89:7]), "intimacy" (Job 19:19, 29:4), "fellowship" (Psalm 55:14), and "secret" (Proverbs 11:13; see Psalm 25:14; Amos 3:7 KJV). Since God's reaction to the **perverse** man is avoidance (Prov. 3:32), perhaps the best word ought to express God's desire to be close to the upright person, such as council, intimacy or fellowship.

3. SUMMARY: GOD CURSES THE WICKED BUT BLESSES THE RIGHTEOUS 3:33-35

Proverbs 3:33-35 concludes this appeal to wisdom by contrasting God's dealings with the wicked and the righteous (see 1:32-33; 2:21-22; Psalm 1:6), especially as it concerns the core social institution, **the home** (Prov. 3:33). How fitting—mockers are mocked while those who have humbled themselves are exalted (**grace** [3:34] is the same term translated **ornament** in verse 22).[4] This call to wisdom concludes with a reminder that God will make a final disposition: The wise will inherit honor, and the fools will inherit shame.

ENDNOTES

[1]A covenant is a solemn promise made binding by a pledge or vow, which may be either a verbal formula or a symbolic action. Covenant often referred to a legal obligation in ancient times. In Old Testament terms, the word was often used in describing the relationship between God and His chosen people, in which their sacrifices of blood afforded them His atonement for sin, and in which their fulfillment of a promise to live in obedience to God was rewarded by His blessings. In New Testament terms, this relationship (the new covenant) was now made possible on a personal basis through Jesus Christ and His sacrifice of His own blood.

[2]Law refers to either the Levitical Code (all God's rules and regulations), the Ten Commandments, or the Pentateuch (the first five books of the Old Testament: Genesis, Exodus, Leviticus, Numbers, and Deuteronomy). It is often capitalized when it means the Pentateuch or the Ten Commandments.

[3]The New International Version and other translations use LORD in small capitals following an initial capital L to denote "Yahweh" in the original Hebrew.

[4]Both James and Peter quote verse 34 (see James 4:6; 1 Peter 5:5).

PROVERBS 4

4:1-27

Once again the invitation to embrace wisdom is issued. The cumulative effect of these frequent and earnest invitations indicates how important it is to become wise. This invitation differs from the preceding in that it reflects a father's advice to his sons based on advice he received from his father. We see a direct quote from this grandfather in Proverbs 4:4-9. It would appear that 4:10-27 (as well as 5:1-6) also reflects "grandfather's wisdom" since "son" (rather than "sons"; see 4:1) is used throughout, and all personal pronouns are singular. By hearing this wisdom, the sons gain time-tested insights, insights they have had opportunity to see practiced by their father. This invitation, like those which preceded it, is predominately positive. That is, instead of laying out a list of prohibitions, the father commands the pursuit of wisdom and offers wonderful incentives to do so. The implications for child rearing are obvious.[1] It should also be noted that although God is not explicitly mentioned in this chapter, His presence is implied throughout as the author of wisdom, the protector of the righteous, and the giver of life— all qualities attributed to Him in previous chapters.

1. A FATHER'S WISDOM 4:1-4a

After inviting his sons to hear and obey his counsel, the father begins to relate, in the form of proverbs, his father's advice given when he was just **a boy** (4:3). By describing himself as **tender, and an only child of my mother** (4:3), he not only relates how special he was to his parents, but he intensifies the importance of the counsel; one takes greater care of what is especially dear. The wisdom this father will relate is divided into four parts: 4:4b-9; 4:10-19; 4:20-27; 5:1-6.

2. GRANDFATHER'S ADVICE 4:4b-9

The acquisition of wisdom should be a top priority because understanding, if gripped wholeheartedly, brings life itself (see Proverbs 4:4b-5). There is a profound irony here in that wisdom, while it is supremely valuable, can be found in the humblest home. More of what is meant by **you will live** (4:4) can be gleaned from verse 6 where protection results from loving wisdom (see 2:8, 11 where the same two Hebrew verbs are used, there translated "guard" and "protect").

The Hebrew of 4:7 is abrupt, perhaps deliberately so. The New International Version translation is acceptable, but requires one to add **therefore.** Another possibility, more blunt but more accurate, would be "The beginning of wisdom is this: Get wisdom." If this is the correct reading, the author is saying that wisdom does not require "brains or opportunity, but decision. 'Do you want it? Come and get it.'"[2] Although the second part of 4:7 could be rendered "Whatever else you get," the NIV is probably correct to translate it **though it cost all you have.**

The first section of advice ends with two verses richly crafted in the original. Both 4:8 and 4:9 are examples of *chiasmus,* where the parallel phrases in the first part of each verse are inverted in the second part. This literary device, meant to heighten the pleasure of hearing these words as well as for ease of memorization, would be literally rendered,

Esteem her, and she will exalt you;
She will honor you, if you embrace her (4:8).
She will set on your head a garland of grace
A crown of splendor she will present you (4:9).

Not only is the description of wisdom beautiful, but wisdom beautifies its possessor (see 1:9).

3. TWO PATHS 4:10-19

The second section of advice (see Proverbs 4:10-19) presents two paths that lie before the **son** (4:10). The first path (see 4:10-13), that of **wisdom,** promises great blessings such as long **life** (4:10). More literally, this verse promises that "words will become to you years of life." While not as clear as the New International Version's translation, such a rendering begins to capture the power that lies within wise words. The path of wisdom is **straight** (4:11; see 3:6) and, therefore, easier to travel. Note that the father giving the advice can speak of himself as guiding the son in the way of wisdom and leading him along straight paths. A good role model and faithful guide is of inestimable worth in teaching others how to walk the path of wisdom. The way of wisdom is not only **straight;** it is smooth, which makes it possible to **walk** or even **run** without difficulty (4:12). It is also the safe path for it is one's very **life** (4:13). The wise hiker remains on the marked path, knowing that that path was laid out by one who knew the best and safest route. The way of wisdom was marked as the best and safest route by no less than the Creator himself, and only a fool would take another path.

That, however, is precisely what some have done. The path of the **wicked** and **evil men** is described in 4:14-17. Under no circumstances should this son even set his foot down on that path because it is a shortcut to disaster. Those who travel this route have a pathological appetite for violence; it is their food and drink. With such fellow travelers, danger lurks around every bend (see 1:10-19). In 4:18-19 **the path of the righteous** is contrasted with that **of the wicked,** a comparison we have seen before (see 1:32-33; 2:20-22; 3:33-35). The difference is, literally, as that of **light** and **darkness** (4:18-19). For the **righteous,** things get clearer the farther they travel. For the wicked, however, the path is shrouded in **darkness** so **deep** they cannot even tell what they stumble over (4:19). This same Hebrew term is used in Exodus 10:22 to describe the plague of darkness God sent on the Egyptians, a darkness so thick it could "be felt" and which kept all the Egyptians prisoners in their own homes (see Exodus 10:21, 23). Little wonder such darkness appears as a symbol of God's final judgment in Zephaniah 1:15.

4. GUARD YOUR HEART 4:20-27

Once again the father calls for his **son** to **pay attention** and **listen** carefully (4:20). By repeating this summons we are reminded that "a major part of godliness lies in dogged attentiveness to familiar truths."[3] A striking feature of this third section of advice in Proverbs 4 is the frequent mention of body parts (occasionally lost in translation). In today's terms, we might understand his advice as "put your body into the pursuit of wisdom." **Listen closely** is really "incline your ear" (4:20), while **your sight** is, literally, "your eyes" (4:21). One's ears, eyes, and heart (see 4:21) should be given over to the pursuit of wisdom. A body so engaged will be a body blessed with **life . . . and health** (4:22; see 3:7-8).

The reference to body parts continues in verses 23 through 27: **Guard your heart** (4:23a). **Wellspring** (4:23b) is, literally, "outgoings," a term usually used in a geographic context to describe the boundaries of a given territory. Here it probably refers to the "source" or "springs" of life. The most important piece of real estate in any town in Israel was the spring that provided water to that town. In ninth-century B.C. Megiddo, an elaborate water system was built including a shaft nearly one hundred feet deep and a tunnel over two hundred feet long, all through solid rock. The purpose for such a costly system was to bring the water from a camouflaged spring safely inside the city walls and secure the city in case of siege. No less diligent effort is needed to protect one's heart and, thereby, one's life from disaster.[4]

The **mouth** and **lips** (4:24) should be engaged in wise speech—that is, speech that is straightforward and not deceptive. Your **eyes** and **gaze** (literally, "eyelids"; 4:25) should be focused on the path ahead, either to watch where you are going or, more likely, to show unswerving determination to your task. Verse 26 could either be a call to **make level paths** or "consider the paths"; the latter is probably to be preferred since this verse and the next call for a person to remain on the right paths (4:27). Not only should your ears, eyes, heart, mouth, lips, eyes, and eyelids be fully engaged in the wise way, but also your **feet** (4:26-27), reminding us that wisdom that does not prove itself in daily practice is not true wisdom.

ENDNOTES

[1]That there is a place for negative prohibitions is indicated by 3:27-35.

[2]Derek Kidner, *Proverbs: An Introduction and Commentary,* Tyndale Old Testament Commentaries, ed. D. J. Wiseman (Downers Grove, Illinois: InterVarsity Press, 1964), p. 67.

[3]Ibid., p. 68.

[4]This verse may lie behind several sayings of Jesus, including Mark 7:15-23; Luke 6:45; John 4:14; 7:38.

5

PROVERBS 5

5:1-23

We see the fatherly wisdom shared in Proverbs 4 continuing in chapter 5.

1. WATCH OUT FOR THAT WOMAN 5:1-6

If we were correct to assign all of Proverbs 4 to grandfatherly advice (see opening remarks of chapter 4 of the commentary), we must see that advice here in 5:1-6 as well.

Having counseled his **son** (5:1) to choose the proper path and remain on it, the father warns against a very dangerous by-path: that which leads to the house of the adulterous woman. After an introductory summons, a description of the adulteress follows. Attention is drawn to her speech rather than to the physical appeal of extramarital affairs, such as the woman's beauty or the delights of lovemaking. Perhaps this is to draw a connection with the reference to **lips** in 5:2. More likely, such a focus is meant to highlight the important role of speech in illicit sexual affairs. Counselors tell us that such affairs are not usually about a desire for sex but result from a longing to be admired, appreciated, understood, and respected. The woman's words are tailor-made for such a task—sweet as **honey,** smooth as **oil** (5:3), and full of the seductive flattery necessary to entice a young man. **Speech** is, literally, "palate" (5:3). This word can be used literally to refer to the place in the mouth where taste is localized (24:13; Job 6:30; 12:11; 20:13; 34:3; Song of Songs 2:3) or figuratively as the capacity of discernment (Psalm 119:103) or breath (Song of Songs 7:9). None of these seem to fit our passage. Palate can also refer to the mouth (Hosea 8:1) or the mouth specifically as the organ of speech (Proverbs 8:7; Job 31:30; 33:2). It can also refer to that place where speech is constricted when the tongue sticks to the roof of the mouth (Psalm 137:6; Lamentations 4:4; Ezekiel 3:26). But nothing like this can happen to the adulteress with her oily palate; she always has just the right word to say.

Such sweetness brings the bitterest results[1]; what was smooth as **oil** will cut like a razor. **In the end** (Prov. 5:4) could mean when she finishes with you, when she reaches her destiny, or idiomatically "when all is said and done." The adulteress is destined for destruction because she does not think carefully about the right paths (**She gives no thought** translates the same verb used in 4:26); she does not even know that **her paths are crooked** (5:6). With these ominous words, the grandfatherly advice concludes.

2. WARNING AGAINST ADULTERY 5:7-14

The father of the **sons** (5:7) continues to warn against adultery. He follows his introductory summons and warning against even going near the house of the adulteress (see Proverbs 5:7-8) with reasons (see 5:9-14). Essentially, the price for such folly is everything: strength, time, wealth, labor, health, conscience, and reputation. **Best strength** (5:9) is usually translated "splendor" or "majesty" when used of God or the king; when used of ordinary people it usually refers to "beauty" (Hosea 14:6; see KJV), "authority" (Numbers 27:20) or, as here, "strength" (Daniel 10:8). The **one who is cruel** (Prov. 5:9) could be the adulteress, her husband, a blackmailer, or society in general; the term is deliberately vague but frightening. Elsewhere it is used to describe a person who lacks the capacity to be kind (see 12:10) and a merciless, marauding army whose arrival produces paralysis, pain, and terror (see Jeremiah 6:23). A closely related word describes those so cruel they refuse to feed their own children (see Lamentations 4:3). Take this course of action, and you have put yourself in the hands of the pitiless. **Strangers** will feast (literally "taking their fill") **on your wealth**[2] while you work as a slave in the household of another, a picturesque description of how adultery impoverishes and puts you at the mercy of others (Prov. 5:10).

At the end of your life (5:11) translates essentially the same Hebrew term as **in the end** in 5:4. "When all is said and done" **you will groan** to realize what you have lost (5:11). **Groan,** usually used to describe the roaring of a lion or the crashing of the sea, is only once used to describe a quieter moaning (see Ezekiel 24:23). Perhaps this **groan** is a loud, grief-stricken cry of remorse. Attracted by the promise of admiration, appreciation, and respect, the adulterer finds himself sucked completely dry, exposed to public humiliation (**whole assembly**), and at **the brink of utter ruin** (Prov. 5:14).

3. FIDELITY: THE ALTERNATIVE TO ADULTERY 5:15-20

Instead of adultery, the sons are encouraged to practice marital fidelity, a delightful alternative as suggested by the choice of metaphor, **water** (5:15). Even today, the Middle East knows no element more essential to life. The **cistern** collects rainwater while the **well** has **running water** (5:15), a term which speaks primarily to the water's refreshing quality.[3] Verse 16 could be interpreted in a positive sense: "Let thy fountains be dispersed abroad, and rivers of waters in the streets" (KJV). Commentator Derek Kidner takes this view, arguing that "strict fidelity is not an impoverishing isolationism: from such a marriage, blessing streams out in the persons and influences of a true family."[4] Given the context, however, the New International Version is probably correct to understand it as a prohibition against sexual activity outside of marriage, warning offenders that **strangers** (5:17, a masculine plural noun as in 5:10) will take possession of all that was theirs (see 5:9-14).

What a contrast with the joys of marital fidelity where one can drink freely at one's fountain, a perpetual source of refreshment and progeny. The phrase, **wife of your youth** (5:18) suggests that marriage can still bring delight long after physical appearance has faded. She remains a lovely and graceful creature whose **breasts satisfy** and whose **love [captivates]** (5:19) or, as the same term is translated in 20:1, intoxicates. Such a marriage remains the best antidote to the boredom that often precipitates extramarital affairs. Only a fool would choose the death-dealing **adulteress** over his life-giving wife (5:20).

4. GOD SEES ALL WE DO 5:21-23

The worst consequence of all is described in Proverbs 5:21-23. Even if your actions go unnoticed by others, "the LORD sees everything you do. Wherever you go, he is watching" (5:21 TEV). By God's design, our actions contain a portion of our punishment. A man is caught and bound by his own sin (see 5:22); he loses all: strength, time, wealth, labor, health, and reputation (see 5:9-14). What looked like the path to greatest pleasure and fulfillment is revealed in the end as a fool's errand, the result of a **lack of discipline** and **great folly** (5:23).

ENDNOTES

[1]Gall is an herb, proverbial for its bitterness and often associated with punishment.

[2]Or strength. Either is possible, although wealth seems more likely since it parallels the result of labor in verse 10b and since strength is included in verse 9.

[3]F. Delitzsch, *Proverbs, Ecclesiastes, Song of Solomon,* Commentary on the Old Testament, by C. F. Keil and F. Delitzsch, vol. 10 (Grand Rapids, Michigan: Wm. B. Eerdmans Publishing Co., 1978 [1872]), p. 127.

[4]Derek Kidner, *Proverbs: An Introduction and Commentary,* Tyndale Old Testament Commentaries, ed. D. J. Wiseman (Downers Grove, Illinois: InterVarsity Press, 1964), p. 70.

PROVERBS 6

6:1-35

Parental instruction continues in Proverbs 6, here warning against guaranteeing the payment of another's loan (6:1-5), against idleness (6:6-11), and against interpersonal discord (6:12-19) before returning to a warning against adultery (6:20-35). Although none of these dangers is directly spiritual, even "secular" activities like our business dealings, our work ethic, our interpersonal relationships and our love lives matter to God.

1. WARNING AGAINST SURETYSHIP 6:1-5

The book of Proverbs has much to say about guaranteeing the payment of another's loan—suretyship—all of it negative (see 11:15; 17:18; 20:16; 22:26; 27:13). Perhaps it is because the Law of Moses[1] is silent on this matter that the writers of Proverbs thought it necessary to emphasize it. The warning in 6:1-5 begins with a description of such a deal, first in the positive light as it appears to those involved (see 6:1), then negatively, as it really is (see 6:2). The handshake (**struck hands in pledge**) which you thought brought security to your neighbor actually **trapped** and **ensnared** you. This is one reason why Proverbs so harshly condemns surety; it violates the connection between one's actions and their results, an important component of this book. Now all your present and future earnings are shackled to the whims of **another,** entirely out of your control. Perhaps another reason Proverbs so harshly condemns surety concerns its connection with one's words, an important indicator of wisdom. The phrase "words of your mouth" occurs twice in 6:2 (translated differently by the NIV in 6:2a), suggesting that the pledge of surety is an example of careless speech.

How does the prohibition against surety fit God's command in Leviticus 19:18 to love one's neighbor? First, the prohibitions of

67

Proverbs are against making a pledge for someone unrelated; one could presumably do so for a family member. Second, one must inquire as to the motive for making such a pledge. Is it love to say yes to a bad idea merely because you lack the courage or forethought to say no? Is it love to say yes in order to be accepted, to make money, or to put someone else in your debt? If you really loved your neighbor as yourself, you could make an interest-free loan or a contribution.

Whatever the reason, surety is so serious that freedom must be obtained at almost any cost (see 6:3-5). The Hebrew word translated **press your plea** (6:3) implies an earnest, even forceful or bullying, appeal. You must be willing to violate social conventions and even sleep (see 6:4) to break the pledge. Your effort must have the swiftness of a gazelle (see 2 Samuel 2:18; 1 Chronicles 12:8) and the intensity of a bird seeking freedom from a trap. Note, however, that one must be released from the pledge. Promises must be kept, in spite of the consequences.

2. WARNING AGAINST IDLENESS 6:6-11

Another danger for the young is idleness, warned against in Proverbs 6:6-11. Either a person other than the son is being spoken to or else the son is addressed as **sluggard** for the purpose of emphasis. He is advised to **go the ant** and learn wisdom (6:6). Because wisdom played such an important role in the creation of this world (see 3:19-20), there is much evidence of wisdom to be found within it, even in some of its smallest inhabitants. The ant needs no one to tell it what to do, while the sluggard refuses the direction offered (see 6:9). The ant knows when it is time to work, while the sluggard seems conscious only of **sleep, slumber,** and **rest** (6:10). The ant is aware of what is coming and prepares for it, while the sluggard seems oblivious to everything, including imminent disaster (see 6:10-11). The tenacity of the ant,[2] implied in this description, contrasts with the wimpishness of the sluggard who "does not commit himself to a refusal, but deceives himself by the smallness of his surrenders."[3] The ant makes a wonderful picture of efficiency, while the sluggard is worthy of ridicule as he lies in bed begging for a little more time to rest. Unlike the ant which can count on food in lean times, the sluggard can only look forward to a surprise visit from **poverty, . . . and scarcity** which will surprise him **like a bandit** (or "vagrant" [NJB]) and an **armed man** (or "beggar" [NJB]; 6:11).

3. WARNING AGAINST INTERPERSONAL DISCORD 6:12-19

Proverbs 6:12-19 provides a warning against interpersonal discord first by pointing out that such behavior brings punishment (see 6:12-15) and second by explaining the reason for punishment: God hates dissension (see 6:16-19). The description of the **scoundrel** and **villain** (6:12; literally, "a worthless man, an evil man" [see 6:24 for a description of "an evil woman"]) contains a series of phrases implying secrecy and subtlety (see 6:12-14) which sharply contrast with the sudden and irreversible disaster that awaits him (see 6:15). Notice how the description moves from **mouth, eye, feet,** and **fingers** to the **heart** of the matter (6:13-14). The focal point for this long sentence (6:12-14) and the reason for all the secrecy is the final phrase: **He always stirs up dissension.** The one who brings discord will be destroyed in an instant without any chance to protect himself.

Disaster comes because sowing discord is something God hates (see 6:16-19). The **six things** . . . no **seven** (a literary device designed to heighten tension) mentioned are sins committed against another person, and they are (literally) an abomination to God's soul. **Haughty eyes** look down from a position of self-elevated superiority on everyone else. Reference to the **lying tongue** reminds us how deeply God cares about truth in our conversation (6:17). The next phrase not only implies violence, but especially violence committed on the innocent.

The progression here may indicate an intensifying of harm: Lies hurt more than proud looks; physical injury against the innocent is worst of all. Such harm begins in the heart, a realm transparent to God's gaze; even the planning of such schemes is abhorrent to Him. Ready inclination and not just action is also implied in **feet that are quick to rush into evil** (6:18). Since deceptive words have already been condemned (see 6:17b), perhaps **false witness** refers to the legal system (6:19). Justice cannot be served when those charged with telling the truth lie "with every breath" (6:19 NJB). The conclusion of this list, number one on God's "Top Seven Things I Hate," is the **man who stirs up dissension among brothers** (6:19). By repeating words from 6:14, the writer has joined these two sections into one warning: God wants people to get along with one another. For those who have become part of the family of God, such a reminder is especially important, whether we are at home or church.

4. CONTINUED WARNING AGAINST ADULTERY 6:20-35

Once again the "parent" warns against adultery (see Proverbs 6:20-35), in part because it is such a serious offense with such dire consequences, and in part because the person who can control his physical appetite has come a long way toward wisdom. Self-control is fostered by listening to parental advice (see 6:20); continual reminders of what is right (see 6:21; also Deuteronomy 6:4-9); and an appreciation for the benefits of righteousness, including guidance (see Proverbs 6:22a), protection (6:22b), counsel (6:22c), illumination (6:23), and life itself (6:23b). Wisdom will also keep you from the adulteress (6:24-35), described here in similar terms to those found in earlier warnings: smooth tongued (2:16; 5:3) and wayward (2:16; 5:20).

Infidelity begins, as does the sin of spreading dissension, in the heart when one becomes too captivated by appearances—the warning in 6:25b is, literally, "Don't let her take you with her eyelashes"—to remember the end result (see 6:26-35). Sleeping with a prostitute is costly enough: loss of money, reputation, health. The cost of an adulterous affair is life itself. The excuse, "That may be true for everyone else, but not me," is at least as old as the book of Proverbs, for the writer answers that excuse with two rhetorical questions. As no one can carry hot coals or walk on them without being burned, so no one can escape the consequences of adultery (see 6:27-29). This is true, in part, because, like contact with hot coals, the punishment is part of the act itself.

As in 5:14, the consequence noted is public disgrace (see 6:30-35). A thief who steals to feed himself must still repay seven times what he stole,[4] even if people can sympathize with his actions (see 6:30-31). The person who "steals" another man's wife clearly **lacks judgment,** for he will never be able to repay that debt (6:32-35). Since the same Hebrew word is rendered **hunger** in 6:30 and **himself** in 6:32, the son is reminded that instead of satisfying his soul, the adulterer destroys it permanently since the offended husband will burn with an unquenchable jealousy.[5]

ENDNOTES

[1]Law of Moses refers to the Pentateuch (the first five books of the Old Testament: Genesis, Exodus, Leviticus, Numbers, and Deuteronomy).

[2]Such tenacity is pictured in this ancient Near Eastern proverb: "When even ants are smitten, they do not accept it passively, but they bite the hand of the man who smites them" (James B. Pritchard, ed., *Ancient Near Eastern Texts Relating*

to the Old Testament, 3rd ed. [Princeton: Princeton University Press, 1969], p. 486).

[3]Derek Kidner, *Proverbs: An Introduction and Commentary,* Tyndale Old Testament Commentaries, ed. D. J. Wiseman (Downers Grove, Illinois: InterVarsity Press, 1964), p. 42.

[4]Since the Law (see endnote 1) does not call for sevenfold repayment, this penalty may be a later modification or the number seven could have been chosen to represent full repayment.

[5]The Hebrew noun translated **fury** can be translated as "heat" (Hosea 7:5) or "hot anger" (Ezekiel 3:14) or with the implication of fire (Jeremiah 4:4; 21:12; Lamentations 2:4; Nahum 1:6), linking this picture with those of Proverbs 6:27-28.

PROVERBS 7

7:1-27

A s a pastor I encountered many people, even professing Christians, involved in adulterous relationships. Their explanations, when confronted, betrayed their shortsightedness. The excitement of the moment had blinded them to the consequences of their actions: broken hearts, splintered families, lost reputations, diseased bodies, divine judgment. However adultery may appear to our society, Proverbs 7 reveals God's perspective: Those who practice it are senseless (verse 7) and deceived (verses 5, 10, 21), and will not escape punishment (verses 22-23, 26-27). Because the truth about adultery is so important and yet so easily obscured in the heat of passion, and because repetition is a good teaching tool, Proverbs returns frequently to this topic.

1. AVOIDING ADULTERY 7:1-5

This warning begins with a summons to wisdom (see Proverbs 7:1-5). The path to sin is not blocked by knowledge; truths, like speed bumps, may slow you down, but they will not stop you. To block the path you need to treasure wisdom, guarding it as instinctively as you would your own eyes (**the apple of your eye** refers to the eye's pupil; 7:2). Wisdom needs to become a constant companion. It must be at your fingertips and permanently inscribed **on the tablet of your heart,** where it can influence decisions when and where they are made (7:3). Wisdom must become as close as a sister (this word can also be translated as lover [see Song of Songs 4:9-10, 12]) and become a close companion (see Proverbs 7:4). This brings life by enabling you to avoid the **adulteress** and the **wayward wife** (7:5), whose "house is a highway to the grave" (7:27).

2. SCENE OF ENTICEMENT 7:6-23

The truth of Proverbs 7:1-5 is driven home by a graphic portrayal of enticement that follows in verses 6 through 23. The victim, "one boy who had no sense" (7:7 NJB), lingers near the house of such a woman, apparently hoping for a rendezvous. It is dark, quite dark; the writer uses four separate Hebrew terms in verse 9 to describe the blackness of the scene. "And look, a woman is coming to meet him" (7:10 NJB) not only announces the arrival of the villainess but also translates a Hebrew word (left out of the NIV) meant to add vividness to the scene. While not a prostitute, this woman resembles one in behavior and appearance ("dressed to kill" is how one commentator describes her[1]). **With crafty intent** (7:10; literally, "guarded of heart") could mean either deceptive or calloused. The next two descriptive terms—**loud and defiant** (7:11)—are also subject to various translations. The first might instead be translated "unstable" or "restless" (like the sea in Jeremiah 6:23); the second could be rendered "rebellious" (see Nehemiah 9:29; Jeremiah 5:23) or "stubborn" (Deuteronomy 21:18). These terms may be ambiguous, but the overall impression is of a woman out of control, her own and God's.

Proverbs 7:11b-12 make clear that this woman has rejected the role and duties society assigned her; she is the reverse image of the woman in 31:10-31. While our society values and encourages such independence, Israelite culture considered it dangerous, and such a woman was a threat to society. Like a hunter **she lurks** until, **with a brazen face** (7:13; literally, "hardened face") to shield her true purposes, she springs her attack by brandishing feigned affection and deceptive words.

What follows in 7:14-20 is a good example of the "smooth speech" about which 5:3 speaks. Cleverly she weaves her words to appeal to the young man's urges and allay his fears. She strokes his vanity by describing him as the sole object of her affections. Three times in 7:15 she uses the pronoun **you** (although verses 12 and 26 make it clear he is not her only interest). With the meat left over from her sacrifices at the Temple, she is having a feast, and she desires the young man to be her special guest (see 7:14). What attractive bait to a young man: a feast with himself as the honored guest. How ironic that food remaining from sacrifices to God, food intended as God's blessing to the offerer, becomes a pretext for immorality.

There is more than meat on the menu, however. This feast would be only the appetizer for a night of lovemaking described in such a way as to appeal to all the senses (see 7:16-18). The woman's **husband** has gone away for a long time so there is no danger of detection (7:19-20).

Her smooth talk succeeds quickly and easily (**all at once** [7:22]) since the young fool lacked the wisdom that would enable him to resist temptation. His destiny is illustrated by three comparisons intended to drive home the seriousness of his situation. He is **like an ox going to the slaughter, . . . a deer stepping into a noose** and **a bird darting into a snare** (7:22-23), each unaware of the doom which awaits it. The second comparison literally reads "as anklets until the chastisement of a fool," a phrase many translators—ancient and modern—have found necessary to modify to something like the New International Version's rendering.[2]

In some ways this scene resembles the description of sexual love in Song of Songs but with several striking differences. In both one drinks deeply of love, and both seek to heighten the pleasure by appealing to the senses of sight and smell. One difference between the scenes in Proverbs 7 and in Song of Songs concerns the roles played by man and woman. In Song of Songs they enjoy a relationship between equals, both initiating and both responding. Here the man never speaks and is passively swept away by the woman's deception. More important, the outcome between the two scenes differs markedly. In Song of Songs the couple experiences unbridled joy while Proverbs 7 speaks of judgment and disaster.[3] Perhaps the writer of Proverbs 7 deliberately crafted his words to resemble the picture in Song of Songs in order to contrast sexual intimacy which is God ordained, with that cursed by God.

3. FINAL WARNING 7:24-27

As if the previous scene were not clear enough, the parent reappears to drive home the point as sharply as possible (**sons** [7:24]). First, keep in mind parental advice (see Proverbs 7:24), an easy thing if it is jealously guarded (7:2) and continually evident (7:3a). Next, watch your heart (7:25), something also made easier when what is right is permanently inscribed where decisions are made (7:3b). Then, watch your actions; do not even walk on "the street near her corner" or "in the direction of her house" (7:8). Finally, think past the "full moon" (7:20); keep the long view, considering the outcome of your choices (7:26-27). Do not be so flattered by temptation you forget to lift up her veil and see how ugly she really is.

ENDNOTES

[1]Derek Kidner, *Proverbs: An Introduction and Commentary,* Tyndale Old Testament Commentaries, ed. D. J. Wiseman (Downers Grove, Illinois: InterVarsity Press, 1964), p. 75.

[2]**A deer stepping into a noose.** For the literal rendering, see Owens, John Joseph, *Ezra–Song of Solomon,* Analytical Key to the Old Testament, vol. 3 (Grand Rapids, Michigan: Baker Book House, 1991), p. 540. One translation retains the original Hebrew and renders it passably: "Like a fool to the stocks for punishment" (NJPS).

[3]For more on the similarities and contrasts, see Daniel Grossberg, "Two Kinds of Sexual Relationships in the Hebrew Bible," *Hebrew Studies,* vol. 35 (1994), pp. 7–25.

8

PROVERBS 8

8:1-36

We have met Lady Wisdom before. In Proverbs 1 she took to the streets to scold the simple, and she appeared in chapters 3 and 4 as the source of rich blessings. The scene in chapter 8 elaborates on these earlier descriptions. In this chapter, Wisdom also serves as a foil to the adulteress of chapter 7. As the wayward wife paraded her offerings, so does Wisdom, although the outcomes are as different as night and day. Proverbs 8 suggests yet another contrast. Israel's neighbors produced literature containing lengthy passages in which their goddesses recommended themselves as worthy of worship. Lady Wisdom is praised, but not as a goddess; Yahweh's superiority to her and all other gods is clear from 8:22-31 and elsewhere.[1] With this literary device, however, the writer has obtained a platform to display Wisdom's wares.[2]

1. INTRODUCTION TO WISDOM'S INVITATION 8:1-3

As seen in Proverbs 1:20-21, Wisdom takes to the streets to make her message known (see 8:1-3). She chooses to move where the throng is thickest so as to gain maximum impact. Such a pedestrian beginning is striking. "A chapter which is to soar beyond time and space," said one commentator, "opens at street level, to make it clear . . . that the wisdom of God is as relevant to the shopping centre . . . as to heaven itself. . . ."[3] Wisdom's aggressiveness here reminds us that our "search" for wisdom is, in fact, a response to wisdom's search for us.

2. WISDOM'S INVITATION 8:4-36

a. Call (8:4-5). Having taken her place among the crowd, Wisdom issues her invitation to all humanity, even the **simple** and **foolish** (8:5; the same ones mentioned in Proverbs 1:22).

b. Testimonial to the Value of Wisdom (8:6-21). Those who possess wisdom gain great advantage both for right living and right decisions. What she has to say is **worthy** (8:6), a striking word usually translated "princes" or "nobility" (see the use of this word in Proverbs 28:16) serving as a reminder of the high value of her **right, true,** and **just** words (8:6-8). At first, her words may not seem right. They may appear restrictive, illogical, and so much less exciting than the words of the adulteress in 7:14-20. **To the discerning** and **those who have knowledge,** however, their value is unmistakable (8:9), for they steer one clear of **wickedness** and perversity (8:7-8). Her words are worth more than **silver, choice gold, rubies,** or anything else one could **desire** (8:10-11) since they not only make it possible to attain **wealth** (see 8:18, 21) but promise something more permanently beneficial, "life" itself (8:35).

Wisdom not only enables right living, but right decisions as well, since she has a close acquaintance with **prudence** and owns **knowledge and discretion** (8:12). To **fear the LORD**[4]—that is, "the beginning of knowledge" (8:13; 1:7)—is to hate evil with the same hatred Lady Wisdom feels toward it (see 8:13). The joining of verse 12's **prudence** with verse 13's hatred of **evil** calls to mind Jesus' words in Matthew: "Be as shrewd as snakes and as innocent as doves" (Matt. 10:16b). **I have understanding** (Prov. 8:14) is, literally, "I am understanding." She is able to give counsel, sound wisdom, and strength because understanding is at the heart of who she is. Those who rule justly do so with the wisdom she gives.[5] By keeping together verse 18 with verses 17, 19, 20, and 21, we avoid the mistake of viewing wisdom as a shortcut to wealth. Those who obtain wisdom must **love** and **seek** her, not just what she brings (verse 17). Yes, Wisdom provides **riches, honor, enduring wealth and prosperity,** but her **fruit is *better* than fine gold** and *surpasses* **choice silver** (8:18-19, my emphasis). You will find wisdom only when you look for her **in the way of righteousness** and **along the paths of justice;** only then will she reward you with full **treasuries** (8:20-21). Wisdom's supremacy over all she has to give is also apparent since in verses 14 through 17a the possessive and personal pronouns, **I, mine,** and **me** are emphatic; "wisdom itself, not its beneficiaries (14-17) nor its benefits (18-21) may dominate the scene."[6] All of this is available for those who love wisdom and make her the object of their earnest pursuit (see 8:20-21).

c. Wisdom's Role in Creation (8:22-31). That wisdom's value is worth pursuing is seen in her role in creation. Any force powerful enough to play a part in creation is worth possessing. If God found Wisdom useful to do His work, how much more will we. These verses not only speak of Wisdom's role in creation, they also show that Wisdom is woven into the fabric of creation. The realization of this is what gives Wisdom so much joy (see 8:30-31). To possess wisdom is to know the code that unlocks life at its best. By comparing this passage with passages like John 1:3, many have seen here a picture of Christ. Paul may have been alluding to this passage in Colossians 1:15-17 and 2:3. Without denying the similarities, it seems more in line with the evidence to say that the writer of Proverbs was not thinking of the Messiah but of a personified Wisdom; we can learn much by reading it in this light. That such passages were later expanded with deeper meaning speaks to the relevancy of the Bible and the creativity of its Divine author.

While the main idea of the passage is clear enough, several phrases are quite difficult and can be understood in different ways. No little debate has swirled around the first line in Proverbs 8:22. Was Wisdom "created . . . at the beginning of his work" (8:22 RSV; see **brought . . . forth** [NIV]) or was she "possessed" (see NIV margin note)? Both meanings make sense but, since "possessed" is the meaning in most other places where this Hebrew verb is used, that may be the preferred reading here as well. Either way, 8:23-26 makes clear that she was born prior to creation. When verse 8:26b is translated more literally—"or the sum of the dust of the world"—it suggests that perhaps humanity is being described.

Wisdom's role in the beginning is also unclear. Was she a **craftsman** (8:30),[7] a "young child" (according to rabbinical interpreters), or a "confidant" (NJPS)? Some have understood this as a noun referring to God: "I was beside the master craftsman" (8:30a NJB). Others have taken it as a verb meaning "make secure": "Then I was beside him binding all together."[8] A recent proposal returns to a variation on the rabbinical interpretation, suggesting that *wisdom* should be taken as a verb meaning "being raised" or "growing up." Now Wisdom is fully grown and serves as guardian and teacher of her pupils.[9] Whichever is the best interpretation, the builder in 8:22-31 is clearly Yahweh,[10] not Wisdom. Her job description includes only rejoicing at what God made, probably because she saw that everything created was "very good," including humanity (8:31; see Genesis 1:31).

d. Call to Listen to Wisdom (8:32-36). Proverbs 8, which has taken us from "street level" to beyond and before time, now returns to a very practical call for wise behavior. (Those of us responsible for preaching and teaching would be well advised to follow this example of relevance.) Instead of lingering near the adulteress's house, wait every day at the house of Wisdom, for there one **finds life and . . . favor from the LORD** (8:35)[11] and shares in the joy (8:34) which characterized Wisdom at creation (8:30-31). Only a fool would choose to do otherwise since wisdom leads to righteousness (8:7-9), is worth more than wealth (8:11, 19), brings good "judgment" (8:14-16), and is the formula for a joyous life (8:30-31). In fact, to reject wisdom means death. It may be more than coincidental that the phrase **fails to find** (8:36) comes from the same Hebrew word elsewhere translated "sin." Those who fail to find wisdom are those who refuse to look for her on the paths of righteousness and justice, and to recognize that she is looking for them. They do not love her, so they **hate** her (8:36) and die as a result.

ENDNOTES

[1]The New International Version and other translations use LORD in small capitals following an initial capital *L* to denote "Yahweh" in the original Hebrew.

[2]R. N. Whybray, *Proverbs,* The New Century Bible Commentary (Grand Rapids, Michigan: Wm. B. Eerdmans Publishing Co., 1994), p. 120.

[3]Derek Kidner, *Proverbs: An Introduction and Commentary,* Tyndale Old Testament Commentaries, ed. D. J. Wiseman (Downers Grove, Illinois: InterVarsity Press, 1964), pp. 76–77.

[4]See endnote 1.

[5]Because other Old Testament passages attribute these same qualities to God, we are reminded that wisdom is, in fact, an attribute of God, not a separate spiritual being (see verse 14 with Job 12:13; Isaiah 11:2-3).

[6]Kidner, p. 78.

[7]It has this meaning in the apocryphal book Wisdom of Solomon 7:21 and 8:5 which dates to the time between the Testaments.

[8]R. B. Y. Scott, *Proverbs, Ecclesiastes,* The Anchor Bible, vol. 18, eds. William F. Albright and David Noel Freedman (New York: Doubleday, 1965), p. 68.

[9]Michael V. Fox, "Amon Again," *Journal of Biblical Literature,* vol. 115, no. 4 (1996), pp. 699–702.

[10]See endnote 1.

[11]Ibid.

PROVERBS 9

9:1-18

The lengthy introduction to the book of Proverbs draws to a fitting conclusion with chapter 9. Wisdom's blessings, promised in Proverbs 8, are here pictured as a banquet (see 9:1-12), in striking contrast with the miserable poison on Folly's table (see 9:13-18). The diligent and thoughtful Lady Wisdom makes careful preparations for the feast while Folly, wanton, careless and loud, prepares nothing. Wisdom offers meat and wine while Folly can only promise bread and water, and stolen at that. The self-centeredness and immaturity of Lady Folly's advice—"Get what you want, even if you have to steal it" (see 9:17)—is far beneath Wisdom's counsel, and the results of such counsel are also quite different (see 9:7-9). Finally, the destiny of the hearers is contrasted; the wise enjoying long and prosperous life while the foolish perish.

1. LADY WISDOM'S BANQUET 9:1-12

Lady Wisdom, her excellence emphasized in the original Hebrew, **has built her house,** and apparently it is quite a showpiece (9:1). Since most Israelite homes were simple, four-room structures with three or four pillars, a seven-pillared house (see Proverbs 9:1) suggests a well-constructed and spacious mansion.[1] **Hewn** (9:1) implies that the pillars were made of quarried stone rather than the normal field stone or wood, and the number seven may suggest perfection. With diligence Wisdom prepares the meat, mixes the wine, sets her table, and issues the invitation. Such preparation implies that wisdom does not come easily but only with hard work. When it comes, however, it brings comfort, satisfaction, and security.

The summons is issued through **her maids** (9:3) perhaps to add color to the scene or to imply that all her household shares in the wisdom of its mistress. The Hebrew of 9:3 leaves it unclear whether she calls through the action of her servants[2] or whether she herself, fervent in her desire for guests, climbs to the highest place in the city where her call will be more widely heard (see NIV). In her summons of the **simple** and **those who lack judgment** (9:4), we are reminded that God calls to those who deserve it least but need it most. Her invitation to **eat . . . and drink** suggests the blessings inherent in obedience to God and the spiritual food which is offered to us in Christ.

Proverbs 9:6a is probably best translated "Forsake the company of fools,"[3] although some have suggested "Forsake, O Fools"[4] or, with a slight change in the Hebrew, "Forsake folly" (or **Leave your simple ways**).[5] **Walk** (9:6b) translates a Hebrew word used only here with this meaning; usually it suggests a state of blessedness. By choosing this word the author conveys the need to proceed toward true understanding where blessedness lies.

At first glance, 9:7-12 seems to bear little relation to what precedes and follows. They represent, however, Wisdom's instructions to her guests, and contrast with the counsel given by Folly in 9:17. These verses clarify the impression that our destiny is determined, not in a single moment of decision—whether one stops at the feast of Wisdom or of Folly—but by our character, whether that of wicked mocker or righteous, wise person.[6] The former, because they do not respect God, mock wisdom's self-discipline and shun the better meal for the titillation of stolen meats. The wise person has an appetite for wisdom, benefits from it, and is grateful even for correction.

The restating of the proverbs' motto in 9:10 reminds us that wisdom and righteousness belong together, just as 9:9 affirmed. Reverence for God is the key which unlocks the mysteries of time and eternity. Although the New International Version translates 9:10 identically with 1:7, a different Hebrew word for **beginning** is used. Given how this word is used elsewhere in the Old Testament,[7] Today's English Version renders it best: "To be wise you must first have reverence for the LORD," a meaning quite similar to what the author meant in 1:7. Reverence for God, the Most Holy One (**Holy** receives special emphasis in the Hebrew in 9:10), brings a long and prosperous life according to Lady Wisdom in 9:11-12. Not only do we thereby avoid the traps into which the foolish fall (9:18), but we also experience the blessings of Wisdom's feast (9:1-5) and the favor of God himself (8:35). Few Old Testament passages emphasize individual destiny as strongly as does 9:12. The meaning is not that we alone will experience the results of our choices for good or ill, since that contradicts other passages which describe how our choices impact others (see 10:1, 21). Rather, 9:12 makes it clear that our destinies rest in our own hands.

2. LADY FOLLY'S BANQUET 9:13-18

Having seen Wisdom's elaborate preparations, we now are shown her counterpart in Proverbs 9:13-18; the contrast could hardly be more striking. Some see Folly pictured here as a prostitute because of similar descriptions given earlier in Proverbs (see 7:11): her summons to drink water (9:17) used earlier as a picture of sexual relations (5:15-20) and the similar destiny for those who visit her (see 9:18 with 7:27). In any case, she is **loud** (9:13), the fault lying not in her volume (Wisdom, too, is loud; see verse 3b) but in her lack of decorum. **Undisciplined** (9:13) could be translated as the adjective "wanton," as the proper noun "wantonness,"[8] or as the noun "simpleton" (this word is related to the Hebrew word translated **simple** in verses 4, 6, 16). Either she is **without knowledge** (9:13) or she "knows no shame."[9]

By picturing her seated at her house door (see 9:14a), the writer emphasizes the contrast. She is idle, having apparently done nothing, while Wisdom never sits still. No maids are mentioned (see 9:3), implying the poverty of her household. She has not gone looking for guests and does not appear to be all that interested in finding any. Today in the Old City of Jerusalem, the more eager a merchant is for business, the further he invades your personal space; desperate ones may even grab your arm. She calls out **to those who pass by, who go straight on their way** (9:15), indicating that, unlike Wisdom, she contents herself with passersby. **Highest point of the city** (9:14) is identical to this phrase in 9:3b. Not only does the repetition of this phrase reveal the contrast between these two women, but something more may be in view. Folly might live in the most prestigious neighborhood, but a prominent address will not make her house any more secure in the end.

She, too, summons the **simple** (9:16)—those like herself (see 9:13)—and offers them this advice: "What is secured illicitly is more attractive" (see 9:17). Her words are more insidious than an invitation to a life of crime. Calling **stolen water . . . sweet** not only contradicts God's precepts (see Exodus 20:15), but calls God's very sovereignty into question, for it denies that His ways are those most blessed. Unlike the "wise" who grow "wiser" (see Proverbs 9:9), those who choose this party get more than they bargained for (9:18). Unlike the wise who experience long and abundant life (9:11-12), those who want water and bread made tasty by deceit find themselves among the dead. Only Wisdom's feast really satisfies.

ENDNOTES

[1]Others have suggested that the seven pillars refer to the seven days of creation; the Holy Spirit (F. Delitzsch, *Proverbs, Ecclesiastes, Song of Solomon,* Commentary on the Old Testament, by C. F. Keil and F. Delitzsch, vol. 10 [Grand Rapids, Michigan: Wm. B. Eerdmans Publishing Co., 1978 (1872)], p. 197); or a temple corresponding to seven-pillared temples found elsewhere in *Ancient Near Eastern Texts Relating to the Old Testament* (3rd ed., James B. Pritchard, ed. [Princeton: Princeton University Press, 1969]; cited by R. N. Whybray, *Proverbs,* The New Century Bible Commentary [Grand Rapids, Michigan: Wm. B. Eerdmans Publishing Co., 1994], p. 142).

[2]Delitzsch, p. 196.

[3]Derek Kidner, *Proverbs: An Introduction and Commentary,* Tyndale Old Testament Commentaries, ed. D. J. Wiseman (Downers Grove, Illinois: InterVarsity Press, 1964), p. 82; ASV margin; Whybray, p. 145; TEV.

[4]ASV; Delitzsch, p. 199.

[5]NJB; R. B. Y. Scott, *Proverbs, Ecclesiastes,* The Anchor Bible, vol. 18, eds. William F. Albright and David Noel Freedman, (New York: Doubleday, 1965), p. 74; RSV; NLT; Crawford H. Toy, *Proverbs,* The International Critical Commentary (New York: Charles Scribner's Sons, 1899), p. 187.

[6]Kidner, p. 82.

[7]The word can be used to speak of something that occurred earlier in time (Genesis 13:3; 41:21; 43:18; 2 Samuel 17:9; 2 Kings 17:25; Isaiah 1:26; Daniel 8:1; 9:21); something which is first in priority and time (Judges 1:1; 20:18; Nehemiah 11:17); or the beginning of an event or activity (Ruth 1:22; 2 Samuel 21:9; Ezra 4:6; Ecclesiastes 10:13; Daniel 9:23; Hosea 1:2; Amos 7:1).

[8]Delitzsch, p. 204.

[9]Kidner considers the latter reading, found in the Septuagint (the Greek version of the Old Testament, translated from the original Hebrew scrolls, and written in the second and third centuries B.C.; often indicated by the Roman numerals LXX in accordance with the legend that it was translated by seventy scribes), to be correct (p. 84).

Part Two

THE PURSUIT OF WISDOM

Proverbs 10:1–31:31

The "introduction" of Proverbs having concluded with the contrast of Ladies Wisdom and Folly (see Proverbs 9), the heart of the book begins in chapter 10.

The proverbs found from here through 22:16 are credited to Solomon (as in 1:1; see comments on authorship in the commentary's introduction) and are mainly pithy, two-line sayings or epigrams meant to drive home important life lessons. At first glance, these verses appear to have been compiled haphazardly with no attempt at thematic development. While they lack the well-arranged nature of chapters 1 through 9, the author has strung together his counsel along carefully considered lines. While each proverb is complete in itself, a close look at the author's themes, choice of words, and means of expression reveals deliberate connections. Such links, while they may appear only cosmetic, suggest deeper connections. Behind and beneath all of life's apparently random experiences is a God who holds this world together and in whom all things make sense.

Not only chapter 10, but the entire first section (10:1–22:16) appears to have been carefully arranged. Chapters 15 and 16 are focused on Yahweh[1] (see especially 15:33–16:9); 10:1 through 22:16 was organized so that, at its very heart, the emphasis would be on Yahweh. The material which begins this section (10:1–11:13) calls the reader to righteous behavior[2] and describes how the upright should behave (see, for example, 10:8, 10, 12) and the effects of such behavior both on others and on oneself (see 10:1-2). Far from random, 10:1 through 22:16 betrays thoughtful arrangement.[3]

There is a pause in Solomon's advice from 22:17 through 24:34, when we hear from unnamed "wise ones," whose counsel appears in two sections (22:17–24:22; 24:23-34). Solomon's advice continues from 25:1 through 29:27, this time preserved and transmitted thanks to the efforts of Hezekiah's court. The last words of Agur, son of Jakeh, are found in 30:1-33, followed by advice from the queen mother on how to be a good king (31:1-9). The book concludes with a poem celebrating the noble wife (31:10-31).

ENDNOTES

[1] The New International Version and other translations render this with LORD in small capital letters following an initial capital *L*.

[2] Much like what we find in Psalm 1, which serves to introduce the book of Psalms.

[3] John Goldingay, "The Arrangement of Sayings in Proverbs 10–15," *Journal for the Study of the Old Testament*, vol. 61 (1994), pp. 75–83.

PROVERBS 10

10:1-32

T his chapter contains many of the themes we will meet throughout the rest of Proverbs: the right and wrong uses of wealth; the benefits of righteousness; and the importance of proper speech, discipline, and hard work.

1. WISDOM: THE HEART OF THE HAPPY HOME (10:1)

This section begins at home, in the parent-child relationship. It balances the individualistic tone of Proverbs 9:12 with the reminder that whether I am wise or foolish affects more than just me. In the family- and group-oriented culture of ancient Israel, such a proverb would provide a powerful influence for good. Children would be reminded that their decisions have consequences, and parents would remember that their own happiness or misery lay, to some degree, in how they raised their children (see 15:20). The Hebrew term translated **brings joy** (10:1) reflects the joy one feels at a wedding (Psalm 45:8), Israel's response when permitted to resume rebuilding the Temple (Ezra 6:22), the response to victory in battle (2 Chronicles 20:27), and how one feels when a son is born (Jeremiah 20:15). In order to continue to experience joy, parents should work diligently to raise wise children.

2. WHAT IS YOUR MONEY WORTH? (10:2)

This and the next three verses speak on the theme of gaining wealth; more specifically, the relationships between money and morality are the concern of Proverbs 10:2-3. How ironic to say that **treasures are of no value** (10:2)! But through this irony the author reminds us that wealth, improperly obtained, cannot bring about lasting benefit (see 11:4). **Ill-gotten treasures** (10:2) is, literally, "treasures of wickedness"—that is, treasures obtained illegally. When the writer says these **are of no value,** he employs a term which can be used in a financial sense (they have no value; see Jeremiah 12:13) or a nonfinancial sense (they do not benefit; see Jeremiah 23:32). Perhaps the author wanted to suggest both ideas as in Habakkuk 2:18; Jeremiah 2:11; and Isaiah 44:9. "Treasures wickedly come by" (NJB), while they can do much, cannot deliver from death, but righteousness can because the righteous person makes choices that avoid deadly consequences (see Proverbs 10:9, 16, 25). When one adds an eternal perspective (which our author did not possess), we see that God's righteousness made available to us in Christ is able to preserve us from eternal death.

3. WHERE DOES YOUR MONEY COME FROM? (10:3)

Exploration of the relationship between money and morality continues in Proverbs 10:3, this time addressing specifically the connection between work and wealth (see similar expressions in 11:6; 13:25). Most people would express that connection according to the axiom, "We get what is coming to us." That is only part of the story, for God has made himself an active partner in the process. He meets the needs of the "soul of a righteous person" even if the person is poor. Those who are wicked, however, will find not only their profit profitless (see 10:2), but their cravings thwarted. The Hebrew word translated **thwarts** (10:3) means more than not letting the wicked have their way. It suggests that God has pushed aside their requests, refusing even to consider them (see Numbers 35:20, 22, where the NIV translates this word "shoves").

4. GOD HONORS THE DILIGENT HAND (10:4)

This and the preceding proverb were meant to be read together. Although Yahweh will provide for the righteous, He also intended the righteous to work for themselves. In fact, He designed the world in such a way that, generally speaking, our reward depends on whether we have **diligent hands** (10:4; reference to the hands continues the allusion to body parts which began in 10:3 and continues through many of the remaining proverbs in chapter 10). Such a careful design reveals God's wisdom; to put it in motion exposes His power; only a loving God would arrange things so fairly. Remember, both verses 3 and 4 must be read together. To take only the first produces lazy followers; if we take only verse 4, we forget that our wealth really comes from God.

5. MAKE HAY WHILE THE SUN SHINES (10:5)

The theme of diligent labor continues, but with a slight shift in focus. Here the contrast is not only between the lazy and the diligent, but between the one who knows when to work and the one who does not. Further, while Proverbs 10:4 spoke of the financial effects of laziness and diligence, 10:5 addresses the moral effects: **wise** or **disgraceful.** The relationship between God's blessing and human diligence, reflected in the combination of verses 3 and 4, is here brought out in one verse. Diligent labor is a by-product of wisdom which flows from a fear of God.

6. CROWNED WITH GLORY OR COVERED WITH SHAME (10:6)

Righteousness and wickedness return to view in this and the next verse. If we take the New International Version reading, the destiny of the two is being contrasted: The righteous wear a crown of blessing, while the wicked are buried beneath an avalanche of violence. The reading in the NIV margin note suggests instead that, while the righteous are clearly blessed, the wicked continue to practice deceitful and destructive speech. In the Hebrew, **overwhelms** or "conceals" (10:6) is, literally, "covers," so either translation is permissible. While the context seems to favor the NIV text, when commentator Derek Kidner describes the wicked one having violence written all over his face, he combines both.[1]

7. WHAT WILL THEY SAY ABOUT YOU WHEN YOU ARE GONE? (10:7)

From the destiny of the righteous and wicked we proceed to their memory. The repetition of **blessing** in Proverbs 10:6-7 emphasizes the favored status of the righteous both during life and after death. Note how the memory of the righteous is a source of blessing for others, while the name of the wicked rots, the result of neglect and disregard. In life the righteous are blessed; in death they bless others. People love to remember them and speak of the good they have done, each reminiscence extending the waves of blessing still further. The wicked live in such a way that after death, most would rather not speak of them at all. If they do, it often rekindles the bitter feelings, which are the legacy of such a life.

8. WILLING HEART OR OPEN MOUTH (10:8)

Contrasted here are two people familiar to all of us (see Proverbs 10:8). To be **wise in heart** is more just being wise; wisdom can be found at the very heart of who that person is. Ironically, characterizing this wisdom is the ability to **accept commands.** In other words, true wisdom is not characterized by a "know-it-all" attitude, but by a teachable, humble spirit which is willing to be directed. The second character is the **chattering fool** (literally, "foolish of lips"). This fool cannot accept commands because he or she is too busy talking. Perhaps the fool chatters about how willingly he accepts the command or how fervently she will carry it out; in fact, nothing will come of the chatter but empty words. The contrast is primarily between a person who lives from the overflow of the heart and someone so shallow that he or she is only talking lips. Such a one will be ruined—that is, pushed down and crushed (see Hosea 4:14), an easy task with someone so hollow. The destiny of the **wise in heart** (Prov. 10:8), while not specified here, is described in the proverb which follows.[2]

9. SOLID FOOTING ON STRAIGHT PATHS (10:9)

According to this proverb, the road of righteousness is the safest path to travel. **The man of integrity** (10:9; literally, "one who walks blamelessly") finds that righteousness helps him avoid pitfalls (see 13:6), while God himself shelters the traveler (see 10:29). **Crooked paths** are chosen because they bypass the moral high ground (10:9). It is easier to lie than to speak the truth and suffer the consequences. Theft is easier than hard work; it is easier to hate than to love. Such compromising shortcuts, chosen to avoid detection, one day **will be found out** (10:9); God will reveal such travelers and punish them accordingly.

10. AVOID THE SUBTLE DECEIVER AND THE LOUD-MOUTHED FOOL (10:10)

Presented here are not two opposites, but two different behaviors to avoid. The winking eye could imply secrecy and deceit (as in Proverbs 6:13; 16:30) or gloating (see Psalm 35:19). Both actions cause **grief** (Prov. 10:10), but the New International Version is probably correct to opt for the former and supply **maliciously** here. We have met the

chattering fool before (10:10; see 10:8); that person is anything but subtle. Both bring about disastrous consequences; the winking eye hurts others, while the chattering lips harm themselves. Although differing actions, both present a clear picture of what the righteous should avoid.

11. IS YOUR MOUTH A SOURCE OF LIFE OR DEATH? (10:11)

The theme of wrong speech and its consequences continues in Proverbs 10:11, graphically portrayed as the difference between a fountain of life and a blanket of death. The righteous enlivens others by what he says, while the wicked brings destruction, both on himself and others. To compare the words of the righteous to flowing water only accentuates their wonderfully refreshing and life-giving nature in a culture where water is absolutely crucial to survival. Verse 11b is identical with verse 6b and is probably repeated here to emphasize the seriousness of wicked words. There is no need, however, to assume the words have precisely the same meaning they had in their earlier use. The author might be saying that, unlike the righteous whose words flow out to bless others, the wicked remains hidden behind his concealment of **violence** (10:11), interested only in harming others.

12. A BETTER TYPE OF COVERING (10:12)

Very likely, this proverb has been placed alongside 10:11 to present a contrast based on the word **covers,** which is found in both (and in 10:6). Because violence and **hatred** cover the face of the wicked, only **dissension** can result, and this is one of the things God hates most (10:12; see 6:14, 19). Although the Hebrew word translated **stirs up** can be used to describe the arousal of romantic feelings (see Song of Songs 2:7; 3:5; 8:4), here it comes closer to stirring up a hornet's nest. Such violence may be concealed, but beneath that covering the hornets are swarming; when the covering is removed by **hatred** (Prov. 10:12), watch out!

Love, on the other hand, truly **covers** potentially divisive faults (10:12). Rather than stirring them up, **love** minimizes those faults and grants the offender another chance. Beneath the covering of **love,** nothing remains to fester, for **all wrongs** are excused. The message of this verse must be balanced by passages like 27:5-6 and 28:13, but its meaning is so profound that several New Testament authors employed it (see 1 Peter 4:8; 1 Corinthians 13:7; James 5:20).

13. DON'T BE A SLOW LEARNER (10:13)

Once again the wise and the fool are contrasted; this time the focus is on how they learn. The wise learn so quickly they can use their new knowledge to help others. Not only can the fool help no one, but he is a nuisance requiring discipline. What the wise obtain almost effortlessly, the fool gains only by pain. Even here God's mercy is evident for He has not abandoned the fool; God continues to call for the fool's attention.

14. HAVE YOU A TREASURY OF WISDOM? (10:14)

The contrast between the wise and foolish speaker continues in this proverb. The **wise** may have wisdom on his lips, but his wisdom keeps those lips from chattering (10:14). Instead, his mind becomes a treasury of wisdom both for himself and others. The **fool,** although bankrupt of wisdom, continues to write checks on an account long since overdrawn. His fate is, literally, "imminent destruction," which stands in striking contrast to the **wise** person whose treasury is amply supplied for years to come.

15. WEALTH HAS ITS PRIVILEGES (10:15)

Aside from the repetition of the word **ruin,** there seems little connection between this proverb (10:15) and the one preceding it. We move from wisdom to **wealth,** a connection with which most of us would be somewhat uncomfortable. Proverbs, however, sees **wealth** as a valuable by-product of righteousness; here it is seen as the source of security. This same chapter also reminds us that **wealth** must be properly gained (see 10:2) so that righteousness, not money, has the greater importance. This verse must be read in company with the next, which makes the moral framework more explicit.

16. SHOW ME YOUR PAYCHECK (10:16)

This proverb continues to use financial language (as in 10:15), but in a broader sense; **wages** and **income** mean more (but not less) than money. The **righteous** (10:16) not only earn a living, but they earn a life by their righteousness. Deliverance from death (10:2), provision (10:3), blessings (10:6), a good reputation (10:7), security (10:9), and the opportunity to enliven others (10:11) are promised to the **righteous** in this chapter. On the contrary, however lucrative wickedness may appear, it actually brings no benefit to **the wicked**. **Punishment** (10:16) is, literally, "sin," which means that **the wicked** person is paid back for the evil he does ("sin is all the wicked earns" [NJB]). Commentator F. Delitzsch suggests that the Hebrew words translated **wages** and **income** are not exact synonyms. The former refers to the reward of labor, while the latter is a more general term for payment, not necessarily what one has worked for. If correct, it is a subtle reminder that **the wicked,** who often appear to get rich at others' expense, have a painful payday coming.

17. DON'T RUN FROM DISCIPLINE (10:17)

Discipline (10:17), a gift from God, falls on the just and unjust. What each does with it determines whether he or she will become better or worse. **Life** (10:17; see 10:16) results when **discipline** is allowed to work its corrective wonders. The New International Version has added **shows** to the very terse Hebrew. Without it the connection between **discipline** and **life** is even stronger. **Heeds** means that discipline, while difficult, must be adhered to for the long run. The wicked also receive **discipline,** but refuse to recognize it as such. Because they miss God's clear directions, they wander from the path of **life.**

18. WHAT IS HIDING BEHIND ONE'S LIPS? (10:18)

Now follow several proverbs addressing the effects of speech. The first concerns the deceptive maligner, whose words are chosen to conceal the poison which lies within. God wants honesty and kindness; He did not endow humanity with the gift of speech to have it used for evil. Ironically, those who lie and **slander** (10:18) often do so to elevate their status. In fact, they only prove what fools they really are.

19. HOLD YOUR TONGUE (10:19)

While **words** (10:19) are powerful tools, capable of bringing life (see 10:11) or ruin (see 10:14), they cannot remove the deadly effects of sin. Those who try to use them this way are not fooling God.

Nor should we be lulled into believing someone by an abundance of his words; **sin** probably lurks within (10:19). Wisdom may be best evidenced, not by what we say, but by what we do not say.

20. BE TRULY SILVER TONGUED (10:20)

The description "silver tongued" is usually reserved for great orators like the eighteenth-century preacher George Whitefield. This proverb applies that accolade to all **righteous** people and not because of what is said or the way it is said (10:20). One is silver tongued when one's words reflect the quality of one's **heart**. Note this is **choice silver—** that is, silver freed from all impurities. So purified, such words, like this valuable metal, can bring great benefit to their owner and others. Perhaps this is why so few words are needed (see 10:19). By contrast, the **heart** and the resulting words of **the wicked** are worthless (10:20). In spite of their abundance, such words will help few and probably harm many.

21. WANT A GOURMET MEAL? (10:21)

Having given a negative example of speech (10:18) and having spoken to the quantity of words (10:19) and their value (10:20), Proverbs 10:21 focuses on their benefit. If words were food, many people could find their dietary needs met at the table of **the righteous** person. This would not be smorgasbord fare, with the emphasis on quantity over quality, for the words of the righteous are few (see 10:19). Yet even with few words, **many** are nourished thereby (10:21). Do not bother sitting down at the table of the wicked, however, for there is nothing there worth eating. In fact, because of (literally) a "senseless heart," the wicked **lack** sufficient nourishment for themselves and are dying of mental malnutrition.

22. THE TRUE SOURCE OF UNMIXED BLESSINGS (10:22)

According to one commentator, this and the next two verses "say that good comes from above, and is as a second nature to the man of understanding."[3] One might read the previous proverb and conclude that the righteous man not only nourishes many with his words, but that he also provides the gourmet food from his own pantry. But when that verse is read together with this proverb, the true source of blessing is clearly God. Another word is added in the Hebrew (left untranslated in the NIV) which emphasizes that it is God's **blessing** and nothing else which makes one truly rich (10:22; see Psalm 127:1-2; Genesis 49:25-26). The second part of this verse does not exempt the righteous from trouble. Instead it describes the **blessing** of God as perfect since "with the possession [of this blessing, God] grants at the same time a joyful, peaceful mind."[4]

23. WHAT IS YOUR SPORT? (10:23)

Ask that question in our sports-oriented culture, and you will likely get a wide variety of answers. But there is a deeper level on which this question can be asked, a level addressed by Proverbs 10:23 and made more evident in the New Jerusalem Bible:

A fool takes pleasure in doing wrong,
the intelligent in cultivating wisdom.

The contrast is not between earthly **pleasure** and more spiritual **delights** as the New International Version translates (10:23), but between two "sports," two behaviors in which people engage with great pleasure. The **fool** enjoys his wrongdoing; this comes as no surprise. But the verse tells us that the wise **man** enjoys **wisdom** just as much as the **fool** enjoys his folly. The wise **[find] pleasure** in fellowship with God, in avoiding the effects of sin, in understanding human nature, and in being able to nourish others. Pursuing **wisdom** may require discipline (see 10:8), but it is nothing less than enjoyable, no less than a beautiful "garland" or adorning "chain" (1:9).

24. GOOD NEWS AND BAD NEWS (10:24)

Much of the joy gained from a happy event like a reunion or birthday occurs well before that event occurs, in its anticipation. Just so, a large part of anguish comes from anticipating dreaded events, a truth reinforced by Proverbs 10:24. **The wicked** have much to dread from those they wronged, from other wicked people, and from God. Not only will these dreaded things most certainly **overtake** them in the end, but they must always be looking over their shoulders. **The righteous,** on the other hand, enjoy the benefits of clear consciences which fear no reprisals from humanity or God. Ahead waits their reward, and along the way they have the joy of anticipation.

25. SWEPT AWAY OR STANDING FIRM (10:25)

This proverb continues the contrast between the destiny of "the wicked" and "the righteous" seen in 10:24, and does so with a metaphor which may have been in Jesus' mind when he told the parable of the wise and foolish builder (see Matthew 7:24-27). When the word translated **storm** (Prov. 10:25) is used in the Old Testament, it almost always speaks of a meteorological disturbance accompanied by a furious wind (see Job 37:9; Psalm 107:25). It is this wind which sweeps away the wicked. Note that their departure is not described; only their vacancy is observed: **. . . the wicked are gone** (Prov. 10:25a). The second half of this proverb differs from the first, not only in content, but also in form, for there is a stately cadence in the Hebrew words. Unlike the sudden and final departure of the wicked, **the righteous stand firm forever** (10:25b). Most of the remaining proverbs in this chapter continue the theme of the permanence of the righteous.[5]

26. SMOKE GETS IN YOUR EYES (10:26)

This proverb needs no explanation to those forced to rely on **a sluggard** (10:26); that person so lazy, slow, and unmotivated he could learn a lesson from the ant (see 6:6). **Smoke** irritates **the eyes,** and **vinegar,** probably a strong variety, apparently irritates the mouth (10:26). To avoid such irritation, choose your messengers carefully.

27. TO WHAT DO YOU ATTRIBUTE YOUR LONG LIFE? (10:27)

The best answer to this question, often asked those who have lived a long life, is found in this proverb: **the fear of the LORD.**[6] We have met this phrase before; in fact, it is the motto of Proverbs (see 1:7). What does reverence for God have to do with long life? It means avoiding life-destroying behaviors and adhering to those attitudes (peace, for example) and practices (love, for example) proven to accompany good health. When one considers eternity (a reality probably beyond even Solomon's understanding), this proverb achieves still deeper meaning.

28. JOY OR DISAPPOINTMENT (10:28)

The permanence of **the righteous** (10:28), addressed in 10:25 and resumed in 10:27, continues as the theme throughout the rest of the chapter. This proverb, in many ways, resembles 10:24. Both, for example, speak of the **joy** of **the righteous.** That verse spoke of what the wicked dread, while this verse addresses their **hopes** and expectations, which will amount **to nothing.** What a sorry picture! Pursuing what they will never obtain, they are pursued by what they dread.

29. REFUGE OR RUIN (10:29)

The key phrase in this verse is placed first in the New International Version: **the way of the Lord.** These words, in the original, appear in the middle of the verse and are meant to be read with both parts. **The way of the Lord is** both **a refuge for the righteous** *and* **the ruin of** the wicked. Both truths, asserted throughout this chapter, are here strikingly combined. The Lord is the only immovable object in our existence, a strong mountain rising out of this swirling sea of life. Either we take refuge in His sheltering harbor or we must be dashed to pieces against His character and will.

30. ANCHORED OR UPROOTED (10:30)

This verse continues the theme of the permanence of the righteous in a way quite similar to what is found in Proverbs 10:25. By mentioning **the land** (10:30), however, it adds an element of profound interest to the Israelites. The land of Canaan had been given to them as a visible expression of their covenant relationship with God. When they arrived, God told them that as long as they were righteous, they could remain there, but wickedness would mean exile (see Deuteronomy 30:15-20). This proverb reasserts God's promise and even sweetens it, for it speaks of purging the wicked elements from the land. It takes on a poignant tone when one looks back at Israel's exile, but a glorious tone when one looks ahead to God's ultimate and final vindication of **the righteous** (Prov. 10:30).

31. WHAT FRUIT DO YOUR WORDS GROW? (10:31)

Once again we return to the subject of speech, an important component of the overall message of Proverbs. The words of the wise, because they flow from one rooted in the land (see 10:30), flourish and bear fruit like a well-tended vine. The wicked, whose **perverse** words[7] are barren (10:31), will be uprooted and thrown aside for burning (see John 15:1-8). We have heard similar warnings before, but, placed within a series of proverbs (see Proverbs 10:25, 27-32) dealing with the permanence of the righteous and the transience of the wicked, this verse takes on a more ominous tone. The ruin predicted earlier for one who speaks wickedly (see 10:6, 8, 10, 11, 14) is here described graphically, conjuring up images of both pruning knife and surgical scalpel.

32. DO YOUR WORDS FIT? (10:32)

Once again we find contrasted **righteous** and **wicked** speech (10:32). The previous proverb called the speech of "the righteous" wise. Here it is termed **fitting** (10:32), a word which could also be rendered "favorable," "good," or "kind." It is the same word used in 11:1, there translated "delight." When one considers how much good the words of the righteous can accomplish (see 10:11, 13, 20, 21, 31), it is no surprise they are described so positively. Once again the wicked are said to speak **what is perverse** (10:32). This word, used several times in the Old Testament, but mostly in Proverbs, can mean unfaithfulness (Deuteronomy 32:20), wickedness (Proverbs 2:14), deception (Proverbs 6:14; 16:30) or what is strange and unexpected (Proverbs 23:33). Because its parallel term means what is appropriate, perhaps **perverse** (10:32) is used here in a general sense to refer to words completely unlike what God would want us to say.

ENDNOTES

[1]Derek Kidner, *Proverbs: An Introduction and Commentary,* Tyndale Old Testament Commentaries, ed. D. J. Wiseman (Downers Grove, Illinois: InterVarsity Press, 1964), p. 85. Two references to the body can be found here as well, namely **head** and **mouth** (see verses 2, 4).

[2]John Goldingay ("The Arrangement of Sayings in Proverbs 10–15," *Journal for the Study of the Old Testament,* vol. 61 [1994], pp. 75–83) also points out a similar construction for the proverbs in 10:8-10. Once again we meet references to the human body (heart and lips).

[3]F. Delitzsch, *Proverbs, Ecclesiastes, Song of Solomon,* Commentary on the Old Testament, by C. F. Keil and F. Delitzsch, vol. 10 (Grand Rapids, Michigan: Wm. B. Eerdmans Publishing Co., 1978 [1872]), p. 222.

[4]Ibid., p. 223.

[5]Verses 25 and 26 are related by a common theme and similar structure (Goldingay, p. 77).

[6]The New International Version and other translations use LORD in small capitals following an initial capital *L* to denote "Yahweh" in the original Hebrew.

[7]See verse 32 for a fuller description of what **perverse** can mean.

PROVERBS 11

11:1-31

This chapter could be titled "Righteousness Pays." Many of its proverbs deal with the benefits that come from being righteous and the problems that arise from folly, a theme found throughout the book of Proverbs.

1. THE NOT-SO-SILENT WITNESS OF EVERY TRANSACTION (11:1)

At the very beginning of Israel's existence as a nation, God warned her against cheating in commercial transactions as seen in passages such as Leviticus 19:36 and Deuteronomy 25:13-16. The latter passage, in fact, reminds them that God detests such behavior, using the same word translated here in Proverbs as **abhors** (11:1). That such deception is warned against elsewhere in Proverbs (see 16:11; 20:10, 23) and criticized in the Prophets (see Amos 8:5; Micah 6:11)[1] indicates that it remained a problem throughout Israel's history. Archaeologists have discovered stone weights which, when weighed, measured just shy of the proper heaviness.

That God would care about something as ordinary as accurate scales is not unusual; like any king in that culture did, God does care about what is just, fair, and honest. Such fairness must exist if society is to be preserved. Note, however, that honest weights are not primarily for the benefit of society; they are for God's **delight** (Prov. 11:1). This term reminds us that God passionately desires honesty among His people.

2. TAKE THE ROUNDABOUT WAY TO WISDOM (11:2)

There is something playful about this proverb. It contains a relatively uncommon example of rhyming in the Hebrew; the word for **pride** *(zadone)* rhymes with the word for **disgrace** *(qadone).* The warning against defrauding others, a practice of the proud who would become rich quickly, is followed by a warning that such a route actually brings disgrace. More fundamental is the irony of suggesting that the way to become disgraced is by choosing its opposite, **pride. Wisdom** is reached by the roundabout route of **humility** since it implies a fear of God, the fountain of wisdom. The word for **wisdom,** used only here and in Micah 6:9, is defined by commentator Derek Kidner as "the biddable spirit," the opposite of the insubordinate attitude of Proverbs 11:2a.[2]

3. THE REWARD OF RIGHTEOUSNESS (11:3)

Throughout Proverbs 11, one learns of the many benefits of righteousness, a theme especially prominent in 11:3-10. Here righteousness and wickedness are pictured carrying their rewards within them. **The upright** are guided by their **integrity** (11:3); it allows them to use a mind uncluttered by deception and guilt, and enables them to trust their own motives. **The unfaithful** ("treacherous" [NJB]; "people who can't be trusted" [TEV]) become entangled in a web of lies, lose the ability to help themselves because they have lost the capacity to trust themselves, and self-destruct.

4. THE ULTIMATE SECURITY SYSTEM (11:4)

Under the broader theme of the benefits of righteousness, this proverb continues the subtheme of the security gained through righteousness begun in 11:3. **Wealth** (perhaps obtained illegally as in 11:1) may be able to bring security, but not *ultimate* security. The fault does not lie in **wealth** (see 10:15); Proverbs is no more antiwealth than it is antibeauty, based on 11:22. Only the foolish depend on money to do what it cannot do. Only **righteousness delivers** (or "snatches away"; 11:4) from death, for only righteousness can guide one through the danger zones of life (see 11:3).

5. TAKE THE STRAIGHT WAY (11:5)

Not only does this proverb continue to highlight the benefits of righteousness, but it closely resembles what is found in 11:3. This repetition is not accidental, but betrays an emphasis of the author. In such instances, it is often enlightening to ask in what ways the two proverbs differ. The path of the upright is illuminated by their righteousness according to 11:3, and that path is actually made smooth and easily passable by **righteousness** in 11:5 (see the same verb in 3:6).

6. CORRALLED BY CRAVINGS OR RELEASED BY RIGHTEOUSNESS (11:6)

Again this theme is sounded (see 11:3, 5) and thereby emphasized; again the proverb takes a slightly different turn. Language drawn from verses 3 through 5 is combined: **righteousness** from verses 4 and 5; **upright** from verse 3; **delivers** from verse 4; and **unfaithful** from verse 3. The righteous, guided in verse 3, traveling smooth paths in verse 5, and delivered from death in verse 4, are here delivered in a general and unrestricted sense (11:6). They may, like Daniel, have to enter the "lion's den," but God will be faithful to free them in the end. The wicked, on the other hand, will be ensnared or taken captive by their **evil desires** (Prov. 11:6). This phrase (literally, "lust of treacherous") can refer to something bad which happens to you (see Job 6:2; 30:13; Psalm 57:1; 91:3; 94:20; Proverbs 19:13), but in this case probably refers to the destructive cravings (see Proverbs 10:3; Micah 7:3).

7. THE HOPELESSNESS OF THOSE WHO HOPE AMISS (11:7)

The previous twelve proverbs employ antithetic parallelism (where a single point is made by stating two opposites; see the commentary introduction). This verse alters the pattern and, as a result, snags the reader's eye and ear. Another attention grabber is the repetition of the same verb in both lines of this proverb (but translated differently by the NIV: **perishes** and **comes to nothing**). By implication, the righteous person is survived by his or her hopes and expectations.

8. WHERE TROUBLE GOES WHEN IT LEAVES THE RIGHTEOUS (11:8)

Commentator F. Delitzsch picturesquely summarizes this proverb by identifying **the wicked** as the lightning rod for **the righteous** (11:8). Such a picture is played out every Saturday morning in cartoon form: The bad guy plots to destroy the good guy, only to be "zapped" by his own device. The humor of such a picture is universal. The use of the passive voice (**is rescued**) implies that God does the rescuing (see Psalm 60:5; 108:6).

9. KNOWLEDGE: YOUR BEST DEFENSE (11:9)

Here Proverbs continues the theme of the deliverance of **the righteous.** The same Hebrew words are used in 11:8 and 11:9 for **righteous** and "deliverance" (translated **rescued** in verse 8 and **escape** in verse 9). Verse 9 develops this theme first by moving from individual to group relationships: **righteous** is singular in verse 8 and plural in verse 9, and one's **neighbor** comes into the picture. Next it shows that **the godless** not only destroy themselves, but attempt to do so to others also, even those with whom they are commanded to live in harmony (10:9; see Leviticus 19:18). Their weapons are their words, probably slander, and they betray their folly through those words. The **righteous** are protected from such attacks by **knowledge** (Prov. 11:9). They know how to avoid behavior which could be slandered and understand how to handle such attacks when they come.

10. A HAPPY CITY (11:10)

Communities easily recognize the difference between **the righteous** and **the wicked,** and understand which is best for society (Proverbs 11:10). Commentator Derek Kidner's assessment is correct, both of ancient Israelite society and our own, when he writes, "However drab the world makes out virtue to be, it appreciates the boon of it in public life."[3] Perhaps this is one reason why righteousness is self-preserving and wickedness self-destroying. People seek out **the righteous,** but would rather be rid of **the wicked.**

11. REASON FOR A HAPPY CITY (11:11)

This proverb helps explain why verse 10 is true. A city is either **exalted** or **destroyed** by the words it listens to. If populated by righteous people, it will benefit from their words of blessing and will share in the blessings **the upright** enjoy. But if words from **the wicked** drown out the words of the righteous, woe to that town. The next several proverbs contrast different types of speech, both edifying and destructive.

12. CRITICISM REVEALS THE TRUE FOOL (11:12)

Speech critical of one's **neighbor** reveals a lack of judgment (11:12). Ironically, the critic intends, by his words, to reveal his discerning eye and the faults of the criticized; instead he reveals his own faults. Specifically, he shows that he **lacks judgment** (literally, is "void of heart"). Based on his use of similarly sounding words, the author subtly connects this phrase to the word "destroyed" in 11:11, thereby suggesting the destiny of the critic. The neighbor may not be perfect, but the wise person knows how little good can come from criticizing and how much can be gained by keeping negative opinions to himself. Furthermore, wisdom makes him capable of doing so.

13. WATCH OUT FOR THE GOSSIP (11:13)

Proverbs 11:13 turns to consider the speech of the **gossip** (the "tittle-tattler" [NJB]). This person would rather talk, even if it means exposing a friend's secret, than be silent. How much better to be **trustworthy,** worthy of the trust you have been given and willing to keep hidden what should remain hidden. How much better to choose the "trustworthy soul" for a friend.

14. THE IMPORTANCE OF GOOD COUNSEL IN ABUNDANCE (11:14)

Once again the topic is wise speech—in this proverb, words of counsel. Without it, a **nation falls** (11:14), a serious problem at any time, but especially in the context where that nation is Israel, God's chosen nation. Had Rehoboam taken this advice in 1 Kings 12, the nation of Israel may not have been torn apart by civil war. Here is one instance where many words are good, for they bring **victory** (or safety; Prov. 11:14). This proverb also reminds us that God often guides us through others.

15. THE DANGER OF HASTY WORDS (11:15)

The problem of pledging to pay the debts of another (discussed at greater length in Proverbs 6:1-5) is also a problem of speech. One secures such costly and destructive obligations by failing to think carefully about the consequences of his words. In 11:14, safety was found in plenty of good advice, while here **security** comes from keeping your words few and carefully considered.

16. THE POWER OF KINDNESS (11:16)

Kindness (literally, "graciousness"), although it appears weak and ornamental, is really a potent force. It can provide a solitary **woman,** in a male-dominated and communally oriented society, great **respect** (11:16). Money cannot do this, nor can violence (**ruthless men**). Graciousness leaves a favorable impression wherever it goes, and it grows in the soil of wisdom (see 13:15).

17. HELP YOURSELF BY HELPING OTHERS (11:17)

While the emphasis on kindness continues, we again return to consider the benefits of wisdom (see Proverbs 11:17-21). From the gracious woman of 11:16, we move to a "man of kindness" whose loving actions, although directed to the benefit of others, pour back in reward to himself. The Hebrew word translated **cruel** (11:17) can describe a merciless army whose attack produces paralysis, pain, agony, and terror (see Jeremiah 6:23). A closely related word describes those so cruel they refuse to feed their own children (see Lamentations 4:3). This person not only acts cruelly, but has lost the capacity to be kind (see Proverbs 12:10). This man, intending to harm others, actually **brings trouble on himself** (11:17).

18. REAL WAGES (11:18)

Some mock kindness for its wastefulness and inability to produce a profit. In fact, says this proverb, the only seed that produces a crop— **a sure reward** *(sheker)*—is the seed of righteous acts, sown in the lives of others. Wickedness appears to produce a crop. There are plants in the field which, from a distance, appear to be lush and productive. Draw closer, however, and you will see that you have been fooled (*shaqer,* **deceptive**). To drive home the point, **deceptive wages** is, literally, "wages of deception," while **a sure reward** is, literally, "a reward of truth."

19. A LIFE-OR-DEATH MATTER (11:19)

Translated more literally, this proverb reads,

He who is genuinely righteous lives;
He who pursues evil does so to his death.

The first man is righteous to the core, solid, stable, and unmoved by temptation, content in God. The latter is on the move, never content, insistent on sinning as long as he lives. The first lives—that is, he experiences the blessings which accompany righteousness. The one **who pursues evil** is actually chasing his own **death.**

20. DO WE HATE WHAT GOD HATES? (11:20)

This is the second time in Proverbs 11 we are told what delights the heart of God. In the other instance (see 11:1) it was honesty in business; here it is a blameless lifestyle. Nor is this the first time we are told what God hates. We learn of seven such things in 6:16-19 (where **detests** is also used) and additional items elsewhere (see 3:32; 12:22; 15:8-9, 26; 16:5; 17:15; 26:25). This and the next verse help explain why righteousness brings blessing, but wickedness brings punishment. They also challenge us to take God's standard as our own.

21. THE RESULT OF GOD'S HATRED AND DELIGHT (11:21)

Because God hates the wicked and delights in the righteous, Proverbs says, **the wicked** will be punished and the **righteous** delivered (11:21). **Be sure of this** is, literally, "hand to hand," an idiom which probably alludes to shaking hands on a matter (see 6:1; 11:15). We would say, "You can shake on it—God will certainly judge the wicked and the righteous." This truth can be the anchor which gives hope to the suffering who can find no justice here.

22. WASTED BEAUTY (11:22)

This proverb reminds me of a young woman in one of the congregations I pastored. She possessed a natural and striking beauty, but she lacked discretion. Without the ability to discern what was best and make good choices, she went from one disaster to another. **A gold ring** (11:22), like this young woman, is beautiful. But when you take that ring and hang it from the nose of a detested animal which wallows in muck, what was beautiful becomes ridiculous, its beauty tarnished and wasted. Physical beauty, unaccompanied by wisdom, is wasted. Instead God wants more "Abigails," those who combine beauty with discernment (see 1 Samuel 25).

23. A PLEASANT ARRIVAL (11:23)

Because "hope springs eternal in the human breast," both **the righteous** and **the wicked** long for what they lack (11:23). Here is where the similarities end. This proverb suggests that the objects of their desire are different. The righteous want **only** what is **good,** what pleases God. **The wicked,** by implication, desire what is evil. **The righteous** receive what they hope for, while **the wicked** fail to realize their dreams. Thus they must not only face disappointment, but eventually come under God's **wrath** as well. Once again we see that righteousness is the most blessed choice.

24. GENEROSITY PAYS (11:24)

This is the first of three proverbs which point out the rewards of generosity. Two men are pictured; one is generous, while the other is frugal. Reason would say that the first will reduce his wealth through his extravagance, while the second will become wealthier through thrift and compound interest. Reason, however, does not always take into account the actions of God. While He has put into our hands great potential for wealth through hard work, economy and common sense, true prosperity lies outside our power. If we will freely share our resources with others, He will bless us with even more. If we refuse to be charitable, we will find ourselves working against Him, and **poverty** will be the result (11:24).

25. A CUP OF COLD WATER RETURNED (11:25)

The theme of generosity, continued in Proverbs 11:25, becomes especially vivid with the mention of water in the second line (literally, "one who waters will himself be watered"). Even today, water in Israel is a precious commodity. The generous person (literally, "soul of blessing") draws freely from his well to refresh others. The well does not go dry, however, but flows even more abundantly, as if God directs underground reservoirs in response to obedience.

26. A CROWN FOR THE GENEROUS (11:26)

While God's response to generosity is presented in Proverbs 11:24-25, verse 26 describes how others respond to generosity. **People curse** the miser who puts gain above the needs of others, but bless the man who values people more than profit. These blessings alight on the head of the generous person, prompting the New International Version to add the word **crowns.** When people **curse** or bless others, they acknowledge that God sees our actions, takes an interest in them, and rewards accordingly.

27. FINDING WHAT YOU LOOK FOR (11:27)

The exact meaning of the first line of this proverb is somewhat uncertain. Today's English Version expresses one possibility: "If your goals are good, you will be respected," presumably by other people. The New International Version is more correct in suggesting that those who look for good find the favor of God. Both the righteous and the wicked find what they are looking for. The latter seek **evil** and find it, but like a letter bomb returned to the sender for insufficient postage, the outcome is disastrous. The righteous look for good and find God's favor; what could be better than God's "well done" (see Matthew 25:21)?

28. TOPPLE OR THRIVE (11:28)

A picture from the world of nature illustrates the truth that righteousness, not wealth, is best. The one who trusts in wealth is like a branch broken off from the tree. That branch may be rich with fruit and **green** leaves, but only for a time (11:28). The Hebrew is emphatic: *"He will fall."* The righteous do not **fall** and die, but flourish because they are connected to the source of true life, to God himself. Wealth is not in itself bad, but was never intended to sustain life, only enrich it. Perhaps Jesus had this proverb in view when he spoke of the vine and branches in John 15.

29. A WINDY INHERITANCE (11:29)

Wealth is inferior to righteousness (see Proverbs 11:28), in part, because wealth can be easily lost through mismanagement. The phrase **he who brings trouble on his family** (11:29) is, literally, "troubler of his house" (see 11:17) which could occur either by mismanaging household resources or besmirching the family name (see NIV; TEV). In either case, the fool has failed to properly steward the resources entrusted to him, whether wealth or reputation. He emerges, in the end, with a handful of nothing and in bondage to the "wise of heart."

30. THE SOUL CATCHER (11:30)

The superiority of righteousness (see Proverbs 11:28-29) can also be seen in its ability to bring **life** (11:30). A **righteous** person is like **a tree** whose "words and actions exert a quickening, refreshing, happy influence" upon others.[4] The meaning of the second line of this proverb has troubled commentators at least as far back as the Septuagint[5] who sought to clarify the obscurity by reading "violent" for the similar-sounding (in Hebrew) **wise.** The Revised Standard Version agrees and translates the line, "but lawlessness takes away lives," thereby presenting a contrast between the life-giving **righteous** and the life-taking violent.

The problem concerns the verb rendered **wins.** This verb usually has a negative connotation, as in 1 Kings 19:4 where Elijah asks God to kill him and in Psalm 31:13 where murder is plotted. Literally, the line reads, "A wise man takes [away] lives," which prompted the Septuagint change. By using a verb which can have a violent meaning, however, the meaning of the first line is intensified in the second, and the life-giving effects of righteousness are graphically portrayed.[6] The New Jerusalem Bible expresses it well: "The sage captivates souls" (11:30b).

31. BAD NEWS FOR THE WICKED (11:31)

Proverbs 11 concludes on a note sounded throughout: the permanence of **the righteous** and the punishment of the wicked (11:31). Both will be requited for their deeds **on earth.** There is some question, however, of the precise meaning of the phrase **receive their due.** Some take it positively, to refer to rewards for good behavior, making the second line ironic: The wicked will get their "rewards," too. The phrase could be taken more negatively, however, and this is the way Peter understood it: "If it is hard for the righteous to be saved, what will become of the ungodly and the sinner?" (1 Pet. 4:18). Since elsewhere this verb (in this grammatical pattern) is only understood positively, perhaps this sense should be read here.

ENDNOTES

[1]The Prophets consist of the biblical Old Testament books of Isaiah, Jeremiah, Lamentations, Ezekiel, Daniel, Hosea, Joel, Amos, Obadiah, Jonah, Micah, Nahum, Habakkuk, Zephaniah, Haggai, Zechariah, and Malachi.

[2]Derek Kidner, *Proverbs: An Introduction and Commentary,* Tyndale Old Testament Commentaries, ed. D. J. Wiseman (Downers Grove, Illinois: InterVarsity Press, 1964), p. 90.

[3]Ibid., p. 91.

[4]F. Delitzsch, *Proverbs, Ecclesiastes, Song of Solomon,* Commentary on the Old Testament, by C. F. Keil and F. Delitzsch, vol. 10 (Grand Rapids, Michigan: Wm. B. Eerdmans Publishing Co., 1978 [1872]), p. 249.

[5]The Septuagint is the Greek version of the Old Testament, translated from the original Hebrew scrolls, and written in the second and third centuries B.C. It is often indicated by the Roman numerals LXX in accordance with the legend that it was translated by seventy scribes.

[6]See Jude 23 for a similar picture.

PROVERBS 12

12:1-28

T his chapter opens with an invitation to embrace discipline and closes with the promise that the resulting path—the road of righteousness—leads to immortality. According to Proverbs, you cannot have one without the other.

1. YOU HAVE TO LOVE DISCIPLINE! (12:1)

Loving **discipline** (12:1), like loving spinach, is not easy. By definition, **discipline** and **correction** are painful because they force us to confront our motives and actions, admit our faults, pay for our missteps, and try again. One might *endure* **discipline,** but *love* it? To be truly wise, however, requires embracing discipline with loving passion, preferring it to the comfort of self-indulgence. Those who prefer the latter are **stupid,** lacking even a minimum of sense ("brutish" [NJPS]).

2. GOD IS WATCHING OUR ACTIONS (12:2)

This verse might be passed by with minimal commentary if it were not so easily forgotten. To say that God rewards all according to their deeds implies God's knowledge of human actions, even those done in secret (**crafty**). That God judges those actions speaks to His authority in the world and His interest in justice. Our path is clearly marked: We must choose to do good for others—not just talk about it—to obtain **favor from the LORD** (12:2; see 1 John 4:8).

3. THE PATH TO TRUE STABILITY (12:3)

We have met this theme many times before in Proverbs. At times it is expressed in similar language: 10:30a speaks directly of the rootedness of the righteous; 11:28 implies it. One of the "perks" of **wickedness** (12:3) is supposed to be security, gained by deceit or violence at the expense of others. Righteousness strives for another goal, choosing to take a risk and do what is right rather than be concerned for self-preservation. Yet it is **the righteous,** not the wicked, who become secure. **Wickedness,** like a live volcano, is inherently unstable and will eventually and assuredly "blow." Righteousness quietly goes about its task of doing the right thing, putting others ahead of itself and God ahead of all. All the while its roots are pushing down into the soil—deeper, wider, stronger—until the fiercest storm **cannot** tear it out.

4. ADORNMENT OR UNDOING (12:4)

The results of righteousness and "wickedness" (see Proverbs 12:2-3) reach out to touch others. For example, a man's wife will either be his adornment or his undoing, depending on her nature. **A wife of noble character** (12:4; described in 31:10), greatly benefits her husband. She becomes for him a **crown** (12:4)—that is, her nobility dignifies his existence. On the other hand, a woman who humiliates her husband, whether through laziness (see 10:5) or foolish decisions (see, for example, 19:26), destroys him. The Hebrew behind **decay** (12:4) describes a moth-eaten garment (see Job 13:28) or wood so rotten it easily crumbles (see Job 41:27; Isaiah 40:20). **A disgraceful wife** (Prov. 12:4) destroys her husband gradually and from within; she is "a cancer in his bones" (NJB). Addressed to the wife because of the cultural context of ancient Israel, this proverb should now challenge both husbands and wives to be a **crown** on the head of one's spouse.

5. HOW DO YOU THINK ABOUT OTHERS? (12:5)

This and the next two proverbs proceed logically: The first speaks of the thoughts of the righteous, the second of their words, and the third of their destiny. The "thoughts" or "purposes"[1] **of the righteous are just** (12:5). **The righteous** think about how to treat others honestly and fairly because they know they must answer to God, even in what they think. **The wicked,** without this conviction and with only themselves to please, think about how to deceive others or be treacherous. As the next two proverbs show, thoughts produce words and destinies.

114

6. WHAT DO YOU SAY ABOUT OTHERS? (12:6)

If one's thoughts are deceitful and treacherous, one's **words** will be also (12:6). **The words of the wicked** are graphically described literally as "lying **in wait for blood**," ready to ambush the unsuspecting. **Words** that spring from just thoughts are equally powerful forces for good. Not only will they help others (implied), but they can even deliver the righteous person from difficulty (see 11:9).

7. THOUGHTS, WORDS, DESTINY (12:7)

This proverb provides insightful commentary on the kings of the Northern Kingdom of Israel (see 12:7a) and the kings of the Southern Kingdom of Judah (see 12:7b). The former were, for the most part, **wicked men** whose dynasties came to a violent and shortened end, sinking into oblivion (they **are no more**). **The house of the righteous,** the dynasty of David, did stand **firm** for over four hundred years. The verse is true in a general sense as well and represents another installment of a consistent theme throughout Proverbs and another summons to righteous living for both king and subject.

8. THE HONOR OF WISDOM (12:8)

To all of the many reasons to choose **wisdom,** another is added (12:8). People prefer to be around someone who is wise, but dislike the "twisted mind" (NJPS). This verse does not specifically identify who does the praising or despising, so God might be assumed as the subject, or the author may imply that "prudence wins praise" (12:8a NJB) both from people and God. Those **with warped minds,** who lack the ability to think straight,[2] are held up to contempt or ridicule (see 18:3) as a laughingstock (see Genesis 38:23).

9. YOU CAN'T EAT AN IMAGE (12:9)

This proverb touches the universal desire to be imagined as better than we really are. To **pretend to be somebody** and starve to death is a ridiculous choice, but one often chosen. Uncertainty remains whether the first line should read with the New International Version or as the Revised Standard Version, which says, "Better is a man of humble standing who works for himself." The latter is better supported, but the point of the proverb is the same either way: Be humble. There is a spiritual application here as well since only those who recognize their need for God will be satisfied by Him.

10. WOULD YOUR DOG GIVE YOU A GOOD CHARACTER REFERENCE? (12:10)

Pictured here are kindness and cruelty at their extremes. The **righteous man** not only cares for other people, he even **cares for his** animals (12:10). His care extends to an understanding of the animal's **needs** ("knows the needs of his beast"; "knows how his cattle feel"[3]). How does this demonstrate righteousness? One who **cares for** animals is considering others besides himself and is doing so without thought of personal gain. By contrast, **the wicked** person is so **cruel** that even his kindness is cruelty. In other words, if it appears he is attempting to be compassionate, a closer look will reveal some ruthless intent.

11. YOU CAN'T EAT A FANTASY (12:11)

Apparently the temptation to chase **fantasies** is nothing new (12:11). If you want something to eat (see Proverbs 12:9), hard work, not **fantasies,** will produce it (see 28:19 for a similar proverb). Hard work implies smart work, as any farmer can tell you, since one must know when and how to work the soil. But the rewards of such labor are abundant: "bread and to spare" (12:11 NJB). The one who **chases fantasies** (12:11) wants to avoid hard work and obtain his dreams the easy way. Ironically, the Hebrew grammar here suggests he may be working just as hard as the diligent farmer, but in "worthless pursuits" (RSV). These leave him, in the end, with nothing to show but his lack of **judgment** and the need to buy his **food** from the one **who works his land** instead of his **fantasies.**

12. SECURE UNDER SIEGE (12:12)

While the interpretation of this verse is somewhat unclear, it "appears to contrast the delusive attractions of evil methods with the quiet rewards of goodness."[4] The first line seems to suggest that **the wicked** employ trickery to trap others.[5] The New Jerusalem Bible translates this, "The godless delights in the snare of the wicked." Such deception cannot harm **the righteous** who are rooted (see 12:3) and flourishing. **Flourishes** (12:12) is, literally, "gives," as in bearing fruit. The fiendish deceit of the first line is eclipsed by the strong, silent, fruit-filled testimony of the second.

13. THE POWER OF WORDS FOR EVIL (12:13)

At the beginning of a cluster of proverbs on the wise use of words is one which concerns their power to either trap or liberate a person. The words of **an evil man** ensnare him (12:13), perhaps through ill-considered promises, empty boasts, or rash curses. The repetition of **evil man** and the theme of entrapment shed light on the trickery in 12:12a. The words of the **righteous man** (12:13) have power as well, for by them he can avoid entrapment (see 12:6). Jesus put this proverb in eternal perspective in Matthew 12:36-37.

14. THE POWER OF WORDS FOR GOOD (12:14)

This proverb continues the theme of words and builds on 12:11. Just as surely as hard work can produce abundant "food," so can good words. The choice is not between hard work and talking, but between diligent and lazy speech, between carefully considered words and those sprinkled liberally more for good effect than to effect **good** (12:14). What **good things** can words bring? They can plant good thoughts and cultivate relationships. They can weed out what is harmful and fertilize with hope. Our words can bring in a harvest of good for us and for others.

15. THE KNOW-IT-ALL FOOL (12:15)

Commentator Derek Kidner has well expressed the thought of the first line of Proverbs 12:15: "The person who always knows best may be the only one unconscious of his real name."[6] The **fool** thinks his path is the right one, and no one can steer him differently. The **wise** person is always willing to take **advice,** not because he is unsure of his direction, but because he is **wise.** He knows that his own judgment is not flawless, that God often leads through others, and that even bad advice is helpful, if only to discern the character of the giver.

16. THE QUICK-TEMPERED FOOL (12:16)

By putting this verse after verse 15, we discover what happens to the **fool** when annoyed, whether by unwanted advice or some other indignity.

He immediately betrays his anger; he has no choice since he lacks the self-control to wait. He may "blow his top" for other reasons, perhaps to impress others, possibly because he likes to quarrel (see Proverb 20:3) or very likely because he considers himself so important that an insult becomes a capital offense. The **prudent man** (12:16) is not spared insults or their pain, but he knows to overlook it. He knows that just because something is spoken does not make it true and that lies have a short shelf life. He knows that retaliation has consequences, but those consequences are usually destructive and rarely erase the insult. He knows that time, not heat, is better at producing clarification and apologies. The wise man **overlooks an insult** because he has self-discipline and a faith in God which trusts the results to Him.

17. THE TRUTH, THE WHOLE TRUTH, AND NOTHING BUT THE TRUTH (12:17)

Words, to be pleasing to God, must also be **truthful** (12:17). His command to tell the truth about our neighbors in Exodus 20:16 is restated simply and directly here in Proverbs. These two witnesses do not merely tell the truth or tell **lies** (Prov. 12:17). The original Hebrew implies that they are characterized by either faithfulness or deceit, and their words reflect their character. "Nothing but his honest thought a lover of truth declares, a false witness nothing but lies."[7] The **truthful witness** more literally "breathes out faithfulness," while the **false witness** "is nothing but deceit" (NJB). God wants truthful words because He is a God of truth and because society cannot survive without it. But He especially wants truthful people whose words reflect what is inside.

18. DO YOUR WORDS HARM OR HEAL? (12:18)

The truth about words continues with another reminder of the power of words both for harm and healing (see Proverbs 12:13-14). **Reckless words** (12:18), those spoken rashly or in haste, can have devastating consequences, just as damaging as the thrust or slash of a **sword.** Reputations can be destroyed, the human spirit can be broken, opportunities can be lost, and friends can be alienated all because of the ill-considered word. Just as rash words harm, **wise** words—that is, those words carefully considered and judged to be necessary—bring **healing.** Such a powerful tool calls for careful and thoughtful control.

19. LONG-TERM LIPS (12:19)

Continuing the theme of words and returning to the matter of truth telling (see Proverbs 12:17), this verse celebrates the enduring nature of truth. On one level, truth itself is eternal, for it usually manages to win out in the end, while lies tend to be revealed and removed (although their impact can be long lasting; see 12:18). But 12:19 suggests that it is not only truth which is eternal; **truthful lips** are also. God will reward the truth teller with security and permanence. The phrase **lasts only a moment** is translated "in an instant" in Jeremiah 49:19 and 50:44. The God of truth will silence this **tongue** instantly (Prov. 12:19).

20. MOTIVATED BY JOY (12:20)

"What we pursue for others, and the way we pursue it, leaves its mark on our cast of mind."[8] Proverbs 12:20 contrasts **those who** seek to deceive others with **evil** intent (continuing the theme found in 12:17, 19) with **those who** act from a spirit of **joy.** The New Jerusalem Bible expresses this contrast even more clearly: "Deceit is in the heart of the schemer, joy with those who give counsels of peace" (12:20). Since **promote peace** probably implies the idea of good counsel (12:20; see 11:14b where the same verb is used), the theme of words continues.

21. DON'T POKE A HOLE IN YOUR OWN BOAT (12:21)

This verse does not promise a trouble-free existence for **the righteous.** The **harm** in view is of the self-made variety. Righteousness protects itself by avoiding those activities which tend to harm the actor. **The wicked** are full of **trouble** because they have chosen a route which takes them by way of the trouble spots. Only a fool would sabotage his own efforts.

22. GOD LOVES TRUTH (12:22)

According to Proverbs 12:19, deceit is short lived, and this proverb tells why. God hates dishonesty, along with perversity (11:20) and several other offenses (6:16-19). He delights in truthfulness, as well as goodness (11:27; 12:2), blamelessness (11:20), honesty in business (11:1), and wisdom (8:35). **Men who are truthful** (12:22) is more literally "doers of faithfulness," suggesting that more is in view here than telling the truth. The New Jerusalem Bible reflects this in its translation of 12:22b: "Dear to him [Yahweh] [are] those who make truth their way of life."

23. WHEN KNOWLEDGE SHOULD BE HIDDEN (12:23)

Sometimes wisdom is best expressed not in what is said, but in what is left unsaid. Leave it to the **prudent man** to know the difference (12:23). Characterized by self-control, he both possesses **knowledge** and knows when and how to use it. **Fools,** lacking self-control, blurt out everything they know, which is not much. **Folly** comes from **the heart** because, at heart, a fool is what he is.

24. ANOTHER BENEFIT OF DILIGENCE (12:24)

As with Proverbs 12:11, diligence and **laziness** are contrasted (12:24). There the end result was either ample "food" or evident folly. Here the end is either authority or loss of freedom. The lazy not only go hungry and reveal their lack of judgment, but they become slaves. In ancient Israel, a person in financial trouble could sell himself into slavery for a limited period after which he would be released. The **diligent** not only thrive, they **rule,** by implication, over the lazy.

25. THE POWER OF A GOOD WORD (12:25)

The first line of Proverbs 12:25a needs no explanation. Medical science and our own experience confirm the burdensome effects of anxiety. The Hebrew word for **anxious** can describe a wide range of emotions from concern which takes precautions (see Joshua 22:24) to despair which abandons hope (see Ezekiel 4:16; 12:18-19). **A kind word** (a "good word"; Prov. 12:25) is good in quality (appropriate to the occasion and morally proper) and good in effect (it lifts the load). "A good word is wider than the good news which would remove the cause of the anxiety but is not always possible; a good word gives courage to face it."[9] To heighten the contrast between **weighs . . . down** and **cheers . . . up,** the author chooses two similar-sounding words. Our words should be chosen with as much care in order to ease someone's **anxious heart.**

26. CHOOSE YOUR FRIENDS CAREFULLY (12:26)

The first line of this proverb requires a great deal of explanation, and the proposed translations in the New International Version are only two of several offerings. Does the **righteous man** choose his friends carefully, guide his friends, make wise decisions, survive misfortune, or turn away from evil?[10] He does all these, in fact, but we are unsure which one is counseled in 12:26a. The reading in the NIV margin note has the advantage of providing a suitable parallel between the lines (guides and goes **astray**) and continuing the themes of responsibility for others (see 12:25) and the value of words (much of chapter 12).

27. TREASURE LIFE (12:27)

The sense of this proverb is clear—diligence is better than laziness—but the details are not. Some suggest that **the lazy man does not roast** the **game** he catches (NIV), others that he catches nothing (see RSV). The end, in either case, is the same. "But the substance of a precious man is diligent" translates the second line more literally. This may mean that **the diligent man prizes his possessions,** that diligence makes a person rich ("A diligent man has precious wealth" [NJPS]), or that diligence is what makes him a man of quality ("Diligence is anyone's most precious possession" [12:27b NJB]). The last option seems to make the best use of the Hebrew as it stands and provides a suitable parallel. **The lazy man** has nothing; **the diligent man,** having diligence, has all he needs.

28. LIFE OR DEATH (12:28)

Proverbs 12 concludes by promoting **righteousness** as the path to life (12:28). Because the second line is difficult to translate from the Hebrew, some modify the original to produce a smooth statement which contrasts with the first: "But [there is] a way [which is] a path to death" (see RSV; TEV). Others make minor modification to the Hebrew and emerge with a more awkward phrase: "And the journey of her pathway is no-death" (see NIV; NJPS). This awkwardness and the switch to synonymous parallelism after so many examples of antithetic parallelism (see commentary introduction) catch the ear and make us attend to its truth. The weight of that truth, which takes us to the doorstep—perhaps over the threshold—of eternity, serves as a fitting conclusion for the section which began at 10:1. The fatherly counsel of the next verse begins a new section which may extend to 15:19 or to 22:16.

ENDNOTES

[1]F. Delitzsch, *Proverbs, Ecclesiastes, Song of Solomon,* Commentary on the Old Testament, by C. F. Keil and F. Delitzsch, vol. 10 (Grand Rapids, Michigan: Wm. B. Eerdmans Publishing Co., 1978 [1872]); NJPS.

[2]Derek Kidner, *Proverbs: An Introduction and Commentary,* Tyndale Old Testament Commentaries, ed. D. J. Wiseman (Downers Grove, Illinois: InterVarsity Press, 1964), p. 96.

[3]Delitzsch, p. 255.

[4]Kidner, p. 97.

[5]**Plunder** is used in this sense in Ecclesiastes 7:26.

[6]Kidner, p. 97.

[7]Ronald Knox in *The Old Testament Newly Translated from the Latin Vulgate* (1949) as cited by Kidner, p. 98.

[8]Kidner, p. 98.

[9]Ibid., p. 99.

[10]NIV; NIV margin note; Delitzsch; R. B. Y. Scott, *Proverbs, Ecclesiastes,* The Anchor Bible, vol. 18, eds. William F. Albright and David Noel Freedman (New York: Doubleday, 1965); RSV.

13

PROVERBS 13

13:1-25

Righteousness not only **guards the man of integrity** (13:6), but it richly rewards him as well, as Proverbs 13 makes clear.

1. FATHER KNOWS BEST (13:1)

A statement like this encouraging a son's attention to parental advice indicates the beginning of a new section (see Proverbs 2:1; 3:1; 4:1; 5:1; 6:1; 7:1; 10:1). **Instruction** (13:1) is often translated "discipline" (see 13:24); this is instruction with reinforcements. **Heeds** must be supplied (13:1) since there is no verb in the first line of the Hebrew. Some suggest that the original verb was accidentally omitted by a copyist in transcribing Scripture (see RSV), others that the author intended the verb in the second part of the verse to serve both lines (see NIV), a difficult but not impossible view. Another possibility takes the verse as it stands:

A wise son—it is through the discipline of his father;
A scoffer—he never heard reproof (NJPS).

In any case, the responsibility rests on both parents and children: The children must listen to direction, and the parents must provide it.

2. WHEN EATING YOUR WORDS IS A GOOD THING (13:2)

We do not often think of eating our words as being something pleasant, but this proverb suggests otherwise. With the right kind of words, anyone can experience **good things** or can eat well (depending on whether the Hebrew word for **good** is translated as an adjective or as an adverb).

Craving is, literally, the noun *nephesh,* commonly translated "soul." Some translators employ less common meanings for this word, such as "desire," "hungry," "delight," "appetite," or "throat."[1] "The soul of the treacherous feeds on violence" (13:2b NJB) or, even stronger, "is violence," makes good sense of the passage and contrasts nicely with the first line.

3. WHEN EATING YOUR WORDS IS A BAD THING (13:3)

Not all words are tasty. This proverb continues the theme of words begun in Proverbs 13:2 and reuses the Hebrew word, *nephesh,* **life** (13:3). Words not only can bring "good things" (13:2), but can determine our destiny. If one **speaks** carefully—avoiding rash promises, preserving confidences, restraining harsh words—security follows (13:3). To speak **rashly** is, literally, to "open wide his lips," used only here in the Old Testament. A similar expression, found in Ezekiel 16:25, refers to careless promiscuity. Such a one, according to commentator F. Delitzsch, "expresses unexamined and unconsidered whatever comes into his mind and gives delight."[2] **Comes to ruin** (Prov. 13:3) is, literally, "ruin to him"; **ruin** becomes his personal possession ("He who opens wide his mouth, it is his ruin" [NJPS]).

4. DESIRE IS NO SUBSTITUTE FOR DILIGENCE (13:4)

This proverb provides a wonderful example of chiasm (see commentary introduction). Translated more literally the verse reads,

> [He] craves and gets nothing,
> > the soul of the sluggard;
> > the soul of the diligent
> Is richly satisfied.

Notice how the first and last lines present ideas opposite to one another, while the second and third lines do the same. Biblical authors loved this literary device; so many passages, even entire books, reveal it in varying degrees of complexity. Translating the second use of *nephesh* as "soul" (as above) rather than **desires** (13:4), emphasizes the importance of diligence and sharpens the contrast between unfulfilled longings and rich supply (see 12:11, 24, 27). **Fully satisfied** (13:4) is related in Hebrew to "fatness" (a positive quality in ancient Israel); this is satisfaction that shows.

5. DO YOU HATE WHAT IS FALSE? (13:5)

This proverb returns to the theme of words and particularly to the importance of honest speech. Because **the righteous hate what is false** (literally, "a word of deceit"), the temptation to speak such words has no hold on them. **The wicked** love deception and prove it by using lies to slander and defame. They **bring shame and disgrace** both on themselves and others. The double object, **shame and disgrace,** is meant to emphasize the evil effects of their speech.

6. THE BEST DEFENSE IS RIGHTEOUSNESS (13:6)

How can the upright protect themselves against the slander of the wicked (see Proverbs 13:5)? **Righteousness** (13:6) provides the surest defense. Those who demonstrate their **wickedness** through deceitful speech and in other ways will be overthrown. The connection between verses 5 and 6 is strengthened if the second line of verse 6 is translated "sin causes the ruin of the wicked" (NJB). **Overthrows** includes the idea of destruction (13:6; see Job 12:19), but can also describe the manipulation of words so that their true meaning is lost. God warns the Israelites against making a bribe which "twists the words of the righteous" and obscures the truth (see Exodus 23:8). God can twist words also, as in Proverbs 22:12 where He "frustrates the words of the unfaithful" (the same Hebrew word stands behind "frustrates"). The threat in 13:6 may be that the deceitful words of the wicked will boomerang and "shame and disgrace" the speaker (13:5).

7. WEALTH: THE ILLUSION (13:7)

This proverb, by itself (though meant to be read with the next), represents an accurate observation about life. We know the observation is true, but are not sure what to do with it except to take people's claims of **wealth** or poverty with a grain of salt. It also reminds us of the warning in 12:9 against pretending to be who we are not.

8. WEALTH: THE DANGER (13:8)

This verse and the preceding, read together, illuminate each other. Together they make the point that wealth is not all it is "cracked up to be."

It does not always match up with appearances, for you cannot really tell who is rich by what a person says or how a person appears (see Proverbs 13:7). Wealth may, in fact, make your life more difficult. Yes, the wealthy have money to ransom themselves out of difficulty, but it may have been their wealth that brought them into difficulty in the first place; the **poor man hears no threat** (or "no rebuke"). The wealthy must not only worry about violent threats such as robbery and kidnapping, but also about tax shelters, investments, and maintaining all those possessions. After hours of fixing, painting, mowing, oiling, inspecting, and replacing, you realize you do not own things; they own you. Together verses 7 and 8 caution against making money your goal, for it is an overpriced investment.

9. THE BRIGHTLY BURNING LAMP (13:9)

This proverb picturesquely contrasts the destiny of **the righteous** and **wicked** by speaking of their **lamp**—that is, their lives (13:9; see Job 18:5-6). **The light of the righteous shines brightly** (Prov. 13:9); literally, it rejoices. How does **light** rejoice? Many scholars see in the flickering flame the dance of joy that characterizes **the righteous** person. **The lamp of the wicked is snuffed out.** One minute it shines brightly, and the next it is dark with only a momentary trail of smoke. Commentator R. N. Whybray points out that a burning light meant family life and activity, "and its (permanent) extinguishing signified the extermination of a household."[3]

10. PRIDE GOES BEFORE A FIGHT (13:10)

If sociologists have correctly described our North American culture as one quick to quarrel, this proverb helps explain why. We have an abundance of **pride,** which can **only** lead to fights. **Pride,** by definition, imagines itself superior to others and, if I am superior, my will must be done. If others also feel this way, we can have "nothing but trouble" (TEV). How much better to admit our need for God and others and **take advice** from them. Who could argue with that?

11. WEALTH: NO FAST TRACK THERE (13:11)

The skeptical view of wealth in Proverbs 13:7-8 is balanced by this proverb which speaks of the right way to wealth (the same Hebrew word for **money** is used in 13:7b, 11a). **Dishonest money** (13:11; literally, "wealth from vanity") could refer to money gained deceitfully (see NIV) or money made in haste (requires the transposition of two Hebrew letters; see the Septuagint[4] and the Vulgate). The right way to make **money** is **little by little.** Literally, the original Hebrew calls for the money to be made "upon the hand," an idiom that implies hard work and patience. Make money the long, hard way, and it will grow. Choose "quick money," and watch it slip between your fingers.

12. WEALTH: WORTH WAITING FOR (13:12)

This proverb serves as a counterpart to 13:11. By taking the long route (see 13:11), one defers gratification and leaves room for despair. Verse 12 counsels **hope** and perseverance; the best is yet to be. **Longing fulfilled** is, literally, "desire coming," which suggests the ongoing nature of the fulfillment. This fits well with the picture of the **tree of life** which continues to produce shade and fruit to sustain the soul. All good things, including wealth, are worth waiting and hoping for.

13. REVERENCE FOR THE WORDS OF THE WISE (13:13)

This and the following proverb counsel obedience to the wise. The scorner will pay for his attitude, presumably with disaster. The one who listens will be paid back for his obedience. Whether to pay for disaster or be paid back in blessing—this is not a tough call. Although not an explicit reference, **command** could include divine as well as human commands (13:13). If so, this would be one of the few places where God's law[5] is explicitly mentioned in Proverbs.

14. THE REWARDS FOR OBEYING THE WORD (13:14)

The rewards promised in Proverbs 13:13 are illustrated here; by altering the pattern of parallelism from antithetic (see commentary introduction), those rewards are emphasized even more. **A fountain** (13:14) or spring of water meant a continual supply to irrigate crops, sustain life, and quench the thirst of man and beast. The ancient Israelite would consider himself blessed to have such **a fountain** of water. The obedient possess **a fountain of life** from which one can always draw instruction and find refreshment. This **fountain,** by opening one's eyes to see the deadly **snares** into which the scorner would fall, could even enable escape from **death.**

15. FAVOR OR FAILURE (13:15)

Commentator F. Delitzsch connects the next four proverbs by the sound of their words in the original Hebrew. A stronger connection seems to exist in that they all (with the possible exception of verse 17) concern the benefits of righteousness. The first line of 13:15 is clear enough: People prefer the wise and righteous person to the fool. This is true at home (10:1), in the city (11:10), and with God (12:2). This favor, according to Proverbs, brings blessing. **The way of the unfaithful** provides a clear contrast to those with **good understanding,** but **hard** may not be the best way to translate the Hebrew at the end of the second line (13:15). This word usually means "perennial" (as a river; see Amos 5:24) or permanent (as a rock; see NIV). Delitzsch takes the latter view, calling the unfaithful "uncultivated," like a stony riverbed. The way such people conduct themselves with others is "stiff, as hard as stone, and repulsive; they follow selfish views, never placing themselves in sympathy with the condition of their neighbour; they remain destitute of feeling in things which, as we say, would soften a stone."[6] The New International Version reading, "The way of the unfaithful does not endure," represents the view that the two-letter word for "not" has accidentally dropped out of the Hebrew. Either reading brings us to the same point.

16. THINK BEFORE YOU ACT (13:16)

When I was younger, after having lost my keys for the umpteenth time, my parents bought me a key chain shaped like a very large light bulb with the one-word message, "THINK." They were trying to reinforce the message of this proverb, which really continues the thought of 13:15 with its theme of wisdom's qualities and benefits. We have met this **prudent man** several times before (13:16). In 12:23 he had knowledge, but knew the right time to speak it. Now the **prudent man acts,** and his actions demonstrate his wisdom. He not only knows how to act, but he also knows when. The **fool** knows neither when nor how to act: "The fool parades his folly" (13:16b NJB; see also 15:2).

17. MAKE WISE CHOICES (13:17)

Evidence of having good understanding (see Proverbs 13:15) and prudence (see 13:16) is choosing wisely those who will help you.

128

Messengers in ancient Israel were essential components in most transactions, whether personal, commercial, or civic (see Genesis 32:3, 6; Job 1:14; 2 Kings 5:19-24; 6:32). Since the wrong **messenger** (Prov. 13:17) could mean miscommunication, lost profits or broken treaties, choosing the right person was essential. Make the wrong choice, and your message might never get through, and you will lose even more time going to the aid of your messenger. Make the right choice, and **healing** results.

18. TREASURE DISCIPLINE (13:18)

This proverb returns to the theme of 13:1, but expands on it by describing what happens when discipline is ignored or obeyed. Ironically, those who ignore **discipline** (13:18; the same word translated "instruction" in 13:1) do not see any need to be corrected. They are in good shape; at least they think they are in better shape than the one who disciplines them, and they see themselves as worthy of honor. When someone accepts **discipline,** he humbly and willingly accepts the authority of the discipliner (literally, he "guards" **correction** [13:18]), admits his need for change and sets about to do so. By viewing himself as undeserving of honor, this person becomes honorable, while those who think they deserve honor get **poverty and shame** instead.

19. WHY TREASURE DISCIPLINE? (13:19)

This proverb may continue the thought of 13:18. A person allows correction out of **a longing** to become better (13:19). Such a hope will not disappoint for **a longing fulfilled is sweet to the soul.** A fool ignores discipline because it is distasteful to him. **Detest** is not too strong a word; the line could read, "turning from evil is an abomination to fools." If only he had enough sense, the fool would see he forfeited a satisfied soul for "poverty and shame" (13:18).

20. YOU WHO WALK WITH WISE MEN, BECOME WISE (13:20)

Parental advice was not the only component in the education of a young person. Your choice of companions also helps to determine whether you become a **wise** person or a fool (13:20). The wisdom of others will rub off on you as you listen to their words, obey their counsel, and observe their actions. Become **a companion of fools,** and you will become foolish. "Fool he ends that fool befriends."[7] Still worse, such a person will suffer the fate of the fool, a destiny emphasized by a word play between the Hebrew for **companion** *(roeh)* and **suffers harm** *(yeroa).*

21. CHASED BY TROUBLE OR PAID BY PROSPERITY (13:21)

This proverb picks up where 13:20 leaves off, with the problems suffered by those who ignore God's direction. Be sure to notice the aggressive tone of these words. The wicked do not just experience misfortune, it pursues them like a wild animal. Although the New International Version makes **prosperity . . . the reward of the righteous,** the original Hebrew makes **prosperity** *the rewarder* **of the righteous** ("good will reward the upright" [13:21b NJB]). This vivid picture suggests a cup "full and running over." Our allegiance to God determines whether we will be chased by trouble or paid by **prosperity.**

22. A LASTING LEGACY (13:22)

Once again the benefits of righteousness are described; here the focus is not on what **the righteous** receive, but what they leave behind. The **good man** has the assurance that he bequeaths **an inheritance** not only for his children, but also for his grandchildren. Either this means that he leaves behind too much wealth to spend in a single generation or, more probably, he leaves behind more than money; he leaves a priceless, godly heritage. Not only does the sinner leave nothing to his children, but his sins continue to haunt him after his death. It is **the righteous** who profit from the fool's estate.

23. GOD BLESSES HARD WORK (13:23)

As it appears in the New International Version, this proverb teaches that **injustice** deprives the **poor** of what they deserve. If this is the right translation, it provides a good reason to leave something behind for one's children and grandchildren (see 13:22) and challenges God's people to battle injustice, a view supported elsewhere in Proverbs. Other translations have been offered, however:

Though the farms of the poor yield much food,
some perish for lack of justice (NJB).

Unused fields could yield plenty of food for the poor,
but unjust men keep them from being farmed (TEV).

Still another, more likely possibility is suggested by commentator F. Delitzsch who argues that the Hebrew behind **field** (13:23) is better translated "fresh land"—that is, previously untilled land which has, by diligent labor, been planted. Because of God's blessing, it yields an **abundant** harvest. The moral: God blesses hard work. The second line speaks not of **injustice,** but of the wealthy who, with all their advantages, lose what they possess because of iniquity.[8] Another translation follows a similar line of thought:

The tillage of the poor yields much food;
But substance is swept away for lack of moderation (NJPS).

24. HAVE THE DISCIPLINE TO DISCIPLINE (13:24)

If obedience to God yields all the blessings promised in Proverbs 13, then parents must properly train their children. This is no excuse to abuse, for abuse is motivated by anger and fear, not love. Unlike earlier proverbs in this chapter (especially 13:1, 18), 13:24 is directed at parents. It takes discipline to **discipline** children. In the hectic pace of life, it is easy to let things slide and not fulfill parental responsibility. But real love makes the effort. Note, too, that **discipline** is not an end in itself, but the means to an end, namely the development of wise children. Parents must know their children well enough to know what it will take to bring about wisdom in each one.

25. THE SATISFIED SOUL (13:25)

We have heard much of the blessings of righteousness in the preceding verses. Once again this theme is sounded in this proverb, which is rich in double meaning. On one hand, 13:25 contrasts the full, satisfied belly of **the righteous** with the empty stomach of **the wicked.** This very practical reality is asserted several times in Proverbs 13 alone (see verses 2, 4, 23). But **to their hearts' content** (13:25) can also be rendered "to the satisfying of his soul" (KJV). Perhaps a satisfaction deeper than physical hunger is also in view, a point made in 13:4, 12-15, 19, and elsewhere. Going God's way means contentment for the whole person—body, mind, and spirit.

ENDNOTES

[1] RSV; TEV; F. Delitzsch, *Proverbs, Ecclesiastes, Song of Solomon,* Commentary on the Old Testament, by C. F. Keil and F. Delitzsch, vol. 10 (Grand Rapids, Michigan: Wm. B. Eerdmans Publishing Co., 1978 [1872]); R. B. Y. Scott, *Proverbs, Ecclesiastes,* The Anchor Bible, vol. 18, eds. William F. Albright and David Noel Freedman (New York: Doubleday, 1965); NJPS.

[2] Delitzsch, p. 271.

[3] R. N. Whybray, *Proverbs,* The New Century Bible Commentary (Grand Rapids, Michigan: Wm. B. Eerdmans Publishing Co., 1994), p. 203.

[4] The Septuagint is the Greek version of the Old Testament, translated from the original Hebrew scrolls, and written in the second and third centuries B.C. It is often indicated by the Roman numerals LXX in accordance with the legend that it was translated by seventy scribes.

[5] Law here refers to the Levitical Code (all God's rules and regulations).

[6] Delitzsch, p. 281.

[7] Ronald Knox in *The Old Testament Newly Translated from the Latin Vulgate* (1949) as cited by Derek Kidner in *Proverbs: An Introduction and Commentary,* Tyndale Old Testament Commentaries, ed. D. J. Wiseman (Downers Grove, Illinois: InterVarsity Press, 1964), p. 104.

[8] Delitzsch, p. 286.

14

PROVERBS 14

14:1-35

From the humble home (see Proverbs 14:1) to the king's palace (see 14:35), wisdom is the way to go. But remember, wisdom requires the **fear of the LORD** (14:27; see 14:2, 16, 26).

1. ARE YOU IN THE CONSTRUCTION OR DESTRUCTION BUSINESS? (14:1)

So many of the proverbs speak to the edification of the household. For Israel, as for our own society, the family forms its backbone. This proverb points to the importance of the wife and mother for a strong and healthy home. **The wise woman builds** is, more literally, "the wisest of women builds" (NJPS). The New Jerusalem Bible takes this to refer to Lady Wisdom herself, thus linking this verse with Proverbs 9 and illustrating what wisdom can do. Lady Folly's actions become even more ridiculous with the addition of **with her own hands** (14:1), for who would willingly destroy her home? Young men benefit from this proverb by seeing the wisdom of choosing a wise wife; young women are shown a good example to follow.

2. GOD IS NOT MOCKED (14:2)

Wisdom and folly are more than intellectual activities, but include right living, a point reinforced by Proverbs 14:2. This verse also makes clear that wisdom is demonstrated by how one walks, not just by one's words. Still more sobering is the assertion that the **devious** person does not merely disobey God; that person **despises,** "scorns" or "displays contempt"[1] for Him. This Hebrew word describes Esau's attitude toward his birthright (see Genesis 25:34); it was worth less to him than a bowl of stew. In this light, to disobey God is just as foolish as tearing down your house with your own hands (see Proverbs 14:1).

3. YOUR WORDS CAN PROTECT YOU (14:3)

Lest Proverbs 14:2 be understood to say that words do not matter, 14:3 reminds us that they do. According to the New International Version, they can mean the difference between punishment and protection. A more literal reading sees the first line as speaking not of the destiny, but of the character of the fool ("Pride sprouts in the mouth of the fool" [14:3a NJB]). **Rod** refers to the branch, which reveals the health of the root; it is used this way in the only other Old Testament passage where this word appears (see Isaiah 11:1 KJV).[2] Instead of contrasting punishment with protection (as the NIV), this reading contrasts the arrogant boasting of the fool with the prudent speech of **the wise** (Prov. 14:3).

4. WORK LIKE AN OX (14:4)

Perhaps the agricultural allusion in 14:3 led to another proverb from the farm. We begin in the stall with an impeccably neat manger. While this may appeal to our sense of neatness, no one can eat neatness. The **ox** (14:4) and the work associated with his care are essential. Wisdom is no substitute for hard work; in fact, wisdom requires that we work with an ox-like attitude.

5. TELL THE TRUTH, PART 1 (14:5)

The power of this proverb lies in its simple call for truth couched in extremities and literary skill. This skill, evident in the chiastic arrangement (see 13:4 for another example; see also commentary introduction), emphasizes the contrast between the faithful and **false witness** (literally):

> A faithful witness
>> does not lie,
>> but he breathes out lies
> A false witness.

Unlike the **truthful witness** (14:5) who "tells no lies," the **false witness** "lies with every breath" (NJB). As 6:19 makes clear, those who fear God must speak the truth.

6. A LEARNING DISABILITY (14:6)

As frustrating as learning disabilities can be, this one is the worst of all. Here we have **the mocker** who looks for **wisdom,** but cannot find it (14:6). The problem lies not in the elusiveness of **wisdom,** but in **the mocker.** He cannot learn because he "does not listen to rebuke" (13:1); his scornful attitude brings him not **wisdom,** but the scorn of God (see 3:34). Wisdom is readily available for **the discerning** for whom it **comes easily** (14:6).

7. AVOID FOOLISH FRIENDS (14:7)

This proverb continues the theme of acquiring wisdom and the contrast between the fool and the wise. In spite of difficulties translating the second line, the general sense of this proverb is clear: The wise person avoids fools for they cannot bring wisdom (see 13:20). Line 2 reads (literally), "for you do not know lips of knowledge." Since this is difficult, Scott alters the line to read "and do not lavish wise words" on the fool. The New International Version is probably correct to retain the Hebrew, and take it as a warning against expecting to learn from a fool.

8. CHECK THE ROAD MAP (14:8)

I hate to admit it when I am lost. I have driven long and fast in one direction to avoid stopping at a gas station and admitting I don't know where I am going. Because this flaw is deadly in the moral realm, **the prudent** man thinks about the right way to go (14:8). In fact, he shows his prudence by checking the map and carefully following its directions. Even if the fool checks the map, he continues on the wrong road: "The folly of the stupid misleads them."[3] In his arrogant stupidity, the fool has torn off the compass rosette and now has no idea which way to hold the map. The fool who cannot learn (14:6) and speaks only folly (14:7), drives determinedly in the wrong direction (14:8), and laughs at oncoming traffic (14:9).

9. LAUGHING AT ONCOMING TRAFFIC (14:9)

Several possible interpretations exist for this proverb. Some see the fool mocking the need to make atonement, or to feel guilt, or to offer sacrifices.[4] Others see the sacrifices mocking the fool.[5] According to the last view (probably closest to the original Hebrew), the sacrifices ridicule the fool who must continually present expensive offerings as the price of folly. **The upright** need not fear such ridicule; instead they enjoy good relationships among themselves and (implied) with God.[6]

10. THE PRIVATE CHAMBERS OF THE HEART (14:10)

Commentator F. Delitzsch sees verse 10 as the first of four proverbs which deal with joy and sorrow in the present and future.[7] In addition, 14:10 provides important truths which a wise person must know. First, while many proverbs speak to human relationships, this one points to the depths which exist in each soul. No book on wisdom is complete unless it acknowledges these depths. Second, do not expect others to fully understand your **bitterness** and **joy.** You will thus be spared the frustration of trying to fully communicate these to others and will be brought, in prayer, to the only one who can understand (see 1 Kings 8:38). Finally, this proverb puts the wise on guard against the manipulator who pretends to unburden his soul or to be able to understand when you unburden yours. "The upright" may enjoy fellowship with each other (see Proverbs 14:9), but only God fully understands your heart (see 17:3; 21:2; 24:12).

11. DON'T BE FOOLED BY APPEARANCES (14:11)

Sometimes the ultimate security of the righteous—a theme sounded often in Proverbs—seems contrary to the facts. After all, **the wicked** live in a **house,** while the righteous have only a **tent** (14:11). Houses are more permanent, more secure; tents can be flattened by strong winds or falling trees. But appearances can deceive, for **the house of the wicked will be destroyed,** while **the tent of the upright will flourish.** In trying to express the permanence of the righteous, the proverb explodes the domestic metaphor. The upright's **tent** becomes a tree bursting into buds whose roots go deep into the soil—too deep to be uprooted (see 12:3)— and whose branches provide shade and fruit and joy for generations to come (see 13:22).

12. ASK SOMEONE WHO HAS BEEN THAT WAY (14:12)

If verses 10 and 13 speak of the private world, this proverb (repeated exactly in 16:25) emphasizes our need for others. The wise person does not trust his or her own judgment, even if it **seems right.** The "wicked" man of 14:11 looks down in scorn from the window of his house on the poor but righteous person in his "tent."[8] Proverbs 14:12 counsels trust in the advice of those who have been down the road ahead of you—God, parents, wise counselors, those who know the road which leads to life and joy.

13. LOOK BEYOND THE LAUGHTER (14:13)

Life contains tragedy which no amount of **laughter** can fully hide (14:13). All the wisdom in the world cannot make it otherwise. Those who remember this will not foolishly expect cloudless skies or be surprised by suffering. Life may begin with birth, in joy, but it always ends at death, with **grief.**[9] The wise will know that the people they meet, even those laughing on the outside, have secret pain. Such knowledge, while it falls short of complete understanding (see 14:10), can guide the wise to more compassionate interaction.

14. "WRONGS WILL BE MADE RIGHT WHEN ASLAN COMES IN SIGHT" (14:14)

In *The Lion, the Witch, and the Wardrobe* by C. S. Lewis, the good inhabitants of the land of Narnia have a proverb about Aslan, the lion who rules their country, but whose absence has brought a time "when it is winter, but never Christmas." They console themselves through the cold nights and dark days with this reminder, "Wrongs will be made right when Aslan comes in sight." This same truth, that there is a God in heaven who will one day right all wrongs, sustained Old Testament believers through exile and centuries of foreign domination and gave hope to the early church during persecution. Vindication is sure and will be complete: The wicked **will be fully repaid** (14:14). Elsewhere this verb is translated "filled" or "satisfied" as if by a large meal. **The faithless** must one day eat his fill from the menu of his own faithlessness. **The good man** will also eat his fill, but from a more appetizing menu. Here is cause for encouragement on cold nights and dark days.

15. BE SENSIBLE (14:15)

Those who told you that "gullible" was not in the dictionary were teasing (really). If they said, however, that "gullible" is not in the

prudent person's dictionary, they would be absolutely right (14:15). The **simple man believes** everything he hears, but the **prudent** one is more careful. He (literally) "gives heed to his step"—that is, he "looks where he is going" (NJPS). Perhaps this is what Jesus had in mind when He instructed His followers in Matthew to be "shrewd as snakes and as innocent as doves" (Matt. 10:16). The next two proverbs continue the theme of folly and sense.

16. BE CAUTIOUS (14:16)

Reverence for God breeds caution which, as we have seen elsewhere, produces rewards.[10] That God designed things this way can be seen on Mount Sinai in Exodus 20. His displays of power which accompanied the giving of the Law were meant to produce reverent fear in Israel[11] ("to keep you from sinning" [Exod. 20:20]). The **fool,** we see here in Proverbs, provides a good example of what happens when reverence and caution are lacking (14:16). **Hotheaded** refers to his fierce anger, perhaps kindled by some supposed slight. **Reckless** means he has total confidence in his own abilities and judgments—he reveres himself, not God. Ablaze with indignation and overconfidence he presses on, only to be burned by his own stupidity. Good examples are Peter before his denial of Christ (see Matthew 26:31-35) and Amaziah with Joash (see 2 Chronicles 25:17).

17. BE PATIENT, PART 1 (14:17)

Both the **quick-tempered** (14:17; see 14:16) and **crafty** want what they want when they want it. The one may demand it with fire in his eye, while the other may try to get it by trickery. Both lack the patience to wait, and neither receives what is sought. The hot-tempered (see TEV) end up with only a pile of problems of their own making (see 14:1). People grow weary of being manipulated and deceived and steer a wide path around the "schemer" (14:17 NJB) who also fails in his pursuit. The moral of the story: Good things come to those who wait . . . on God.

18. BE PRUDENT (14:18)

The previous three verses are well summarized in Proverbs 14:18. The gullible (14:15), "hotheaded" (14:16), overconfident (14:17) fool will **inherit folly** (14:18). That is, the stupid will only become more stupid. Those who exercise prudence—thinking ahead (14:15), avoiding "evil" (14:16), being patient (14:17)—inherit a crown of **knowledge, visible proof of one's wisdom (14:18).

19. VINDICATION WILL COME (14:19)

As prudence is rewarded with honor (see Proverbs 14:18), so is righteousness. Such honor may not come immediately (see 14:9, 12). But someday everyone, even the wicked, will have to publicly—**at the gates of the righteous (14:19)—acknowledge the superiority of God's ways and His people. With their poorly developed understanding of an afterlife, the Israelites spoke of a day in this life, on this earth. As the light of God's revelation dawned more brightly, New Testament believers realized that Judgment Day would come after this life at the end of this earth. This hope for justice has sustained God's people from the Old Testament to the present hour (see 14:14).

20. POOR AND WISE (14:20-21)

The next two proverbs should be interpreted together, for they complement one another. Verse 20 states the obvious: People prefer the company of **the rich** to that of **the poor.** A perceptive glance around the room at any social gathering will prove the point. While this proverb contains a warning to the lazy who bring poverty on themselves, it also sets the stage for verse 21.

Most people ignore the poor because they see no benefit to be gained by associating with them (see 14:20). Such behavior is out of place for the righteous, for it is sinful (although we must wait until 14:31 for a clear explanation why). Instead, we should be **kind** to all, even **the needy** (14:21), and thereby receive a blessing from God (see 19:17). Some translate the second line more generally—"He who shows pity for the lowly is happy" (NJPS)—but this happiness comes ultimately from God. God blesses us for treating others the way He treats everyone.

21. PLOT GOOD (14:22)

We do not usually think of "plotting" good, but this is what Proverbs 14:22 instructs us to do. The same Hebrew word is translated **plot** in line 1 and **plan** in line 2. Instead of plotting to harm another, plot something good for them. This suggests we should work as hard at being kind as some do at being cruel. Those who **plot evil** get lost, while those who plot **good find love and faithfulness. Love and faithfulness** are often found together in Hebrew poetry and represent God's gift of lasting love. The previous proverb promised God's blessing when we treat others as He does; this verse describes that blessing.

22. NO EASY WAY TO WEALTH (14:23)

Proverbs neither considers **poverty** a punishment from God nor condones behavior which leads to **poverty,** such as **mere talk** (literally, "words of lips"; 14:23). Words can do many things, but they cannot create wealth out of nothing. Wealth takes **work,** something any farmer laboring to live from Israel's soil would have understood. The contrast in this proverb is heightened by the use of similar sounding words for **profit** *(motar)* and **poverty** *(machsor).*

23. HARD CURRENCY OF WISDOM (14:24)

As seen with 14:20-21, a "secular" proverb is built upon and interpreted along more spiritual lines by the verse which follows. Wealth may result from "hard work" (14:23), but really comes as God's reward for diligence. **Wealth** crowns the **wise** (14:24) as "knowledge" crowns "the prudent" (14:18). "Mere talk" is really the sound fools make (14:23), and it produces not **wealth,** but only more **folly** (14:24; "fools get stupider by the day" [THE MESSAGE]).

24. TELL THE TRUTH, PART 2 (14:25)

This proverb looks very much like 14:5. Closer examination reveals development from that verse to this. There he is (literally) a faithful witness, here a **truthful** one. In verse 5 he "does not deceive"; in verse 25 he **saves lives.** In the earlier passage, the **false witness** "pours out lies," while in verse 25 he "is nothing but deception."[12] How does the **truthful witness** save lives? Quite literally, his testimony can make the difference between life and death for one falsely accused.

25. A SECURE FORTRESS (14:26)

This and the next proverb picture the fear of **the LORD**[13] first as a **fortress** (14:26), then as "a fountain" (14:27). The fear of **the LORD** surrounds us with sheltering walls, walls which keep out self-destructive behaviors (14:3, 16, 27) and harmful relationships (7:1-27) and places us safely in His hands (18:10). These walls surround not only us, but our **children** as well (14:26), for they are protected by our reverence as they grow up in good homes, with healthy relationships and an easy familiarity with things that really matter.

26. A FLOWING FOUNTAIN (14:27)

Not only does the fear of God provide a place to hide from danger, but it also offers a positive, nourishing source **of life** (14:27). Water means life in the arid climate of Israel, and **a fountain** meant flowing water, the best kind. Such **a fountain** also means protection, but of a different kind. The strong walls of the "fortress" (14:26) keep out unwanted elements, but the **fountain** presents a positive alternative to the temptation of deadly snares (14:27). Eugene Peterson puts it this way: "The Fear-of-GOD is a spring of living water so you won't go off drinking from poisoned wells" (THE MESSAGE). Together, 14:26 and 14:27 describe how "Godliness protects the soul by its solidity (verse 26) and its vitality (verse 27). Both aspects are necessary, since evil not only attacks, but attracts us."[14]

27. EVIDENCE OF SUCCESS (14:28)

As with 14:20-21 and 14:23-24, this verse belongs together with the preceding proverb. That verse spoke of the life-giving and life-preserving benefits of reverence for God. If the fear of God can preserve one person's life, a nation which fears God will be a secure and prosperous nation indeed. That nation which does not fear God will be weak and ridiculous, like a leader without a following. Verse 34 is another proverb with a national application.

28. BE PATIENT, PART 2 (14:29)

Although we have already learned the value of patience in Proverbs 14:17, the importance of that truth prompts the placement here of another reminder. The wise person not only avoids the disastrous consequences implied in 14:17a, but he demonstrates his wisdom.[15] The **quick-tempered man displays** what a fool he really is (14:29). More literally, he "exalts" his folly—that is, even as he raises his voice in impatient anger, he lifts up his foolishness for everyone to see.

29. HAVE A HEALTHY HEART (14:30)

The connection between tranquility and physical health is not a modern discovery. This proverb, continuing the theme of peaceable living from 14:29, describes how "peace of mind makes the body healthy" (TEV). **Envy,** on the other hand, **rots the bones** (14:30). **Envy** translates a Hebrew word which can have either a positive, a neutral, or a negative sense. It is used positively of Phinehas (see Numbers 25:11) and in a neutral sense of the jealous husband in Proverbs 6:34. Some translations take it this way here as the opposite of tranquility, without reference to whether the reason for the passion is right or wrong.[16] Perhaps those translations which translate the word as **envy** (14:30) have observed the destructive qualities of this emotion which destroys body and soul, and how it acts like "a cancer in the bones" (14:30 NJB).

30. INDIRECT PRAISE (14:31)

Proverbs speaks often about human relationships, but this verse stands out among such statements. It makes clear that how we treat others not only affects them, but indicates our attitude toward God. When we oppress a **poor** man, we treat his Creator with **contempt.** Kindness **to the needy** is actually indirect praise ("an act of worship" [TEV]), for in so doing we honor the God who created them. God singles out **the poor,** not because they are especially favored, but because they are especially vulnerable. Our kindness not only protects them, but helps to move them out of poverty into comfort. What a difference it would make in our relationships if we kept this truth in mind! So often we are tempted to treat people according to what they can do for us. This proverb teaches that everyone, even the person unable to repay us, deserves our kindness simply because God made him or her.[17]

31. REFUGE IN DEATH (14:32)

We have met this theme many times in Proverbs: the ultimate vindication of **the righteous** and defeat of **the wicked** (14:32). Its repeated mention implies how difficult it is to remember and how important it is to God. He sees our actions, discerns between righteousness and wickedness, and will bring justice on the earth. Many proverbs make it clear that the wicked bring their **calamity** on themselves. The Hebrew of the second line appears to speak of **the righteous** having **a refuge** in **death**—that is, in personal immortality. Because such a belief seems too advanced for ancient Israel, some translators have modified the Hebrew slightly to read "in his integrity," a reading which can be supported by the Septuagint.[18] The Hebrew should not be discarded so quickly, however. This may be one of the glimpses of eternity given to ancient Israel by God (see Psalm 49:15). Commentator F. Delitzsch points out as well that even without a clear picture of eternal reward, the dying righteous would still put their hope in God, trusting Him in the darkness.[19]

32. WISDOM AT HOME (14:33)

Wisdom is at home in the heart of **the discerning** person (14:33). She belongs there where she is appreciated and applied. The second line (literally), "but in the heart of fools [wisdom] is known," disagrees with other statements, which describe the fool as completely lacking wisdom (see 14:7). Early versions (the Septuagint, for example[20]) added "not," assuming the small word had dropped out, and many modern translations have followed (see the NIV margin note; CEV). If we leave the Hebrew text unchanged, it may mean that the wise man does not parade his knowledge as a fool does (see 12:23). Or the verse could be understood to say that although wisdom's true home is among the wise, she can sometimes be found **among fools** (14:33), more to the credit of wisdom's persistence than to the credit of her host.

33. RIGHTEOUSNESS MAKES A NATION GREAT (14:34)

Righteousness brings rewards, whether on an individual or national level (14:34; see 14:27-28), while sin dishonors wherever it goes. The Septuagint[21] correctly modifies the Hebrew from *chesed* to *cheser* ("want," "poverty") a change of only a minute pen stroke. Otherwise, one is forced to interpret *chesed*, usually translated "lovingkindness," as violent love. Sin disgraces **people** by causing them to act disgracefully, examples of which can be found any day in any newspaper. When **a nation** no longer sees such behavior as disgraceful, ultimate **disgrace** in God's eyes inevitably results.

34. HOW TO GET AHEAD (14:35)

This and the preceding proverb are equally at home in the throne room and hut. Because the **king,** whether human or divine, finds pleasure **in a wise servant,** be wise. The "incompetent" (NJPS) have only themselves to blame for their failure. Eugene Peterson puts this "royal" proverb in working clothes:

Diligent work gets a warm commendation;
shiftless work earns an angry rebuke (THE MESSAGE).

ENDNOTES

[1]NIV; NJPS; R. B. Y. Scott, *Proverbs, Ecclesiastes,* The Anchor Bible, vol. 18, eds. William F. Albright and David Noel Freedman (New York: Doubleday, 1965).

[2]Derek Kidner, *Proverbs: An Introduction and Commentary,* Tyndale Old Testament Commentaries, ed. D. J. Wiseman (Downers Grove, Illinois: InterVarsity Press, 1964), p. 106.

[3]Scott.

[4]NIV; Scott; NJB.

[5]F. Delitzsch, *Proverbs, Ecclesiastes, Song of Solomon,* Commentary on the Old Testament, by C. F. Keil and F. Delitzsch, vol. 10 (Grand Rapids, Michigan: Wm. B. Eerdmans Publishing Co., 1978 [1872]).

[6]The Contemporary English Version appears to despair of any reasonable translation and, after extensive modifications, translates,

Fools don't care if they are wrong,
but God is pleased when people do right.

[7]Delitzsch, p. 295.

[8]Another connection between this and the preceding verse is the Hebrew word translated **right** in verse 12a and **upright** in verse 11b.

[9]**End in** repeats the Hebrew phrase translated **in the end** in verse 12b.

[10]Because the New International Version adds **the LORD** after **fears,** it is permissible to translate this line, "The wise fears evil and avoids it" (NJB).

[11]Law refers to either the Levitical Code (all God's rules and regulations), the Ten Commandments, or the Pentateuch (the first five books of the Old Testament: Genesis, Exodus, Leviticus, Numbers, and Deuteronomy). It is often capitalized when it means the Pentateuch or the Ten Commandments.

[12]Delitzsch.

[13]The New International Version and other translations use LORD in small capitals following an initial capital L to denote "Yahweh" in the original Hebrew.

[14]Kidner, p. 110.

[15]This is probably better than seeing patience as a source of wisdom: "Patience results in much understanding" (NJPS).

[16]NJPS; Scott; RSV.

[17]For other verses dealing with a proper attitude to the poor, see Proverbs 14:20, 21; 17:5; 19:17; 22:2; 28:8; 29:13; also Job 31:15.

[18]The Septuagint is the Greek version of the Old Testament, translated from the original Hebrew scrolls, and written in the second and third centuries B.C. It is often indicated by the Roman numerals LXX in accordance with the legend that it was translated by seventy scribes.

[19]Delitzsch.

[20]See endnote 18.

[21]Ibid.

PROVERBS 15

15:1-33

Although the proper use of words and the importance of discipline are themes found throughout Proverbs, much of chapter 15 focuses on these themes.

1. ARE YOUR WORDS HARD OR SOFT? (15:1)

This proverb reminds us that words are powerful weapons for healing or hurt. In particular, it speaks of how we respond to provocation. **A gentle answer** is sensitive and compassionate (see Job 41:3); such words accomplish good by mildness and patience (see Proverbs 25:15), not by brute force. The **harsh** reply causes pain (Prov. 15:1; see Genesis 3:16 where the same word is used to describe Eve's punishment), and pain stirs up a hornet's nest of **anger** (Prov. 15:1). That it is singular (**harsh word**) rather than plural emphasizes that **anger** requires only a little provoking.

2. ARE YOUR WORDS CAREFUL OR CARELESS? (15:2)

The theme of words continues in Proverbs 15:2, this time addressing how carefully we speak. **Commends knowledge** is, literally, "makes knowledge good," which is taken by some to refer to the quantity of knowledge spoken by the wise ("produces much knowledge" [NJPS]), its quality ("showeth great knowledge"[1]), or how this knowledge is communicated to others ("makes knowledge welcome" [NJB]; "make knowledge attractive" [TEV]). The second line may refer to how many stupid things **the fool** says (**gushes**). More likely the contrast is between the **wise** person's carefully chosen and appealing words and the careless babbling of **the fool.**

3. BE CAREFUL, HANDS, WHAT YOU DO (15:3)

The Sunday school chorus that encouraged you to be careful what you see, hear, and do could have come from this proverb. God is watching us all—good and bad. He misses nothing, for His **eyes . . . are everywhere** (emphasized in the Hebrew); theologians call this omniscience. There is both comfort and warning here. The one watching is **the LORD** (Yahweh)[2] with whom Israel had an especially close relationship. He stands guard as the divine watchman at His post (the Hebrew for **keeping watch** is used in several other passages to speak of the man who guards a city). His scrutiny is not casual observation, but has greater purposes: protection of the righteous, and punishment of **the wicked.** So, be careful, hands, what you do.

4. BE CAREFUL, MOUTH, WHAT YOU SAY (15:4)

Proverbs 15:1 spoke of the power of words to provoke or calm a quarrel; 15:2 speaks of how the wise carefully consider what they say. This proverb describes the power of words to heal or harm. Those words which bring **healing** because they are gentle, wholesome, and soothing are **a tree of life,** fruitful, vivacious, nourishing (15:4). John provides a beautiful description of such trees in Revelation 22:2. **A deceitful tongue** (Prov. 15:4) not only speaks dishonestly, but destructively. It twists the truth with perversity and treachery intending only to "wound and maim" (THE MESSAGE).

5. PAY ATTENTION TO CORRECTION (15:5)

Proverbs speaks often of correction and discipline in chapter 15. This, the first such reference, locates **discipline** in its rightful place, the home. The **fool** sees no value in such correction and **spurns** it. **Spurns** implies more than ignoring; the **fool** hears, rejects, then rebels against authority (see examples in Psalm 107:11; Proverbs 1:30; 5:12). The wise son, recognizing that **discipline,** while unpleasant, implies a **father's** love and produces good results, yields to it and becomes wiser.

6. PROTECT YOUR INVESTMENT (15:6)

This proverb not only contrasts **the righteous** with **the wicked,** but what the former have in their houses with what the latter earn as **income.** Go into the home of a **righteous** person, and you will find **great treasure:** tranquility, happiness, and other signs of God's blessing securely on display. Since **house** can be translated "heritage," this verse may speak of how righteousness cultivates a godly heritage. **The wicked** possess no such **treasure** because they cannot afford it. Their paycheck either **brings them trouble,** such as those who squander their income by drinking or gambling, or it *is* trouble (see Romans 6:23). The sad example of Achan in Joshua 7 illustrates this truth.

7. DO YOUR WORDS MAKE OTHERS WISE? (15:7)

Wisdom deserves to be shared, and words are one important way to do so. Not all words are wise, however; they can only be found on the **lips of the wise** and originate in their hearts (15:7). **The hearts of fools** do not **spread knowledge,** only folly (15:7; see 15:2—the verb is used of scattering something like seed). Verse 7, while quite similar to verse 2, moves beyond it. The outcome of verse 2a ("commends") is found in verse 7a (**spread**). Verse 2b describes what fools do; verse 7b what **fools** are.

8. WHAT MATTERS TO GOD, PART 1 (15:8-9)

God not only sees what we do (see Proverbs 15:3), but He sees what is in the heart. He is unimpressed by sacrifices if the one offering them is **wicked** (15:8). The prayers of a righteous person, even though less costly than a sacrificial offering, go farther with God. Why this is so is found in the next proverb.

Not just **the sacrifice of the wicked,** but their **way** of life is detestable to God (15:8-9). While pleased with the prayers of the righteous, **He loves those who pursue righteousness** (15:9). Note that they *pursue* **righteousness** rather than merely *being* righteous (my emphasis). This avid pursuit of **righteousness** recalls Jesus' instructions in Matthew to "hunger and thirst after righteousness" (Matt. 5:6) and is captured in this translation: "He loves those who run straight for the finish line" (THE MESSAGE).

9. WHAT TO DO WITH DISCIPLINE (15:10)

God not only "detests the way of the wicked" (15:9), but He disciplines and punishes them. The New International Version renders this proverb as a promise of **stern discipline** and a warning against resisting such **correction** (15:10). A different reading of the first line suggests, "Discipline seems bad to him who forsakes the way." Resistance to **discipline** then ripens into hatred of it which leads, ultimately, to death. **Discipline** comes to the wicked. Those who hate it lose their chance to profit from it.

10. NOTHING HIDDEN (15:11)

God is capable of punishing the wicked because everything lies open before Him. **Death and Destruction** translate the Hebrew terms Sheol and Abaddon (15:11). The Old Testament writers believed that all the dead went to Sheol, both the righteous and the unrighteous. It involved neither torturous punishment nor eternal bliss, but was, instead, a shadowy existence. The combination of Sheol and Abaddon (also found together in Proverbs 27:20 and Job 26:6) probably suggests domains understood to lie far beyond human gaze and human control. That these are "wide open to the Lord"[3] implies that God knows what goes on there (see Proverbs 15:3) and controls it. With such knowledge and power, He can surely read **the hearts of men** (15:11).

11. AFRAID TO BE WRONG (15:12)

No one loves to be corrected, at least no normal person. The **mocker resents correction,** however, because correction implies authority (15:12). To him, authority represents limitation and restriction; he has moved beyond limitations to freedom. Beneath his fearless resentment lies the fear of being wrong, a fear which keeps him from consulting **the wise** (15:12; see 1 Kings 22:8 for a good example). The meaning of this proverb is reinforced by the careful construction of the Hebrew, with verbs placed at the beginning and the end, and by the use of alliteration.

12. A HAPPY HEART (15:13)

Have **a happy heart** (15:13)! The benefits will appear on your face, but also on the faces of others as your happiness lifts their spirits.

Heartache not only makes for sad faces, but it **crushes the spirit.** God is not commanding happiness, for He knows there are times for sobriety (see Ecclesiastes 3:4). The call to happiness here in Proverbs is a call to the behavior which makes one **happy** and avoids **heartache,** and a reminder that our attitudes are contagious (Prov. 15:13).

13. MAN OR BEAST (15:14)

This proverb contrasts **the discerning heart** which **seeks knowledge** with the **fool** who **feeds on folly.** The former demonstrates the human and God-given capacity for self-improvement by seeking to know more ("An intelligent mind is avid for knowledge"[4]). The **fool** is more animal than human. He grazes (the word is used elsewhere for the feeding habits of cattle and sheep as in Genesis 41:18 and Ezekiel 34:14) in the field of **folly,** or among "fast-food fads and fancies" (THE MESSAGE).

14. PULL UP A CHAIR (15:15)

The return to the theme of cheerfulness suggests the importance of this quality. Proverbs 15:13 spoke of the benefits of cheerfulness, both to the cheerful and those around him. The benefits of **the cheerful** (literally, "good") **heart** flow from the banquet within, **a continual feast** (15:15). The preceding proverb also spoke about eating. There the fool ate, while "the discerning" learned. Here the picture expands to point out that the wise one does eat and eats well.

15. LITTLE IS MUCH (15:16)

It does not seem like a fair comparison. **Great wealth,** even **with turmoil,** is still great wealth (15:16). Think of all you can do with it: vacation home, boat, beautiful car, top-quality education. With all that **wealth** you can even buy your way out of **turmoil.** What is all that compared to **the fear of the LORD?**[5] You cannot see that fear or cash it in at the bank. It is not a fair comparison, for **the fear of the LORD** is far more valuable. The bearer is entitled to come expectantly and daily to God's throne to receive the wisdom and other resources for that day, blessings untainted by trouble (see 10:22). Having **little** does not matter if you know where to get more (15:16). Wealth seems to bring with it a large supply of **turmoil** which money cannot remove. Those who **fear the LORD** can deposit their **turmoil** with God, trusting Him for relief. "Little is much when God is in it."

16. LOVE: PERFECT WITH ANY MEAL (15:17)

A second "better . . . than . . ." proverb continues the contrast between wealth and poverty (see 15:16) by picturesquely comparing what money can buy. Even the simplest of menus, if eaten in harmony and with loved ones, is better than gourmet fare in a rotten, hateful atmosphere (see 17:1). **Love** (15:17), the perfect side dish with any meal, results from "the fear of the LORD" (15:16) since a reverent relationship with Him (see 1:7) requires us to treat His children well.

17. A FLAMETHROWER OR A FIRE EXTINGUISHER (15:18)

We can either speak like flamethrowers or fire extinguishers. The words of the **hot-tempered man** not only kindle conflict, but they spread it by ill-chosen and self-centered words spoken at the wrong time. The opposite of the **hot-tempered man** is a cool-tempered one, but this proverb calls us to more than self-control. We must be peacemakers, slow to become angry and able to calm **a quarrel.** Instead of ill-chosen, ill-timed words, ours should be carefully considered and spoken for the good of others. We must be sure our words extinguish fires rather than spread them.

18. THE HARDEST WORK IS AVOIDING WORK (15:19)

Why is **the way of the sluggard . . . blocked with thorns** (15:19)? Land left untilled can be quickly overrun with thorns; perhaps these **thorns** result from the sluggard's neglect. **Thorns** could also describe the sluggard's path, a difficult route as anyone who has tried to take a shortcut through the brier patch can testify. Some commentators take this statement as an excuse, made up by the lazy person, explaining why he cannot work. By any reading, **the sluggard,** to avoid work, has actually taken the most difficult **path.** The easiest route belongs to the righteous who travel on a highway, "a properly constructed road from which obstacles have been removed."[6] Note also how a "wisdom" term (**sluggard**) is contrasted with a moral term (**upright**). This contrast illustrates the close connection between wisdom and righteousness and reinforces that laziness is a moral offense, for the **sluggard** shirks responsibilities, shifting them to another's load.

19. DON'T BREAK YOUR MOTHER'S HEART (15:20)

It is a truth which needs as much emphasis in our day as it did in ancient Israel: Our actions affect others. While not responsible for their reactions, we are responsible for the impact we have on them. One son, choosing wisdom, not only brings blessings on his own head (see Proverbs 1:10, 22), but showers his parents with **joy** (15:20). **A foolish man** (15:20; he hardly deserves the title "son"), by choosing folly, brings a myriad of disasters onto his own head. He does not suffer alone, however, for his parents must bear the shame of his folly. By his actions, the fool shows his scorn for his parents and ultimately for God (see 14:2).

20. A GOOD TIME? (15:21)

Twice in Proverbs 15, joy is described as the result of wisdom (see 15:13, 20). The fool also seeks joy (same word in verses 13 and 20), but in the wrong place (**folly** [15:21]). As one translator put it, "To act the idiot is fun to the empty-headed."[7] The wise person is not so easily diverted. He **keeps a straight course,** a strong phrase in the original Hebrew which suggests a resolute determination to stay on track ("he forges straight ahead"[8]).

21. WISDOM DOESN'T MEAN KNOWING EVERYTHING (15:22)

Sometimes the wisest thing to do is to ask advice. The fool refuses, imagining his ideas are flawless simply because they are his. The wise seek advice and not from one source only, but from many. Many counselors mean many avenues down which God will bring wisdom. God has designed us to work together, blending our individual perspectives into a clearer picture of His plan.

22. THE VALUE OF THE RIGHT WORD (15:23)

Two themes which have each appeared several times in Proverbs 15—words and joy—are combined in this proverb. The **apt reply** (using the same Hebrew word rendered "answer" in 15:1 and "reply" in 16:1) brings **joy** (15:23; using the same Hebrew word as in 15:13, 20-21) not only to the speaker, but also to the other conversationalist. An example of how a **reply** might bring **joy** can be seen in the council chambers of the previous verse. The New International Version has supplied **apt** in the first line because of the strength of the second; literally, "A word in its time, how good!"

23. GOING UP? (15:24)

Proverbs 15:24 speaks of two ways, one ascending, one descending. In view is not simply the contrast between where one goes after death—up to heaven or down to hell—although that perspective is not completely foreign to what we find here. The one who ascends proceeds upward to blessing and prosperity in this life. Descent takes one down Folly Boulevard to self-destruction and **the grave** (Sheol). Heaven and hell, as we have come to understand them through New Testament eyes, just trace these same paths into eternity. This proverb also affirms that these paths are mutually exclusive; you cannot go up and down at the same time.

24. HE WATCHES OVER WIDOWS (15:25)

In Israelite society, the **proud** man and the widow (15:25) stood at opposite ends of the social spectrum—he, with his (presumed) strength and security; she, vulnerable and weak. When **the LORD**[9] enters the picture, however, the roles are completely reversed. God destroys **the proud man's house,** referring not only to his residence, but also to its occupants and thus his posterity. God himself **keeps the widow's boundaries intact,** preventing others (like the **proud** man) from stealing her land by moving the boundary markers. Her opponent is devastated, but she is not even defrauded; his **house** is destroyed, but even the outskirts of her property are patrolled. While God's appearance as defender of justice is quite explicit in this proverb, His appearance in real life is not so prominent. This may be due to His strategy of indirectness; He designed this world so that sinners self-destruct, and He entrusted to His people the security of the defenseless (see Exodus 22:21-22, 25).

25. WHAT MATTERS TO GOD, PART 2 (15:26)

Not only does God despise "the way of the wicked" (15:9), but He even hates their **thoughts** (15:26; using the same Hebrew subject and verb in both verses). Since **thoughts** translates the Hebrew word translated "plans" in 15:22, in view is probably "wicked scheming" (15:26 NJB). The New International Version contrasts **the thoughts of the wicked** which God hates with **those of the pure** with which He is pleased (15:26). The Hebrew of the second line is rendered more accurately, "But gracious words are to Him pure."[10]

26. THE ROOT OF ALL KINDS OF EVIL (15:27)

To balance those proverbs which seem to take an overly positive view of riches, 15:27 shows how wealth can bring trouble and even death. The **greedy man** may bring **his family** many treasures, but ultimately what he brings home is **trouble. Greedy man** in Hebrew is a play on words *(bozayah bazah)* which is difficult to represent in English. The second line provides one example of greed (bribery), offers counsel ("Do not just avoid it—hate it"), and promises reward (**will live**).

27. WEIGH YOUR WORDS (15:28)

As a child, I was sobered by Jesus' warning in Matthew that I must "give an account on the day of judgment for every careless word" I had spoken (Matt. 12:36). I resolved to say only what was necessary, a resolution which lasted for the better part of the quarter-hour. However weak my resolve, this proverb makes clear that my motive was right. **The righteous** person carefully considers his words, weighing them in his **heart** and speaking them only after careful consideration (Prov. 15:28; **weighs** is translated "think" in Psalm 63:6). Judging from the volume of his words, **the wicked** person imagines that God counts rather than **weighs** what he says (Prov. 15:28; see 15:2). His words devoid of content and value, **the wicked** are only "sewers of abuse" (THE MESSAGE).

28. DOES GOD DESIRE YOUR COMPANY? (15:29)

To say that God, who is everywhere (see Proverbs 15:3), is also **far from the wicked** (15:29) is not contradictory. The first is true, as can be seen by how He rewards **the righteous** and punishes **the wicked.** God is also far from **the wicked,** such as the person in 15:28b where the same Hebrew word is used. Just look at how He does not answer their prayers. That **the LORD is far from the wicked** (15:29)[11] rather than **the wicked** far from Him implies that He *has* seen what they have done (see 15:3) and removed himself from their presence, a good example to follow (see Psalm 1:1). God's nearness to **the righteous** can be assumed from the way **He hears** their prayers (15:29). The verse does not specifically say He always answers those prayers; the Old Testament believer knew the silence of God. But because they knew they were God's people living according to the law of the Lord and because they knew God was pleased with their prayer (see 15:8), they spoke those prayers with "covenant confidence" and left them in the hands of a loving God.[12] That the New Testament believer can also share this confidence is clear from Hebrews 4:14-16.

29. BE A HEALER (15:30)

Once again we return to the theme of **joy** (15:30; see Proverbs 15:13, 20-21, 23). **A cheerful look** (15:30) is, literally, "the eyes of light," which speaks more of wholesomeness and integrity than it does "a twinkle in the eye" (THE MESSAGE). The meaning of the proverb is closer to what Jesus spoke about in Matthew 6:22: "The eye is the lamp of the body. If your eyes are good, your whole body will be full of light." A "lightened" body is a joyful body and, by implication, a body which brings **joy** to others (Prov. 15:30). We communicate this joy, in part, through our words. **Good news** brings health to our body (literally, "makes fat bones") and to others, as 25:25 illustrates.

30. BE TEACHABLE (15:31-33)

Proverbs 15 concludes with three proverbs on teachability, a subject touched on earlier (see 15:10, 12). The first describes the teachable person, the second contrasts teachability with its opposite, and the third reveals the quality of what makes a person teachable. Teachability requires "hearing ears," a willingness to listen to correction and accept it for what it is, **a life-giving rebuke** (15:31). The teachable not only find life, but they find life among the wise where joy and health abound.

Although the teachable must admit their shortcomings (see 15:31), they do so because they see themselves as worth correcting. The unteachable refuse **correction,** imagining themselves to be without need of it (15:32). In fact, **he who ignores disciplines despises himself** (he "holds himself cheap"; he "lacks self-respect"[13]) because he has refused life itself. The teachable person **gains understanding** (literally, "gains heart"), revealing him to be superior to the fool of 15:21 who "lacks judgment" (literally, "lacks heart").

What makes a person teachable? He or she must have **the fear of the LORD** (15:33),[14] what we saw in chapter 1 as a reverence for the Lord experienced in relationship with Him. When I revere the Lord, I am acknowledging that He is God, not I. I admit He knows me better than I know myself. I accept whatever correction I receive as ultimately from Him and for my good. **Humility comes before honor** (15:33). But I humble myself, not before a distant, fearsome despot, but before a God with whom I enjoy a covenant relationship.[15] My humility springs not from a sense of unworthiness, but from the awareness that this relationship means I am worth correcting. It is the unteachable one who "lacks self-respect"; the teachable person respects himself enough to humble himself. The unteachable may think they are rejecting their teacher; in fact they reject themselves and, ultimately, God.

ENDNOTES

[1]F. Delitzsch, *Proverbs, Ecclesiastes, Song of Solomon,* Commentary on the Old Testament, by C. F. Keil and F. Delitzsch, vol. 10 (Grand Rapids, Michigan: Wm. B. Eerdmans Publishing Co., 1978 [1872]).

[2]The New International Version and other translations use LORD in small capitals following an initial capital *L* to denote "Yahweh" in the original Hebrew.

[3]R. B. Y. Scott, *Proverbs, Ecclesiastes,* The Anchor Bible, vol. 18, eds. William F. Albright and David Noel Freedman (New York: Doubleday, 1965), p. 68.

[4]Ibid.

[5]See endnote 2.

[6]R. N. Whybray, *Proverbs,* The New Century Bible Commentary (Grand Rapids, Michigan: Wm. B. Eerdmans Publishing Co., 1994), p. 232.

[7]Scott.

[8]Ibid.

[9]See endnote 2.

[10]Delitzsch.

[11]See endnote 2.

[12] Law refers to either the Levitical Code (all God's rules and regulations), the Ten Commandments, or the Pentateuch (the first five books of the Old Testament: Genesis, Exodus, Leviticus, Numbers, and Deuteronomy). It is often capitalized when it means the Pentateuch or the Ten Commandments.

A covenant is a solemn promise made binding by a pledge or vow, which may be either a verbal formula or a symbolic action. Covenant often referred to a legal obligation in ancient times. In Old Testament terms, the word was often used in describing the relationship between God and His chosen people, in which their sacrifices of blood afforded them His atonement for sin, and in which their fulfillment of a promise to live in obedience to God was rewarded by His blessings. In New Testament terms, this relationship (the new covenant) was now made possible on a personal basis through Jesus Christ and His sacrifice of His own blood.

[13]Scott; NJB.

[14]See endnote 2.

[15]Ibid.

PROVERBS 16

16:1-33

Proverbs 16 begins with a series of proverbs on the sovereignty of God (verses 1-9) and ends on the same theme (verse 33), with two more which specifically mention Yahweh (verses 11, 20).[1] According to one commentator, the cluster of proverbs which focuses directly on God (15:33–16:9) places theological concerns at the center of the book. Immediately following the opening series of proverbs are several which specifically refer to the king (16:10-15, except verse 11). Clearly, relating to Yahweh and the king were matters of crucial importance in that society, as was the relationship between the Divine King and the human sovereign.[2]

1. LORD OF OUR WORDS (16:1)

Proverbs 16:1 is not intended to minimize the importance of planning, but to emphasize God's sovereignty over our words. Humans are free to carefully arrange their thoughts like soldiers in battle (see the use of a related word in Genesis 14:8), but the ability to answer appropriately (**reply of the tongue** [Prov. 16:1]) comes from God. Commentator F. Delitzsch explains this process—how, out of a state of confusion "like that of chaos before the creation," God gives us the right answer. The answer was not our own, but came to us as a gift.[3] Following 15:33 (remember, chapter divisions are manmade), 16:1 emphasizes that this ability results from reverence for Yahweh,[4] not human ability.

2. LORD OF OUR WAYS (16:2)

We are adept at justifying our failures (the inclusiveness of **all** [16:2] would be humorous if it were not so true), but God is not fooled. He weighs our **motives** on the scales of His perfect knowledge and discerns exactly why we do what we do. We must watch the motives for our behavior and let Him be **LORD**[5] of our **ways.** Understanding this proverb—as it speaks both to our tendency to self-justification and to God's perfect insight—will also curtail a critical spirit in us.

3. LORD OF OUR PLANS (16:3)

As suggested in Proverbs 16:1, God has no problem when we plan; 16:3 even promises success. For this to happen, however, you must **commit to the LORD whatever you do** (16:3).[6] **Commit** is, literally, "roll," and is found with this meaning in Genesis 29:3 where a stone is rolled across the mouth of a well. Used metaphorically, the verb can be translated "remove" (see Joshua 5:9) or, as here, "entrust to God" (see Psalm 37:5). We may not think of "rolling" our actions on God (although we speak of "casting our care on God"), but this may be just the word picture to get us to entrust the totality of our lives to Him.

4. LORD OF THE FUTURE (16:4)

It is a truth easily forgotten when nothing seems to be working out for you and success is showering those who do not care about God: **The LORD** is in control (16:4). He has a purpose for **everything** He made and will bring each thing to accomplish that purpose. **For his own ends** is, literally, "everything for its answer," meaning that "there are ultimately no loose ends in God's world: Everything will be put to some use and matched with its proper fate."[7] The wise person believes in the sovereignty of God.

5. LORD OF THE HUMBLE (16:5)

This proverb and the next two elaborate on "the wicked" of 16:4; 16:5 pictures him more clearly as **the proud of heart,** 16:6 describes his opposite, while 16:7 carries the contrast still further. Some have mistakenly understood verse 4 to argue that the wicked are predestined for destruction without any choice in the matter. Verse 5 implies, instead, that they have a choice and have chosen to be **proud of heart** instead of humble (see verse 6). The term **all** (translated "everything" in 16:4) appears three times in the first five verses to emphasize the completeness of God's power. God **detests all the proud of heart** (16:5), putting them in the same category as those in 6:16-19, the adulterer (6:29), the liar (19:5), "and similar scarlet sinners whom he [the proud man] doubtless thanks God he does not resemble."[8] **Be sure of this** (16:5) is, literally, "hand to hand," an expression which apparently meant something like "you can shake on it" (see 11:21 KJV).

6. LORD OF OUR FORGIVENESS (16:6)

Go as far as you can from "the proud of heart" (16:5), and you will come to the character of Proverbs 16:6. Whose **love and faithfulness** is being described here, ours or God's? Since the second line refers to human actions, many commentators understand the first that way as well. Our faithful love does not actually atone for sin, they argue, but demonstrates repentance and forgiveness as in 10:12. It makes more sense, however, to see the **love and faithfulness** as God's. Because human actions are in view in the second line does not mean they are required in the first, and it makes more sense to speak of God's providing atonement. The Hebrew verb translated **is atoned for** is commonly used in a sacrificial context; it is not the verb used in 10:12. The Israelites would not be surprised by the news that God forgives their sins by His **love and faithfulness.** The psalmist could speak of being forgiven through God's love (see Psalm 25:7; 51:1-2). Even the sacrificial system, with its "sliding scale" of sin offerings—bull for high priest, male goat for leader, female goat or lamb for commoner, pigeon or dove for poor, small quantity of flour for very poor—suggests that it is not the sacrifices but God's mercy which atones for sin. Not only are sin's effects covered by God's love, but those who **fear . . . the LORD**[9] find sin's power minimized (Prov. 16:6). He is Lord of our forgiveness.

7. LORD OF OUR RELATIONSHIPS (16:7)

Proverbs 16:7 illustrates well why the proverbs should be taken as principles rather than promises. Righteousness does not eliminate persecution, as the lives of David, Solomon, Paul, Jesus, and countless other believers have demonstrated. Instead, this proverb continues the theme begun in 16:4 by describing the power of Yahweh[10] and further illustrating the life of the righteous (see 16:6). He can make the righteous so winsome that their **enemies** become allies (16:7; see NJPS). We often try to make this happen on our own, working to please others and make them like us. God says, "Follow me, and let me work out your relationships" (see 29:25; Matthew 6:33).

8. LORD OF OUR NEEDS (16:8)

While Proverbs 16:7 calls us to trust God for our relationships, 16:8 makes the same appeal in the area of our resources. This proverb describes the person who seeks his own interests in spite of what it might cost someone else. Hope for happiness is vain with such a person. In addition to a guilty conscience, "the enjoyment which it **[gain with injustice]** affords is troubled by the curses of those who are injured, and by the sighs of the oppressed."[11] **A little with righteousness** is the better choice, according to God. There is no mention of how the righteous will be supplied, perhaps to remind us that faith must trust God in the dark. Let there be no doubt, however, which is the better choice.

9. LORD OF OUR STEPS (16:9)

This companion to Proverbs 16:1 concludes the section of Yahweh proverbs.[12] Both emphasize the sovereignty of **the LORD;** He is **LORD** of our words in 16:1 and our **steps** in 16:9. How He can be sovereign over our paths without eliminating our free will is a mystery this proverb does not explain. It merely asserts both truths with no attempt to reconcile them. Let us do what we should do: "plan the way we want to live" (THE MESSAGE), recognizing God's power to direct our steps. If our way is "rolled onto Him" (see 16:3), God can direct our plans toward success.

10. LORD OF OUR LORD (16:10)

At this point begins a series of proverbs which refer to the **king** (16:10; see Proverbs 16:12-15). God and the king were, at least in principle, closely related. Israel was a theocracy, a nation ruled by its God, but He had chosen a human to rule as His representative. "The primary function of an earthly king is to administer justice within his realm, protect the weak from exploitation, and ensure security to his subjects. Precisely so is it with God, the King of the earth."[13] The king was to regularly read a copy of the Law in order to obey its principles[14] (see Deuteronomy 17:18-20). These proverbs, meant to be read by the king and others, summon the human sovereign to become more like the Divine whose image is stamped in these verses. By picturing the nation's first citizen, they set a goal for the rest of Israel.

Oracle (Prov. 16:10) refers to divine wisdom given to a human; it is usually translated in the Old Testament with the idea of divination. According to this proverb, when the **king** speaks (ideally), he speaks a message from God. As God's spokesman and representative, a literal rendering reads, "In judgment, his mouth should not sin." The standard of justice set in heaven is to be maintained in the throne room in Jerusalem and among God's people everywhere.

11. LORD OF THE MARKETPLACE (16:11)

While this proverb does not specifically mention the king, it continues the theme of justice from Proverbs 16:10 and makes explicit Yahweh's connection with Israelite society.[15] There may be a further royal connection in that some weights and measures were standardized by the king's authority, according to 2 Samuel 14:26 and archaeological evidence. This proverb clearly calls God's people to honest business transactions because **all the weights in the bag are of his making** (Prov. 16:11). Commentator Derek Kidner points out that even the "humblest device to promote fair dealing is God's."[16] He who made the weights (usually stones) watches how they are used.

12. A MATTER OF NATIONAL SECURITY (16:12)

One of the most important themes in the Old Testament historical books[17] is found here in Proverbs: "Righteousness exalts a nation" (14:34a). When Israel obeyed God, she prospered, but she was punished when disobedient. Since the ultimate responsibility for **righteousness** (16:12) rested with the king before being extended to all Israelites, this proverb is meant for everyone. As was mentioned in 16:11, the standard being upheld is the standard of godliness. As God **detests** wickedness (the same Hebrew word is used in 16:5 and 6:16-19), so should the king and his people. The righteous throne (and nation) **is established** by God (16:12; using the same Hebrew verb in 16:3b where it is translated "will succeed"). The second line of this proverb appears again in 25:5.

13. HONESTY IS THE BEST POLICY (16:13)

From the general principle in 16:12, this proverb specifies one type of righteous behavior (**honest lips** [16:13] is, literally, "righteous lips").

A king should prefer honesty because here is where his best counsel originates (see 15:22). As one translation puts it,

> Good leaders cultivate honest speech;
> they love advisors who tell them the truth (THE MESSAGE).

For an example of a king who preferred dishonesty and the disastrous consequences, see 1 Kings 22. Once again, king and nation are called to be like God. As the Lord blesses those found **pleasing** to Him (16:13; see 16:7), so does the king (same Hebrew verb in 16:7, 13).

14. HELP HANDLING HEAT (16:14-15)

Proverbs 16:14-15 counsel wisdom when dealing with the king whose anger could mean death. **A wise man will appease** (16:14) that anger with well-chosen words and a proper humility. Because he is wise, he also knows how *not* to offend the king to begin with. The proverb implies that what is true for the king's wrath is also true for God's. As God's representative, the king was supposed to be angered by the same things which would anger God. **Appease** is the same Hebrew verb translated "atoned for" in 16:6 where God is the implied forgiver. The original Hebrew words for "king" and **messenger** are nearly identical; the word play suggests that the king is God's **messenger** (16:14). This message is for both the king and his subjects: Avoid arousing God's wrath; be quick to appease it when necessary.

Just as a king's anger means **death** (16:14), the **favor** of the king **means life** (16:15); the **wise** person knows how to avoid the former and cultivate the latter (16:14). **A rain cloud in spring** (16:15) meant not only refreshment, but adequate moisture for the ripening crops. These latter rains were preceded by clouds whose arrival brought joy and relief.[18] Those who pleased the king enjoyed both present and future blessings. **When a king's face brightens** is, literally, "in the light of the face of the king." Because "the light of the face" is usually used in reference to God, reference to the king's **favor** here also implies God's favor for which the king and his subjects should strive.

15. THE GREAT WORTH OF WISDOM (16:16)

Although the connection between verses 16 through 20 is less obvious than the common theme in verses 1 through 9 or 10 through 15, some connection does exist—"Five proverbs regarding wisdom, righteousness, humility, and trust in God, forming, as it were, a succession of steps, for humility is the virtue of virtues, and trust in God the condition of all salvation," observes F. Delitzsch.[19] He notes, as well, that three of these proverbs contain the same Hebrew word, usually translated "good" (**better** [16:16, 19]; "prospers" [16:20]). Further, three proverbs (see 16:16-18) demonstrate an especially high level of literary skill. The opening proverb in this series of five (16:16-20) returns to a theme sounded earlier in Proverbs, the favorable comparison of **wisdom** to precious metals (16:16; see 8:10-11, 19). **Wisdom,** regardless of the cost to obtain it, more than repays the effort. This is a useful reminder given the challenges ahead (for example, the need to be "upright" [16:17] and humble [see 16:18-20]).

16. TAKE THE HIGH ROAD (16:17)

This proverb encourages us to take Interstate Upright rather than any other route. By this route, **evil** is not just more manageable, but we avoid it entirely (16:17; see the same Hebrew expression in 16:6b), just as the interstate bypasses city traffic. **Highway** (16:17) refers to a public road which connects cities, but is never used for the road which passes through the city. Similar ideas can be found in Proverbs 2 and 11:3. The second line is a masterpiece of brevity and balance. The Hebrew phrase is only four words long; grammatically the first two words find their mirror image in the second two. Eugene Peterson catches both the meaning and the form: "Watch your step and save your life" (THE MESSAGE).

17. "BLESSED ARE THE POOR IN SPIRIT"[20] (16:18-20)

Proverbs 16:18-20 deals with **pride** and humility. Verse 18 shows the disadvantages of **pride,** the next reveals humility's superiority to pride, and verse 20 describes the benefits of humility. We have been prepared for the message of verse 18 by verse 5. **Pride goes before destruction** (16:18a) because God hates them both. **Haughty spirit** uses the same noun used in verse 5 where it is translated "proud." Experience also confirms that "the bigger the ego, the harder the fall" (THE MESSAGE). The proud man is at odds with himself (8:36), his neighbor (13:10), and God (16:5); destruction could come from any quarter.[21]

Humility is much better than pride. How much better? Let's say you allowed **the proud** to oppress the humble (16:19; see **among the**

oppressed), so that the humble lost their wealth and the proud became prosperous at their expense (**share plunder with the proud**). Even then it would still be better to be humble. That verses 18 and 19 form a pair is evident from the repetition of a very similar word for pride in both verses. Also note the word play in these verses between the **haughty spirit** in verse 18 and those **lowly in spirit** in verse 19. An even more obvious connection? Verse 18 provides the reason why verse 19 is true: It is better to be humble because **the proud** will one day be destroyed.

Humility, according to 16:20, is shown by a willingness to listen to instruction and trust **in the LORD. Instruction** (literally, "word") could be a word from God or another person. By the latter reading, those who are humble in their relationships with people and God prosper (literally, "find good") and are blessed. The poverty experienced in 16:19 is only temporary, another reason why it is better to be humble than proud.

18. THE WINSOMENESS OF WISDOM, PART 1 (16:21)

Proverbs 16:21-24 conveys the common theme of human speech. A good reputation and influence with others result from well-chosen words, according to 16:21. Such words must come from a **wise . . . heart**—that is, they represent the overflow of a **wise** person; these are not accidental insights. They should also be **pleasant words** (those "sweet to the lips"), words which are appropriate, well said, and helpful. Whether one reads **promote instruction** or "make a man persuasive," the effect is clear: When the wisdom of the heart is expressed properly, people listen.

19. THE BENEFITS OF WISDOM (16:22)

While Proverbs 16:22 does not mention speech and clearly applies beyond that realm, its location in a cluster of proverbs on this theme, and especially its placement between two closely related proverbs, suggests some connection. If so, the **fountain of life** is pouring out delightfully refreshing words, words which produce **life** for the speaker and all who listen. In contrast, the fool wanders in a desert of his own design. Who would choose a beating over a cup of cool water? A fool.

20. THE WINSOMENESS OF WISDOM, PART 2 (16:23)

This proverb, a companion to 16:21, continues to address the theme of how people listen to **wise** speech (16:23). Verse 22 may have been placed between them for two reasons: first, to show how that proverb applies to speech; second, because verse 22 adds the element of "understanding," which is taken up in verse 23 where the same Hebrew word is translated **guides.** The connection with 16:21 is much closer: Both use the words **heart, wise,** and **lips,** and both contain the identical phrase, **promote instruction.** Verse 21 implies that "pleasant words" come from a wise heart, while verse 23 makes that connection explicit. Words, like dollar bills, need something of real value behind them or they are worthless.

21. HOW SWEET ARE YOUR WORDS? (16:24)

Continuing the theme of our words, this proverb explores how those words extend our influence. More specifically, 16:24 expands on the phrase "pleasant words" from 16:21. Although **pleasant words** in 16:24 comes from a different Hebrew phrase, **sweet** translates the same word rendered "pleasant" in 16:21. **Pleasant words** drip like honey, strengthening the listener's soul and body (literally, "bones").

22. ASK SOMEONE WHO HAS BEEN THAT WAY (16:25)

This proverb is repeated exactly as it appeared in 14:12. There it spoke in its context of the superiority of the wise way over the foolish. Here, the proverb supplements and balances the preceding series of proverbs on the subject of the power of words to influence others. **Right** words are sweet, but sweet words are not necessarily **right;** the cost of failing to know the difference is **death** (16:25). The wrong road (to change the metaphor) often **seems right** or "is straight before a man," but ends disastrously. **Leads to death** is more literally, "ways of death"; all wrong roads lead to the same place—**death.** With so much at stake, we had better follow the directions of someone who knows, someone who has been down that road before.

23. WHAT MOTIVATES YOU? (16:26)

While many proverbs, such as 16:26, make straightforward observations about life, they were included in the book of Proverbs because those observations illustrate a truth about the life of wisdom. Yes, a laborer works to avoid **hunger** pains, but this proverb was meant to say something more, as evidenced when read against its immediate context. The preceding proverb spoke to the importance of following the right guide. Since our **appetite** is hardly the best guide to follow, this proverb may be calling us to a higher motivation than our physical needs. A laborer led by his **hunger** (literally, "mouth") is to be pitied, while the "scoundrel" of the next proverb is one to be avoided.

24. WATCH OUT! (16:27-29)

This and the next three proverbs form a small collection describing evildoers, reminiscent in theme and vocabulary to 6:12-19. Verses 27 through 29 all begin the same way—literally, "A man of . . . "—each one extending evil: worthlessness (16:27), to perverseness (16:28), to violence (16:29). Although 16:30 differs in form, it continues the same theme and points out external signs by which such evildoers can be spotted. A **scoundrel** [or worthless person] **plots evil** (16:27), a word which literally refers to the digging of a pit in order to trap someone. His words (literally, "upon his lips; see 16:21, 23) "smart and burn" (THE MESSAGE).

Worse than a worthless man is **a perverse** one (16:28)—that is, a liar. By his lies he brings dissension even to the closest relationships (**close friends**). His approach may be subtle—**gossip** is, literally, "whisperer." The outcome, however, is devastating; **stirs up** is used to describe Samson's releasing the flaming foxes in the fields of the Philistines (see Judges 15:5). As in Proverbs 16:27, and as was emphasized in verses 21 through 24, the devastating weapon is speech.

Worst of all is the **violent man** (16:29). **He entices his neighbor**— that is, he lures him to a secluded place to harm him. He **leads him down a path that is not good,** while a very literal rendering, misses the violence these words imply. The first part speaks of the allurement alluded to above. The path that **is not good** is not merely bad; it is the very opposite of the good path. Eugene Peterson comes much closer to the meaning:

Calloused climbers betray their very own friends;
they'd stab their own grandmothers in the back (THE MESSAGE).

25. HOW TO SPOT A BAD APPLE (16:30)

Although this proverb does not begin like the previous three (see 16:27-29), it was clearly intended to stand with them. Prominent terms found in the previous three proverbs appear in verse 30, terms such as "perverse" (verse 28), **lips** (translated "speech" in verse 27), and **evil** (verse 27). The purpose of 16:30 is to make it easier to identify evildoers. Look for subtle clues, we are told. Watch for a wink of the **eye** or a pursing of the **lips,** and you will not be deceived.

26. A NOBLE EXAMPLE (16:31-32)

After such a rogues' gallery, two proverbs describing admirable members of the human family are fitting and welcome. Verse 31 pictures the aged, **righteous** person; and verse 32 the **patient man.** The principle in view is that since righteousness brings long life, and long life usually means **gray hair,** then **gray hair is a crown of splendor** or glorious crown (16:31). Age alone is not being celebrated, but rather age as the reward of righteousness.

Verse 32 prizes patience over power, even successful power. While righteousness (see 16:31) obviously deserves to be celebrated, why choose to celebrate patience? Perhaps because the element missing among the rogues of 16:27-30, aside from righteousness, is patience. Since they cannot wait to obtain their desires by legitimate means, they pursue them by deception and force. They choose the route of the **warrior,** and although they may have "taken their city" by brute force, they choose foolishly (16:32). One **who controls his temper** (literally, "who rules his spirit") has chosen the better path (see 14:17, 29; 25:28; 29:11; James 1:19-20).

27. LORD OF THE LOT (16:33)

Chapter 16 ends where it began, by emphasizing the sovereignty of God. Casting lots was one way of discovering God's will in the Bible. Part of the wardrobe of the High Priest (see Exodus 28:30) was to be the Urim and Thummim, a lot-like device used to determine God's will. Joshua used the lot to parcel out the land of Canaan (see Joshua 14:1-2), and Temple service was assigned in this way (see 1 Chronicles 25:8). This proverb does not mean that God predetermines all our choices. If this were so, why would He have given the Urim and Thummim? How can we be held accountable for our choices if they are not our choices after all? God is sovereign. Like a master chess player who knows my move before I make it, He always responds perfectly.

ENDNOTES

[1]The New International Version and other translations use LORD in small capitals following an initial capital *L* to denote "Yahweh" in the original Hebrew.

[2]R. N. Whybray, *Proverbs,* The New Century Bible Commentary (Grand Rapids, Michigan: Wm. B. Eerdmans Publishing Co., 1994), p. 238.

[3]F. Delitzsch, *Proverbs, Ecclesiastes, Song of Solomon,* Commentary on the Old Testament, by C. F. Keil and F. Delitzsch, vol. 10 (Grand Rapids, Michigan: Wm. B. Eerdmans Publishing Co., 1978 [1872]), pp. 334–35.

[4]See endnote 1.

[5]Ibid.

[6]Ibid.

[7]Derek Kidner, *Proverbs: An Introduction and Commentary,* Tyndale Old Testament Commentaries, ed. D. J. Wiseman (Downers Grove, Illinois: InterVarsity Press, 1964), p. 118.

[8]Ibid.

[9]See endnote 1.

[10]Ibid.

[11]Delitzsch, p. 339.

[12]See endnote 1.

[13]A. Cohen, *The Psalms,* Soncino Books of the Bible, ed. by A. Cohen (London: Soncino, 1950), p. xiv.

[14]Law refers to either the Levitical Code (all God's rules and regulations), the Ten Commandments, or the Pentateuch (the first five books of the Old Testament: Genesis, Exodus, Leviticus, Numbers, and Deuteronomy). It is often capitalized when it means the Pentateuch or the Ten Commandments.

[15]See endnote 1.

[16]Kidner, p. 119.

[17]The historical books consist of the biblical Old Testament books of Joshua, Judges, Ruth, 1 and 2 Samuel, 1 and 2 Kings, 1 and 2 Chronicles, Ezra, Nehemiah, and Esther.

[18]Whybray, p. 246.

[19]Delitzsch, p. 344.

[20]Matthew 5:3a (NIV).

[21]Kidner, p. 120.

PROVERBS 17

17:1-28

While there is no clear arrangement of these verses, a number concern foolish behavior (see Proverbs 17:2, 7, 10, 12, 16, 18, 21, 24-25, 28) and the question of justice (see 17:5, 8, 15, 23, 26). Verses 1 and 2 are set in a domestic scene, verses 17 and 18 appear to have been paired, and verses 18 through 21 refer to sources of trouble. The chapter concludes with two proverbs on proper speech (verses 27-28).

1. WHAT IS ON THE MENU? (17:1)

This proverb brings an important message to our society, a society consumed with prosperity at any price. Far better than abundant prosperity (**full**) is peace, even if peace means a meal of only "bread and water." "House of peace offerings," a more literal rendering of **house full of feasting,** refers to the practice of bringing a portion of a sacrificial animal to the Temple as a voluntary expression of thanksgiving, then consuming the remainder of the animal at a banquet. Simplicity **with peace** is superior to abundance, even "spiritual" abundance **with strife.**

2. WISDOM AND THE LADDER OF SUCCESS (17:2)

Although you might feel locked into a particular situation—perhaps at work—this proverb makes clear that wisdom allows for advancement. An "incompetent son" (NJPS), lacking wisdom, loses his position of advantage to the **wise servant** who comes to be regarded as "one of the family" (THE MESSAGE). A good illustration of this proverb can be found in 1 Kings 11:28 through 12:33 where Solomon's son, Rehoboam, loses ten of the twelve tribes to Jeroboam, a former employee of Solomon.

3. "A REFINER'S FIRE"[1] (17:3)

Our worth in God's eyes is not dependent on our station in life; the previous proverb makes this clear. Verse 3 suggests that God determines "our metal" by subjecting us to **tests.** Fire not only **tests** the metal, however; it refines it. This is the role of **the crucible for silver and the furnace for gold**—to improve the quality of the metal. This proverb teaches that God seeks to improve **the heart** of His people, that part which controls all thoughts, choices, and desires. The metaphor implies that God intends to do something in us which we cannot do in ourselves. Further, it leads us to expect that God's work will involve some unpleasantness.[2]

4. BE CAREFUL, EARS, WHAT YOU HEAR (17:4)

In sharp contrast to God who, in Proverbs 17:3, examines "the heart" and seeks to improve it, the **wicked** and the **liar** do not want the truth (17:4). Instead they look for lies and what will destroy others. They listen to such talk because of the benefits it brings: like learning what they can use against others and finding ways to advance themselves. Those who are wise will remember that God "tests the heart" (17:3), and they will steer clear of such characters.

5. WHO DO YOU THINK YOU ARE? (17:5)

A proverb like 17:3 casts a long shadow, long enough to make us think more carefully about 17:5. Our attitude toward **the poor** (and toward all people) reflects our attitude toward God who created all people, and God is perfectly aware of what we think of others. While 14:31 forbids the oppression of the poor, here we are told not to mock them or gloat over (see 17:5; literally, "rejoice at") their misfortune. To do so is to mock God; **shows contempt** is a particularly strong verb in the Hebrew. The last line makes clear that God will not take such ridicule quietly (see 16:5). He allows poverty and calamity to come; our responsibility is not to distance ourselves through ridicule, but to respond as generously as if we are giving to God, which we are (see 14:31).

6. PROUD OF YESTERDAY, TODAY, AND TOMORROW (17:6)

The grandparents I know prove the truth of Proverbs 17:6a. They are as proud of their grandchildren as any king could be proud of his **crown.** This line is also true in a different sense: To see your grandchildren means you have been given long life, a mark of success in Israel. The second part of the verse moves to the opposite end of the generational spectrum. Not only are grandparents proud of their grandchildren, but **children** are proud of their **parents.** Both lines speak to the importance of being praiseworthy. Be the kind of grandchild your grandmother would be proud of; be the kind of parent your child can look up to.

7. NOBLE SPEECH (17:7)

Wisdom is a matter of the mouth as well as the mind. This is true for anyone, but especially for a person in authority; here "nobility is made a title to be lived up to."[3] The phrase **arrogant lips** might be better rendered "fine speech" or "eloquent" (17:7; see NIV margin note). This translation captures the sense well:

Lofty words are not fitting for a villain;
Much less lying words for a great man (NJPS).

8. MONEY TALKS, BUT NOT TO GOD (17:8)

This proverb should not be taken as a recommendation of bribery, for such a reading would run counter to the clear character of God and other passages (see 17:15, 23). It is true that bribery often succeeds and, in some cultures, is essential to success. However, the placement, wording, and ironic tone of this proverb reveal the sordidness of bribery. Since the preceding verse speaks of one quality of nobility—honesty—it makes more sense to see this proverb as one warning against dishonesty among officials. **Charm** (17:8) is, more literally, a "magic stone," "talisman," or "golden key" used by some to open the door of success.[4] Those beguiled by it rely on their "magic charm" (CEV) instead of honesty and hard work.

9. FORGIVE AND FORGET (17:9)

In a world like ours, slights and offenses will come. What we do with them makes the difference between friendship and alienation, Proverbs affirms. **Covers** (17:9) refers to the ability to keep a secret (see 11:13) or hide what should not be seen (see Genesis 9:23). It is the opposite of repeating an **offense** or returning to past injuries at the slightest provocation (Prov. 17:9). The **offense** that has been covered is no longer visible, not even to the one offended, and **love** results (17:9; see 10:12b).

10. THE QUICK STUDY (17:10)

The wise person has not arrived at a point beyond need of correction, this proverb says, but where correction benefits most. A mere **rebuke impresses** a wise person (17:10; see Psalm 38:2b for a similar use of this verb). It can do what beating **a fool** nearly to death cannot (Prov. 17:10). Aside from appealing to the wise to be teachable, this proverb also discourages association with fools who are exasperatingly slow learners.

11. CRUELTY REPAYS THE CRUEL (17:11)

Commentator R. N. Whybray notes that, in most of the uses of **rebellion** in the Old Testament, rebellion against God is in view,[5] **only** emphasizing the great extent to which the rebellion has gone (17:11). If this is true here, **merciless official** might better be rendered more literally as "cruel messenger." God may use the government to punish evil men, but the point of the parable is broader: God will punish **rebellion,** and His agent will show no pity. Like many of the proverbs, this one contains a delightful word play between the words for **only . . . rebellion** (*ak mari*) and **a merciless official** (*malaak achzari*).

12. BEWARE THE FOOL (17:12)

While we meet many proverbs dealing with the fool, several in chapter 17 alone, meeting **a fool** is dangerous business (17:12). This verse compares him to a mother **bear robbed of her cubs** with the encounter just as disastrous. Although bears do not appear often in the Old Testament (only twelve times), they are usually presented as creatures to be feared, especially if a she-bear has lost her cubs (see 2 Samuel 17:8;

Hosea 13:8). In Hosea, God uses this same picture to describe the punishment He will inflict on the rebellious (see Proverbs 17:11).

13. EVIL FOR GOOD (17:13)

This verse could have hung as a motto over the doorway of the palace of King David from the time of his adulterous affair with Bathsheba until his death. Although Uriah was a loyal soldier in David's army, the king rewarded his allegiance with murder (see 2 Samuel 11) with the direct result that evil never left David's house (see Proverbs 17:13). Why is it true that if you repay **evil for good, evil will** always be around? The God who punishes rebellion (see 17:11) sees all and will repay all. He may, however, carry out this punishment through very natural means. The offended party or his representative seeks revenge, and the chain reaction is difficult to stop. As well, the person who can stoop to this level of treachery is likely to stoop again, multiplying the **evil.**

14. DROWNING IN QUARRELS (17:14)

The animosity which leads to the treachery of Proverbs 17:13 might begin with just a small **quarrel** (17:14). Once a quarrel begins, however, it is hard to keep it small as one comment leads to another and then another; each time the tension, volume, and animosity rise. Finally, the **dam** bursts, and no one knows what might happen. The Israelites constructed small dams of water for irrigation, releasing the precious substance in just the right quantities and to just the right places to water their crops. A burst dam has wasted its contents, and the long-term consequences could be devastating. Verses 9 and 27 of this chapter make it clear that to **drop the matter** (17:14) does not mean compromise.

15. GOD OF JUSTICE (17:15)

This proverb reminds us that God is fair. Those who are **guilty** should pay for their crime, and those who are innocent should never be condemned. We like to speak of the latter, but are more reluctant to call for punishing **the guilty.** God has no such reticence; when **the guilty** are released and **the innocent** convicted, God is angry. Thankfully, He is also merciful. He expressed that mercy, however, not by overlooking our guilt, but by paying for it himself. God will do more than hate injustice, He will eliminate it and bring justice in its place, as the book of Revelation makes plain.

16. WASTED WEALTH (17:16)

Although many proverbs speak of **wisdom** bringing wealth, 17:16 makes clear that dollars are no certain indicator of sense. It makes equally clear that **money** does the **fool** no good for **he has no desire to get wisdom** or, more literally, "he has no mind" to become wise. This verse brings three conclusions to mind. First, do not be troubled at the sight of a rich fool. He is more to be pitied than envied. Second, do not imagine that giving money to a fool will solve his problem. It will not, and it will only add to yours (see 17:12). Third, folly must be serious if money cannot help.

17. BE A FRIEND (17:17)

This and the next proverb present two aspects of friendship. Verse 17 sets the standard: Friends should be friends through all experiences (**at all times**), especially times of trouble. Such **a friend** (literally, "neighbor") becomes like **a brother.** He may not have been born my sibling, but his faithfulness makes it seem like he was **born** to help me. Such friends are priceless; we all have at least one who was born to help us with our **adversity.**

18. ... BUT DON'T BE A FOOLISH FRIEND (17:18)

This proverb balances the sentiments of 17:17 by warning against what might be thought the friendly thing to do. It is also the first of four proverbs which describe causes of trouble: pledging surety (17:18); quarrelsomeness (17:19); perverse heart (17:20); foolish son (17:21). Pledging surety is soundly condemned in Proverbs (see 6:1-5 for a prominent example), which provides a limit on what you should do for your **neighbor** (using the same word as the one translated "friend" in 17:17). There is no contradiction here; "a friend" must love "at all times" (17:17), but folly is no expression of love.

19. WHAT BRINGS TROUBLE: PRIDE (17:19)

Just as surely as pledging surety leads to trouble, so does pride. Explicitly, this proverb condemns quarrelsomeness, a vice warned against in 17:14. The tendency to argue, however, betrays a deeper problem revealed in a more literal reading of the first line: "He who loves transgression loves strife." In other words, the person who likes **sin** tends to be more quarrelsome (17:19). What **sin** is involved is suggested by the second line. **Gate** could also be "door" or "doorway," while **high** comes from the same root word translated "haughty" in 16:18. One who has built a **high gate** or door has proudly set a high standard for others to enter into fellowship with him. Strife and quarrels result when the wrong type of person seeks admission.

20. WHAT BRINGS TROUBLE: DECEIT (17:20)

This, the third of four proverbs on the causes of trouble, is intended to warn against perversity or deception. Note the digression from a **perverse heart** to a **tongue** that **is deceitful.** What is located in the first can be expected to show up in the second. In the same way, one who for this reason **does not prosper** eventually **falls into trouble** because he is engaged in an activity which God hates (see 11:20).

21. WHAT BRINGS TROUBLE: A POOR START (17:21)

This proverb fittingly appears last in the series on what causes trouble, for it returns to the source of trouble, the home. But why remind a parent of the **grief** involved in having a foolish **son?** The parents of such a child know that **grief** more acutely than anyone. These words are less an indictment than a warning to present and future parents: If you want to avoid the trouble just described in the preceding proverbs, bring up your child properly. To see the sorry results of neglect may provide the needed motivation to face the challenges of child rearing.

22. HAVE A HAPPY HEART (17:22)

How fitting to place a proverb dealing with happiness following the sobering message of 17:18-21. God desires our happiness; He even designed our physical bodies to respond positively to "joy" (17:21; the same Hebrew word is here translated **cheerful**). By avoiding trouble and raising our children to do the same, we provide the best chance for happiness to result. **Bones** (17:22) translates a Hebrew word which might also be rendered "strength"; Eugene Peterson creatively combines these as "gloom and doom leave you bone-tired" (THE MESSAGE).

23. GOD VALUES JUSTICE, PART 1 (17:23)

This proverb returns to a theme familiar in chapter 17—God's passion for justice—and puts 17:8 in proper perspective. **Bribe in secret** (17:23) is, literally, "bribe from the bosom" ("Under cover of his cloak" [NJB]). Such behavior, while it goes on **in secret,** will be punished publicly, for God is a God of **justice** (17:23; see 17:15). The proverbs from this verse to the end of the chapter replay the important themes of the book (folly, justice, trouble) and conclude with a word about words.

24. TURN YOUR FACE TO WISDOM (17:24)

This verse calls for a focused life, one lived purposefully and wisely. It employs a contrast between the face of the wise man (as seen in a more literal rendering of **keeps . . . in view**) and the **eyes** of the fool. The first is fastened in one direction, toward **wisdom,** the focus of his attention and the chief object of his desire. He sees it directly in front of him and never changes course. The fool, on the other hand, drifts from one thing to another, looking for what he would not recognize or even want (see 17:16) if he found it.

25. BROKENHEARTED PARENTS (17:25)

While Proverbs 17:24 describes the fool, 17:25 concerns itself with the results of his folly. It conveys the same sentiments as 17:21 (as well as 10:1 and 15:20), but expands it by introducing the mother. Both parents suffer with a fool for a son:

A surly, stupid child is sheer pain to a father,
a bitter pill for a mother to swallow (THE MESSAGE).

As with 17:21, the intent here is to encourage parents to do what they can to raise wise children.

26. GOD VALUES JUSTICE, PART 2 (17:26)

The perversion of "justice" was caught in the act in Proverbs 17:23. Here such perversion has brought punishment to the **innocent,** something God hates (17:26; see 17:15). **To punish** (17:26) is, more literally, "to charge a fine." **Officials for their integrity** is, literally, "noble men," using the same word in 17:7 where it is translated "ruler"; this term need not refer to government officials. In Hebrew, the verse begins with a word often translated "also." The New International Version and some translations omit it, while others explain this was originally the second in a pair of proverbs, perhaps joined with 17:25 (although there seems to be no connection) or with 18:5 (with which it shares a similar theme). A simpler and better approach translates the word as "even." The verse then might read like this:

Even to fine an innocent man is bad;
[much more,] to flog noble men for their uprightness.[6]

27. CONTROL YOUR SPEECH (17:27-28)

Proverbs 17 concludes with two proverbs which counsel self-control in speech. According to 17:27, the **man of knowledge** (literally, "one who knows knowledge") speaks few **words** and chooses those **words** with self-discipline (literally, "with a cool spirit"). That cool spirit characterizes more than just his words, but never less (see James 3:1-12).

Proverbs 17:28 begins with the same small word which begins 17:26 in the original Hebrew; this time it is translated by the New International Version as **even.** The purpose here is to show the power of the kind of speech described in 17:27. Verbal self-control is so influential that it can even make **a fool** look **wise,** although 18:2 displays the fool in his natural habitat (see Ecclesiastes 10:12-14). Similar thoughts are ancient—even found in literature earlier than Proverbs—and more contemporary, as in this quote from Lincoln: "It is better to be silent and be thought a fool than to open one's mouth and remove all doubt."

ENDNOTES

[1]Malachi 3:2 (NIV).

[2]The first line of this proverb is found in 27:21, but in another context.

[3]Derek Kidner, *Proverbs: An Introduction and Commentary,* Tyndale Old Testament Commentaries, ed. D. J. Wiseman (Downers Grove, Illinois: InterVarsity Press, 1964), p. 124.

[4]RSV; NJB; F. Delitzsch, *Proverbs, Ecclesiastes, Song of Solomon,* Commentary on the Old Testament, by C. F. Keil and F. Delitzsch, vol. 10 (Grand Rapids, Michigan: Wm. B. Eerdmans Publishing Co., 1978 [1872]).

[5]R. N. Whybray, *Proverbs,* The New Century Bible Commentary (Grand Rapids, Michigan: Wm. B. Eerdmans Publishing Co., 1994), p. 257.

[6]Kidner, p. 127.

PROVERBS 18

18:1-24

While most of the proverbs in chapter 18 stand apart from one another or cluster into very small groupings, many take the theme of public behavior—how one relates to others. Commentator F. Delitzsch titles this chapter, "Exhortations to Fidelity and Other Social Virtues."[1]

1. THE DANGERS OF ISOLATION (18:1)

The subject of this proverb would not agree with the observation of seventeenth-century poet John Donne that "no man is an island." He is **unfriendly** (18:1)—more literally, "is separated"—suggesting broken relationships (see 19:4). Whether or not the separation was of his choosing, he relishes his isolation in order to satisfy **selfish ends** (18:1; literally, "desire"). The second line marks his character as rebellious and antisocial for **he defies** (literally, "breaks out") or quarrels with **all sound judgment,** "what everyone else knows is right" (TEV).

2. EMPTY PLEASURE (18:2)

Like the isolationist of 18:1, the fool in this proverb has a rather high opinion of himself. Both express their views boldly without regard for what others see as sensible (the Hebrew words for "defies" [18:1] and **airing** [18:2] are similar). Neither **finds . . . pleasure in understanding** or humbly learning from others. Imagining himself to have already obtained all the wisdom one could possibly possess, the **fool** opens his mouth only to reveal how little he knows. How much better for him to go back and listen to 17:28.

3. WICKEDNESS IS NOT PRETTY (18:3)

This proverb puts **wickedness** on parade. Trotted out in broad daylight, we can see it for what it is. Instead of the clever, exciting, satisfying, attractive life it advertises itself to be, we see it as contemptible, shameful, and disgraceful. Thus revealed, we see that **wickedness** is not a private affair. By sinning we show **contempt** for ourselves and others, and we always become more contemptible and disgraced. After witnessing such a parade, who would choose **wickedness?**

4. DRINK DEEP AT WISDOM'S WATER (18:4)

While this proverb makes it clear that **wisdom** brings refreshment, it is unclear whether the first and second lines are meant to be read as contrasting or synonymous. The New International Version takes the former view, suggesting a contrast between the **deep waters** of concealed **wisdom** and a gushing **fountain of wisdom** (18:4; see 20:5). However, if 18:4 wants to describe concealed **wisdom,** why speak of **the words of a man's mouth?** Further, given water's special importance to the Israelites, it is hard to imagine them speaking of it negatively, as the NIV implies. Perhaps it is better to read these lines as synonymous, rather than in contrast:

Deep waters, such are human words;
a gushing stream, the utterance of wisdom (NJB).

5. JUST BE JUST (18:5)

In the original Hebrew, both lines of this proverb rotate on the phrase, **It is not good.** Although the New International Version has moved these words to the beginning of the verse, originally they stood like a pivot between the lines, as seen in the following literal rendering:

To be partial to the wicked
it is not good
to deprive the innocent of justice.

By its design, this proverb emphasizes that injustice—whether by pardoning the guilty (literally, "lifting the face") or refusing to clear the name of **the innocent**—is wrong. No reason is given, but **not good** has an ominous ring; injustice violates the very order of the universe and invites divine judgment.

6. PLEASE HIT ME (18:6)

This proverb is the first of three devoted to the theme of words, especially wrong words. There is more than a thematic connection between 18:6 and 18:7; these two verses are arranged chiastically (see commentary introduction). The first line of 18:6 is meant to pair with the last line of 18:7 (**lips** and their ill effects), while verses 6b and 7a form another pair (**mouth** and the harm it can bring). As the title suggests, the fool's words so often land him in trouble that every time he opens his mouth he is begging for a beating.

7. ENSNARED IN HIS OWN TRAP (18:7)

Not only does the fool invite pain when he speaks (see Proverbs 18:6), but he also traps himself by his words. The irony is unmistakable; who would be foolish enough to lay a trap for oneself (literally, his soul)? Note also how matters have grown increasingly serious. Only beaten in verse 6, the fool is ruined in verse 7.

8. DON'T SPOIL YOUR APPETITE (18:8)

This proverb (repeated exactly in 26:22) focuses on gossip, one particularly harmful use of words, and especially on its attractiveness. **Choice morsels** (18:8) comes from the Hebrew word translated "to swallow greedily." Far from an advertisement, this is a warning: **Gossip** is seductive, resist it. By linking this verse with the two preceding, **gossip** becomes an example of foolish speech, and those warnings can be applied here.

9. DILIGENCE OR DEMOLITION (18:9)

Just as foolish speech brings disaster, so does laziness. "Slack habits and sloppy work" may not seem that bad, but laziness is "as bad as vandalism" (THE MESSAGE). There is no place for sluggards in God's economy. This proverb begins with the Hebrew word *(gam)* usually translated "also" or "even" (see 17:26, 28). Here it probably is used to strengthen the comparison.[2]

10. ETERNAL SECURITY FOR THE RIGHTEOUS (18:10)

Another trio of proverbs begins here, each of which deals with the theme of security. Perhaps mention of demolition in Proverbs 18:9 was intended to set the stage for what follows. **The name of the LORD** (18:10)—that is, Yahweh's nature as revealed in creation and in Israel's history[3]—means security. Towers would have been a part of any of Israel's fortified cities. Often built into the walls, the **tower** served as observation post, superior defensive position from which to repel assaults, and secure refuge in time of attack (see Judges 9:46-52). Because of the protection it offered, it would likely be the last structure in the city to fall into enemy hands. Yahweh's nature **is a strong tower** (see Psalm 61:3) to which His people **run** (Prov. 18:10) in time of trouble and where they find safety. **Run** implies urgency and exclusivity; they rely only on Yahweh and no one else. Only **the righteous** can enter because God is holy; only **the righteous** will seek entry, for all others will shrink from His demands.

11. ETERNAL INSECURITY FOR THE WICKED (18:11)

Standing alone, Proverbs 18:11 might be taken to celebrate the security of the righteous. Joined with 18:10, this proverb reveals the weakness of trusting in anything or anyone other than Yahweh.[4] That the two proverbs belong together is clear from their similar theme and vocabulary. The same word translated "strong" in verse 10 is rendered **fortified** in verse 11. "Safe" (verse 10) and **wall** (verse 11) also translate the same Hebrew word. Instead of relying on Yahweh, **the rich** are tempted to rely on their **wealth** to provide security (18:11; see 10:15). "The world thinks that the unseen is the unreal," says Derek Kidner. However, it is not the righteous person but **the rich** who must rely on his "imagination" (18:11; see RSV margin note on this verse) in order to feel secure.[5]

12. "WHOEVER EXALTS HIMSELF WILL BE HUMBLED"[6] (18:12)

Reading this proverb brings to mind Jesus' words in Matthew, "For whoever exalts himself will be humbled, and whoever humbles himself will be exalted" (Matt. 23:12). Proverbs 18:11 describes those who trust in themselves, not Yahweh,[7] for security. Verse 12 makes explicit both the motive of such people—pride (the same Hebrew word for **proud** is translated "high" in 17:19b)—and their destiny—**downfall.** To be exalted one must first be humble; to be humble means trusting in God rather than oneself (see 15:33). The destruction of one's city (see 18:11) may be God's gracious invitation to true **honor** (18:12).

13. TWO EARS, ONE MOUTH (18:13)

When Charles Caleb Colton wrote, "If God gave us two ears and only one mouth, He must want us to listen twice as much as speak," he may have been inspired by this proverb. According to the fool, **listening** is unnecessary because he already knows everything (18:13; see 18:2). All that is needed, he imagines, is for people to listen to his opinion and be enlightened. His answer, because it is usually wrong, reveals **his folly** ("intellectual indiscipline"[8]) and brings him disgrace (18:13). If he blurted out his answer while someone else was talking, **shame** might refer to the way he insulted the speaker.

14. STRENGTHEN YOUR SPIRIT (18:14)

That this proverb makes a true observation, few would doubt. "What can you do when the spirit is crushed?" (THE MESSAGE) "Short of outward resources, life is hard; short of inward, it is insupportable."[9] The purpose of 18:14, however, goes beyond mere observation to help the reader avoid **a crushed spirit.** God has designed the way of wisdom to bypass problems. The more we walk in this path, the less chance of having our spirits **crushed.** Broken hearts do happen, sometimes by our mistakes and sometimes through no fault of our own. Knowing this, God endowed others with the capacity to bring us joy (see 17:21-22; 12:25).

15. INQUIRING MINDS (18:15)

Perhaps this proverb was placed alongside 18:14 because it addresses an important way to avoid heartache: through **knowledge** (18:15). This verse also begins a series (see 18:15-19) which describes the value of discernment. To the Israelite, **the heart** (18:15) was the place where decisions were made, where wisdom was stored, and from which wisdom was dispensed. Unless **the heart** was involved, no learning would occur. Reference to the ear, the organ by which wisdom is obtained, recalls the oral nature of this fatherly advice. Note that the ear does not passively listen for this wisdom, but aggressively searches for it (see NJB).

16. THE KEY TO INFLUENCE (18:16)

Numerous illustrations of this proverb can be found in the Bible. Jacob proved it true in his encounter with Esau (see Genesis 32:20), as Abigail did with David (see 1 Samuel 25:27). As with Proverbs 18:14, however, this proverb is intended as more than an observation on how things get done. If our resources are capable of producing such powerful effects, we had better use all of them wisely. Such an interpretation is more likely, since **gift** (18:16) represents a more neutral term than the Hebrew word translated "bribe" in 17:8, 23. One such **gift** is the subject of 18:15: discernment. Acquire it, develop it carefully, and it will open doors into **the presence of the great** (18:16). The next proverb demonstrates why discernment is so valuable.

17. WHY DISCERNMENT IS NEEDED (18:17)

How many times, when listening to an argument, have we proven this proverb true? Just by hearing this proverb and learning of our tendency to agree with the most recent voice, we become more discerning. Because truth is not always easy to discover, hasty decisions are discouraged (for the third time in Proverbs 18; see 18:2, 13),[10] and discernment is seen as all the more important (see 18:15-16).

18. PUT THE MATTER IN GOD'S HANDS (18:18)

Although human wisdom is essential and helpful (see Proverbs 18:15-17), sometimes even this is not enough to resolve disputes. God must be appealed to directly; in biblical times, this could be done by **casting the lot** (18:18; see 16:33). Mostly scorned by contemporary Christians, **the lot** may be as biblical a means of discovering God's will as a democratic vote. It openly acknowledges God's ability to affect the outcome of the process and His right to do so. Casting lots, however, does not really move us away from the theme of discernment since it takes wisdom to put the matter in God's hands. Ultimately, whether you cast lots or make a decision conscious of God and using your God-given reason, you have relied on God for the answer.

19. THE IMPORTANCE OF RECONCILIATION (18:19)

Placed at the end of a series of proverbs dealing with discernment (see 18:15-19), we are reminded of its value for reconciling the alienated, an important theme in Proverbs. Although the Hebrew of this verse is difficult to translate, most versions speak of permanent alienation between brothers (see 18:19). Alienation of any kind is unfortunate, but a falling out between blood relatives or close friends is even more so. Many tragic tales could be told to illustrate how family conflicts are some of the most irreparable; wounded pride builds insurmountable gates of self-protection. Discernment can go a long way toward preventing such alienation and healing it when it arises.

20. WELL NOURISHED BY WORDS (18:20)

This and the next proverb focus our attention on words, a topic of considerable importance in Proverbs and a prime cause for alienation (see 18:19). Verse 20 emphasizes the power of words to satisfy one's soul—both **filled** and **satisfied** reflect the same Hebrew verb. This word can mean "happily content" (see 12:11), the result of good words, or "miserably gorged" (see 1:31), the result of bad words. The proverb also emphasizes that the one satisfied is not the hearer, as we might expect, but the speaker.

21. WORDS: A POWERFUL WEAPON (18:21)

Words not only have the power to satisfy (see Proverbs 18:20), but also the power to kill or make alive (see 18:21). Their **fruit** might be life giving, such as that which hangs on the trees flanking the river flowing from God's throne (see Revelation 22) or it may be poisonous, such as that which hung on the tree in the Garden of Eden. **Those who love it [the tongue]** (Prov. 18:21) sounds as strange in English as it does in Hebrew. Some suggest that the phrase refers to those who show their **love** for **the tongue** by exercising it often; others see a **love** which only employs **the tongue** in the best way and at the right time. The phrase is neutral, neither negative or positive. The New Jerusalem Bible puts it well: "Those who indulge it must eat the fruit it yields" (18:21b).

22. GOD'S GOOD GIFT OF MARRIAGE (18:22)

Commentator R. N. Whybray notes that a theme common to Proverbs 18:22-24 is that of relationships: that with one's spouse (18:22), the isolation one experiences without friendship (18:23), and the importance of finding the right friend (18:24). If a connection exists with 18:21, it may be in the reference to love. Earlier passages spoke of a good wife as a cause for joy (see 5:18) and the "crown" of her husband (12:4). Here she is pictured as a source of prosperity (**finds what is good** [18:22] elsewhere means "to prosper"[11]) and a symbol of God's **favor.**

23. THE LONELINESS OF ISOLATION (18:23)

Money adds an edge to a person's voice, an edge that seems to be missing among those whose resources are more limited than their needs. Take 18:23 by itself, and one has an accurate (albeit cynical) observation on life. Keep it in context, however, and we hear something more. We hear about the importance of relationships as our hearts go out to the pleading **poor** (18:23; see 18:22, 24). We are reminded of the importance of justice as we see how "money talks" (see 18:5). We hear a warning against wealth as we listen to the strident, proud tones of the **rich** (18:23; see 18:11). Those harsh **answers** (18:23; the word is used in Exodus 14:21 to describe wind strong enough to blow a path through a sea) remind us of the power of words (see Proverbs 18:20-21).

24. TRUE FRIENDSHIP (18:24)

What the "poor" person of Proverbs 18:23 needs is **a friend who sticks closer than a brother** (18:24). With one such **friend,** he is no longer poor. The rich person, who somehow manages to retain **many companions** in spite of his rudeness (18:24; see 18:23), **may come to ruin** (18:24; literally, "is to be shattered"). That such a destiny awaits the wicked, other proverbs make clear. This Hebrew phrase (actually a single word built on the root *ra-ah*) may also have been chosen because it sounds like the words for **friend** *(ray-ah)* and to "make friends" *(ra-ah;* 22:24). Proverbs 18:24 does not so much decry having many friends as it discourages one against making many friends carelessly. Or it may contrast different kinds of friends, as in the New Jerusalem Bible:

There are friends who point the way to ruin,
Others are closer than a brother.

ENDNOTES

[1]F. Delitzsch, *Proverbs, Ecclesiastes, Song of Solomon,* Commentary on the Old Testament, by C. F. Keil and F. Delitzsch, vol. 10 (Grand Rapids, Michigan: Wm. B. Eerdmans Publishing Co., 1978 [1872]).

[2]R. N. Whybray, *Proverbs,* The New Century Bible Commentary (Grand Rapids, Michigan: Wm. B. Eerdmans Publishing Co., 1994), p. 267.

[3]The New International Version and other translations use LORD in small capitals following an initial capital *L* to denote "Yahweh" in the original Hebrew.

[4]See endnote 3.

[5]Derek Kidner, *Proverbs: An Introduction and Commentary,* Tyndale Old Testament Commentaries, ed. D. J. Wiseman (Downers Grove, Illinois: InterVarsity Press, 1964), pp. 128–29.

[6]Matthew 23:12a (NIV).

[7]See endnote 3.

[8]William McKane, *Proverbs,* The Old Testament Library (Philadelphia: Westminster Press, 1970), p. 515.

[9]Kidner, p. 129.

[10]Ibid.

[11]Whybray, p. 274.

PROVERBS 19

19:1-29

W hile most of the proverbs in chapter 19 stand alone or as part of small groupings, several themes recur: riches and poverty (19:1, 4, 6-7, 10, 14, 17, 22), domestic concerns (19:13-14, 18, 26) folly and wisdom (19:2-3, 8, 11, 19-20, 27), justice (19:5, 9, 25, 28), discipline (19:16, 18, 25, 29), and laziness (19:15, 24). Three proverbs make specific reference to Yahweh[1] (19:3, 21, 23), a fairly uncommon occurrence in Proverbs.

1. WEALTH HAS ITS DANGERS (19:1)

Proverbs 19:1 actually continues the theme with which the preceding chapter concluded, that of relationships. It sets the tone for the several proverbs in this chapter which deal with the issue of wealth and poverty, especially those which appear to give unqualified approval to wealth (see 19:4, 6-8).[2] For some reason the New International Version condenses the second line, thereby obscuring its meaning. Commentator F. Delitzsch renders it more literally, "Than one with perverse lips, and so a fool."[3] The point of this line is that, although this man is presumably wealthy (given the contrast with line 1), by **perverse** speech he shows what he really is—**a fool** (19:1).

2. HASTE MAKES WASTE (19:2)

Wisdom involves patience, an element easily neglected by youthful **zeal** (19:2). This verse follows naturally after verse 1, for what that proverb implies, verse 2 makes clear: **Knowledge,** not money, represents true wealth. Of course, since poverty has no virtue of its own, a reality some might forget in their **zeal** for righteousness, be sure your **zeal** is guided by **knowledge.** The connection between verses 1 and 2 is strengthened by the appearance, at the beginning of verse 2, of the Hebrew word often translated "also" or "even" (left untranslated by NIV).

3. DON'T TRY TO BLAME IT ON GOD (19:3)

Folly's consequences may arise from haste (see Proverbs 19:2) or some other source, but they are always disastrous. Because the fool has only enough sense to realize his ruin, but not enough to see that he brought it on himself, he blames God for it. After all, it could not have been his fault (see 12:15; 14:8). The noun form of the verb, **rages** (19:3), is compared to the roaring "of a lion" in 19:12. It is rendered "be dejected" in Genesis 40:6 which comes closer to one translation of Proverbs 19:3b: "yet he is bitter against the Lord."[4]

4. WEALTH HAS ITS PRIVILEGES (19:4)

Proverbs takes a very realistic view of **wealth** (19:4). **Wealth** can open doors (18:16) and bring us many **friends** (19:4), but it can also take us away from a trust in God (18:11). In addition to making a valid observation on the power of **wealth** (19:4; see 14:20) and encouraging the proper attainment of **wealth,** this proverb warns of the difficulties one should expect if the choice of integrity brings poverty (19:1). After all, we are often reminded that neither friendship nor **wealth** are the primary goals, but obedience. Coming so soon after 18:24, it also encourages the kind of friendship which does not so easily end. Finally, 19:4 serves to remind future rulers of a sobering reality of human nature.

5. GOD OF TRUTH, PART 1 (19:5)

It is no surprise that proverbs on the importance of justice are found amidst proverbs about money. The latter is so often used to twist the former; this connection is made more explicitly in 19:6. God cannot be bought nor does He wish His representatives to be, for justice is too important. All dishonesty will be punished, even that known only to the liar and to God. Similar warnings are issued in 19:9; 6:19; 12:17; 14:5, 25; and 21:28.

6. USE WEALTH WISELY (19:6)

In addition to pointing out the obvious—how money brings influence—Proverbs 19:6 also cautions us to be careful about those who only want what we have to give. Seen more positively, 19:6 encourages wise and generous use of resources. It sounds like Jesus' words on wealth in Luke 16:1-15 when, after telling the parable about the shrewd manager, He counseled, "use worldly wealth to gain friends for yourselves, so that when it is gone, you will be welcomed into eternal dwellings" (16:9).

7. THE LONELY, HELPLESS POOR (19:7)

Several features of this proverb stand out immediately. All of the proverbs since chapter 10 have been of two lines, so the four-line structure is unusual. We are struck by the pathetic situation of the **poor,** who are left alone because of their poverty. Plead as they may, even their **relatives** avoid them. By being unwilling to associate with their **poor** brother, the shallowness of these **friends** and **relatives** also stands out. The last two lines (only one line in the original Hebrew) are very difficult to translate. Some commentators believe they may have originally been part of another proverb, now lost. F. Delitzsch turns to the Septuagint[5] to supply the lost line and translates,

He that hath many friends is rewarded with evil,
Hunting after words which are nothing.

Other translations render the existing Hebrew literally, but without much clarity: "He goes in search of words, but there are none to be had"; "He who pursues words—they are of no avail"; "When he follows them they speak angrily to him."[6] Sufficiently clear is the proverb's warning against poverty and its reminder to those who will be leaders that they must come to the aid of the friendless, for no one else will.

8. THE PATH TO GOOD THINGS (19:8)

Appropriately enough, after a proverb which speaks of hate (a more literal translation of the Hebrew for "shunned"), comes a proverb which speaks of love. The tragedy of friendlessness (see 19:7) prepares us to hear counsel on how to be your "own best friend" (NJPS). Wealth may be an uncertain foundation on which to build relationships, but **wisdom** is not (19:8). **Wisdom** brings prosperity (literally, "finds good"; see 15:32b) to those who not only acquire it, but cherish it.

9. GOD OF TRUTH, PART 2 (19:9)

This proverb repeats 19:5 almost word for word; such repetition suggests how important honesty is to God. Verse 9 does not actually repeat, but develops the thought of its near twin. "Will not go free" has become **will perish;** imprisonment has become punishment. The stronger expression in 19:9 suggests inevitable judgment for deceivers.

10. JARRING ABSURDITIES (19:10)

This proverb has to do with things which do not belong together—"jarring absurdities" to use Derek Kidner's phrase.[7] Some things are inappropriate and potentially serious. **A fool** has no business with money since he does not use it for what he needs most, wisdom (19:10; see 17:16). Instead he spends it acquiring many friends (19:4), dragging them into the ruin he is preparing for himself (19:3). Nor should **a slave . . . rule over princes** (19:10). While it might work in some situations (see Genesis 37–50), such rulers would tend to be ill suited to the demands of true nobility (see Proverbs 30:22-23; Ecclesiastes 10:7). Note the example of Zimri (see 1 Kings 16:8-20; he is described in 1 Kings 16:9 using the same Hebrew word here translated **slave**) who assumed the throne of Israel by killing King Elah and ruling for seven bloody days.

11. "FOR THEY WILL INHERIT THE EARTH"[8] (19:11)

In Proverbs 19:8, "wisdom" promised prosperity; 19:11 speaks of the wise attaining **glory** by responding patiently in the face of **an offense.** Usually we think of **glory** coming as the result of vindication. Here **glory** comes by "overlooking an offence" (NJB; see 12:16)—that is, leaving revenge to God. Jesus taught a similar message in the Beatitudes of the book of Matthew: "Blessed are the meek, for they will inherit the earth. . . . Blessed are those who are persecuted because of righteousness, for theirs is the kingdom of heaven" (Matt. 5:5, 10).

12. SEEK THE KING'S FAVOR (19:12)

If an angry king resembles **a lion** (19:12; see Proverbs 20:2), his subjects should seek his **favor.** If an earthly king demands such a response, how much more the heavenly King who is elsewhere compared to a lion (see Jeremiah 25:38). That the **rage** (Prov. 19:12) of the earthly king should be controlled, like that of his heavenly counterpart, is clear from its placement after 19:11. Contrasted to the king's anger is his **favor.** The one is terrifying, even at a distance; the other welcome. One suggests death; the other life.

13. HOUSE OF HORROR (19:13)

This verse begins a series of proverbs (see Proverbs 19:13-21) which address, directly or indirectly, the domestic sphere, offering practical advice any family could use. Pity the man in 19:13. Look at the house of horror he must come home to. His **foolish son** is a walking time bomb, capable at any moment of destroying his father. **Ruin** implies serious consequences. Job used this word to describe his desperate circumstances (Job 6:2; 30:13). For the psalmist, the term can describe what happens to an animal when caught by the hunter (Psalm 38:12; 91:3) or the harm inflicted by a razor-sharp blade (Psalm 52:2). He cannot turn to his **wife** for consolation, for she is **quarrelsome;** her **constant dripping** drives him insane (Prov. 19:13). Can anything be done to prevent such a horrible home? The proverbs which follow suggest a remedy.

14. A GIFT FROM GOD (19:14)

An important step to avoiding the "house of horror" in Proverbs 19:13 is found in seeking one's wife from Yahweh.[9] This proverb suggests the value of praying for God's will about whom to marry. Examples of courtship in the Old Testament, however, say little about individual choice in the matter of marriage, for most marriages were arranged. Parents can provide **houses and wealth**—they can even arrange the marriage—but only **the LORD** can provide **a prudent wife** (19:14; **from the LORD** is strongly emphasized in the Hebrew). The young man should ask God to send His choice and thank Him when she arrives.

15. GET A JOB (19:15)

The message of Proverbs 19:15 is meant to be heard by more than just the "foolish son" of 19:13. With that sad example so close by, however, one wonders how this advice might have made a difference to such a boy. To say that **laziness brings on deep sleep** (19:15) is somewhat surprising; we would expect it to say that sleep brings on laziness. The emphasis, however, is not on what causes **laziness,** but on the disastrous cycle that laziness perpetuates: first greater sloth, then hunger.

16. OBEDIENCE BRINGS BLESSING (19:16)

A proverb which speaks of obedience and the cost of disobedience fits well in the section on parental advice which began in Proverbs 19:13. **Instruction** could refer to the Law of Moses[10] (see Exodus 20:6) or to the teaching of a parent. The latter is probably in view here, although, ideally, parental commands should be specific applications of God's commands. Note that one **who obeys . . . guards his life** (Prov. 19:16)—that is, he protects himself by his choices. The reverse is also true. The one who disobeys dies, but not as the direct result of divine punishment. He dies of acute carelessness, a disregard for the path of safety. The form of the verb **guards** speaks of ongoing action, while **will die** refers to future consequences. Obedience brings present and (implied) future blessings; disobedience may seem harmless now, but disaster waits around the corner.

17. MONEY WELL SPENT (19:17)

Of all the investments one could make, this one is a sure thing. Be **kind to the poor,** and you, in fact, make a loan to God, who never defaults (19:17). But this investment is not as easily made as one might think, for the proverb counsels kindness **to the poor,** and not just charity. This implies a change in attitude; charity is given to those beneath me, kindness to those alongside. The Hebrew word translated **lends** is used several times in the Old Testament. One such instance presents an interesting point of comparison with this verse. In Exodus 22:25, the Israelites were instructed to loan money to other Israelites. They were not, however, to charge interest nor were they to retain collateral if that would present undue hardship on the borrower. As if to allay the fears such a command would create, this proverb assures them that interest is unnecessary and default impossible—for **the LORD . . . will reward him for what he has done** (Prov. 19:17).

18. KILLING WITH KINDNESS (19:18)

Apparently the temptation to withhold **discipline** (19:18) from a child is not new. Parents, out of kindness, feel the urge to overlook a child's waywardness. Such a choice is not kind, but cruel, for it makes the parents accessories to the murder of their child. **Do not be a willing party to his death** is, literally, "On his destruction do not set your soul." The crime is premeditated. What Proverbs 19:16b says to the individual, this proverb directs to the parent. Translations differ on whether the last part of the first line of 19:18 should be **for in that there is hope** or "while there is hope" (NJB). The latter pictures a limited window in time during which **discipline** is effective; the former makes **discipline** a reason for **hope.**

19. A HARSH KINDNESS (19:19)

Proverbs 19:19 may have been placed here partly as an illustration of the preceding verse. Parents might be tempted to spare their son the trouble of cleaning up the mess he made by his hot temper. When they do, they poison him with kindness by depriving him of the opportunity to be disciplined by consequences. When he erupts again, as he surely will, and when his temper makes a mess, as it always does, guess who is left to clean up the mess? **You will have to do it again** is, literally, "and again you will add." This may refer to how the lack of discipline only makes matters worse: "Spare him, and you aggravate his crime" (19:19b NJB).

20. THE WISE BECOME WISER (19:20)

The series of proverbs which began at 19:13 and which seems so at home in the domestic arena draws to a conclusion with a general injunction to pursue wisdom. **Advice** and **instruction** (19:20) have been offered (such as that found in the preceding verses, but ultimately in the next), but one must **listen to** and **accept** it to become **wise.** Becoming **wise,** according to this verse, differs from the process implied in other passages in Proverbs. There one is told to "call out" and "cry aloud" for it—

Look for it as for silver
and search for it as for hidden treasure—

before one can "understand the fear of the LORD" (2:3-5).[11] No contradiction exists, only the realization that, while wisdom must be diligently pursued, God has graciously provided it more directly through godly, parental counsel (see 19:21). While it may burst upon my mind in "eureka moments," it also lies before me as a pathway only fully attained

in the end (19:20). The alternative to wisdom remains the same: death (see 19:16).

21. LISTEN TO GOD'S ADVICE (19:21)

The "advice" (19:20) which brings wisdom originates in the Lord. He demonstrates His superior wisdom by always bringing His **purpose** (**purpose** [19:21] and "advice" [19:20] translate the same Hebrew word) to fulfillment. We are not wrong to plan, even prolifically (**many** [19:21]), but our wisdom will never surpass His. Therefore, we must "listen to . . . and accept" the "instruction" He gives. His perfect wisdom provides sure footing for our walk of faith.

22. WANTED: A TRUE, BLUE FRIEND (19:22)

While both lines of Proverbs 19:22 are very difficult to translate, the overall meaning seems clear: Honesty is very important. The obscurity of the first line (literally, "the desire of a man, his loyalty") has fostered many attempts at translation. The New International Version and others take "loyalty" as the object of the desire ("Faithful love is what people look for in a person" [19:22a NJB]). Some find another Hebrew word here, spelled very much like the one for **unfailing love,** but meaning "shame." "Desire" is then taken in a negative sense, as "greed" (see NIV margin note). The second line is more clear and makes honesty, even when it leads to poverty, better than dishonest wealth. The reading of the NIV margin note contrasts greed and honesty; the NIV, which makes slightly better sense, promotes both loyalty and honesty, an important reminder in light of the truth of 19:4, 6-7.

23. SATISFIED AND SAFE (19:23)

Obedience requires more than following advice; it takes **the fear of the LORD**[12] (19:23), a key phrase in Proverbs. Such reverence not only represents the fountain from which wisdom flows (see 1:7), but it **leads to life** (19:23). This claim, already made implicitly in 19:3, 16, 18, is easily illustrated. Just as a proper respect toward electricity prevents electrocution and adds convenience to life, so a proper respect toward God brings blessings and old age. **Then one rests content**—more literally, "he shall continue satisfied"; the one who fears **the LORD** leads a life of continual satisfaction. Such a person is not only free from need, but free from danger as well (literally, "not be visited by harm"). Eugene Peterson captures the meaning well:

Fear-of-GOD is life itself,
a full life, and serene—no nasty surprises (THE MESSAGE).

24. TOO LAZY TO EAT (19:24)

Proverbs 19:24 (repeated in 26:15 almost exactly) provides a comical picture of **the sluggard,** picking up the thought from where 19:15 left off. The table has been set and plates filled with food; the lazy person is seated and has forked a load, but lacks the motivation to feed himself. More stupid than the simplest animal, which knows it must eat, this fool will die because it is too much trouble to live. The humor of this caricature may be just what is needed to prompt the young to be diligent.

25. THE BENEFITS OF DISCIPLINE (19:25)

Three characters gather in the courtroom to show how, under the right circumstances, a little discipline (see Proverbs 19:18) goes a long way. **Flog a mocker** (19:25), and the simpleton "may learn a lesson"[13]; the response of the **mocker** is implied in the silence. No beating is needed for the **discerning man** who "gains knowledge" after only a rebuke (see 17:10). A word play, lost in translation, helps to explain the different effects. Because the same Hebrew word is used in the noun (**discerning man**) and the verb (**will gain**), the second line of 19:25 originally suggested that the man of discernment would discern the purpose of the rebuke and learn from his mistake.

26. UNNATURAL AFFECTIONS (19:26)

While the moral of Proverbs 19:26 is painfully clear (respect one's parents), its second line appears anticlimactic, for we expect stronger condemnation of such unnatural behavior. Commentator Derek Kidner thinks otherwise, "for the ruin and eviction are overshadowed by the special bitterness of receiving them from a son."[14] Another way to resolve the anticlimax is to see the first line as describing the real significance of what happens when we commit the second line. That is, when **a son** brings **shame and disgrace** on his parents by any means, it is as bad as if he has robbed **his father** and thrown **his mother** out of the

199

house. By reading this proverb immediately after verse 25, we are reminded of the importance of discipline in producing obedient children, a sentiment reinforced by the following proverb.

27. DON'T REFUSE CORRECTION (19:27)

Proverbs 19:27 drips with irony. The father commands the son to **stop listening** so that he can **stray from the words of knowledge.** Taken at face value, this counsel is the mirror opposite of the advice given in 19:20.   The father has employed irony to make his point more memorable: Keep **listening to instruction** (19:27; literally, "correction," related to the word translated "discipline" in 19:18). Placed immediately after the sobering example of just such a son (see 19:26), this advice is even more ominous. The irony in the original Hebrew is too strong for most translators who change the imperative (**stop listening** [19:27]) into a statement and emerge with something innocuous (see NIV).

28. A FOUNTAIN OF LIES, A VORTEX OF EVIL (19:28)

While at first the two lines of Proverbs 19:18 appear dissimilar, they have much in common. Both refer to actions of **the mouth.** The first describes the **corrupt witness** whose words mock **justice** in a fountain of lies.   The second describes **the wicked** whose appetite for **evil** is voracious. In Hebrew, the second word of the first line and the second to last word of the second line have been chosen for their similarity (**corrupt** *[beliyaal]* and **gulps** *[yibalah]*)—a word play intended to emphasize what liars and **the wicked** have in common. Taken together, this proverb encourages **justice** through honesty and righteousness.

29. THE INEVITABLE (AND PAINFUL) OUTCOME (19:29)

Proverbs 19:29 continues the theme of justice (see 19:5, 9, 25, 28) and also refers to **mockers** (the same Hebrew word translated "mocks" in 19:28). The punishment of **mockers** and **fools** (19:29) is emphasized by the chiastic structure of this verse in the original (see commentary introduction). It is translated more literally,

Is ready for mockers, condemnation
and flogging for the backs of fools.

The proverb does not merely observe that these things happen, but rather that **fools** and **mockers** deserve what they get.

ENDNOTES

[1]The New International Version and other translations use LORD in small capitals following an initial capital *L* to denote "Yahweh" in the original Hebrew.

[2]Line 1 recurs at Proverbs 28:6.

[3]F. Delitzsch, *Proverbs, Ecclesiastes, Song of Solomon,* Commentary on the Old Testament, by C. F. Keil and F. Delitzsch, vol. 10 (Grand Rapids, Michigan: Wm. B. Eerdmans Publishing Co., 1978 [1872]).

[4]R. B. Y. Scott, *Proverbs, Ecclesiastes* in The Anchor Bible, vol. 18, eds. William F. Albright and David Noel Freedman (New York: Doubleday, 1965), p. 36.

[5]The Septuagint is the Greek version of the Old Testament, translated from the original Hebrew scrolls, and written in the second and third centuries B.C. It is often indicated by the Roman numerals LXX in accordance with the legend that it was translated by seventy scribes.

[6]NJB; NJPS; Scott.

[7]Derek Kidner, *Proverbs: An Introduction and Commentary,* Tyndale Old Testament Commentaries, ed. D. J. Wiseman (Downers Grove, Illinois: InterVarsity Press, 1964), p. 132.

[8]Matthew 5:5b (NIV).

[9]See endnote 1.

[10]Law of Moses or Mosaic law refers to the Pentateuch (the first five books of the Old Testament: Genesis, Exodus, Leviticus, Numbers, and Deuteronomy). Law used this way is often capitalized.

[11]See endnote 1.

[12]Ibid.

[13]Scott.

[14]Kidner, p. 135.

PROVERBS 20

20:1-30

Proverbs 20 opens with the observation that **wine** and **beer** lead to brawling (20:1) and closes with the benefits of physical discipline (20:30). Avoid the lifestyle which produces pointless pain (20:1) and embrace the painful correction which purges **the inmost being** (20:30).

1. TWO COMPANIONS TO AVOID (20:1)

The subject of the **mocker** continues from 19:29 to this proverb (20:1), which personifies **wine and beer.** These two drinking buddies should be avoided. **Wine** mocks the drinker, while **beer** provokes fights; **whoever** (literally, "everyone who") consumes them invites abuse. Associate with them, and you will be **led astray**—more literally, you will stagger, unable to control yourself. The theme of avoiding conflict continues through 20:3.

2. THE RIGHT SIDE OF THE LAW (20:2)

The first line of Proverbs 20:2 against arousing the **wrath** of the king is repeated almost verbatim from 19:12, except that this verse substitutes **wrath** for "rage." The shift puts more emphasis on what the king does as a result of his anger. As we noted in 19:12, if angering the earthly king meant disaster, how much more disastrous angering the Divine King he was to represent. By reading **forfeits his life** (20:2) more literally as "sins against his life," more emphasis is placed on how one brings disaster on himself. By avoiding alcohol and exercising the self-control encouraged in 20:1, one is much more likely to stay on the right side of the law, both human and divine.[1]

3. THE HONORABLE PACIFIST (20:3)

We are to **avoid strife** (20:3), a common theme in Proverbs 20:1-3, not merely to keep the law or to keep your nose unbroken, but because it is the honorable thing to do. Associating **honor** and avoiding fights sounds strange; most consider **honor** something one must fight to defend (20:3). But the one **quick to quarrel** is really the fool—he who is characterized by a quarrelsome disposition (**every fool**). The wise person knows that **honor** is lost, not gained, in a fight (see 17:14).

4. THE PUZZLED SLUGGARD (20:4)

When we last met the **sluggard** (20:4), he was starving at a table spread with food because he was too lazy to lift the food "to his mouth" (19:24). Here he appears equally ridiculous, for though he has not even plowed his soil, he still looks for crops "at harvest time." The humor of this scene is well captured by the New Jerusalem Bible (20:4):

In autumn the idler does not plough,
at harvest time he looks—nothing there!

In season is, literally, "in the autumn," after the fruit harvest was completed and the early rains had softened the soil, between October and December. **Harvest time** begins in April and extends through the spring and into the summer. Wisdom does the hard work, knowing that otherwise there are no rewards.

5. HOW LONG IS YOUR ROPE? (20:5)

Proverbs 20:5-7 describes three exceptional people—a wise person, a faithful person, and a righteous person—each intended as an example for the son to follow. The wise man, or **man of understanding,** has the capacity to discern **the purposes** of others, although they lie far beneath the surface (20:5). **Draws them out** is used other times in the Old Testament, all in Exodus 2 (see verses 16, 19). Each refers to the process of drawing water from a well (a fitting companion to the proverb on farming in Proverbs 20:4). The wise man has a long rope which enables him to draw out **deep waters** (20:5), the purposes of others which lie hidden from view. Jesus was such **a man of understanding;** "He did not need man's testimony about man, for he knew what was in a man" (John 2:25).

6. THE VALUE OF A FAITHFUL FRIEND (20:6)

The **faithful** person who lives up to his profession of friendship is the second example worth following (20:6; see Proverbs 20:5). Many a man or woman "proclaims" (better than **claims**) **unfailing love,** but, for one reason or another, that love fails (20:6). How fortunate to find **a faithful man,** one whose love does not fail. This proverb, in addition to encouraging us to be **faithful** friends, also cautions us against believing every promise of friendship we hear.

7. THINK OF YOUR GRANDCHILDREN (20:7)

Proverbs 20:5 presented the example of the "man of understanding," and 20:6 the "faithful man." This proverb speaks of **the righteous man who leads a blameless life** (20:7).[2] Such a man obtains God's blessing not only for himself, but also for **his children.** He has eliminated harmful attitudes and behaviors which would damage the family's reputation and diminish the family's resources. Instead, his wise choices and diligent effort have produced tangible evidence of God's blessing which the whole family can enjoy. How true it is that righteous fathers "make it much easier for their children" (THE MESSAGE)! How welcome it is to meet a person who lives not for himself, but for a future generation. While this verse concludes the trilogy of good examples (see 20:5-7), it also begins a string of proverbs (see 20:7-12) alike in style—all composed of single sentences—and alike in theme: righteousness.

8. JUSTICE'S ALL-SEEING EYE (20:8)

Proverbs 20:8 seeks to encourage righteousness by showing the earthly (and, by implication, heavenly) dangers of disobedience. An important function of Israel's king was to maintain justice for all people; **his throne** served as the judgment seat (20:8; see 1 Kings 3:16-28). Winnowing is the process by which grain is separated from the husk, its inedible covering. Nothing escapes, for the **king . . . winnows out all evil** (Prov. 20:8). **With his eyes** represents a literal translation from the Hebrew, well rendered by the New Jerusalem Bible as "with one look scatters all that is evil."

9. BEWARE SELF-RIGHTEOUSNESS (20:9)

Against the ability of the human king (and certainly the heavenly King) to see so clearly, claims of sinlessness stand out as hollow and naive. There is no contradiction between Proverbs 20:9 and the description of someone as "righteous" (20:7) or God's pronouncement of us as "perfect" (Hebrews 10:14). Only pride would say, **I have kept my heart pure** (Prov. 20:9); this is something God alone can do (see Psalm 119:9). Righteousness is commendable, but you must do more than claim it. You must obtain it from the King who sits on the heavenly throne of judgment.

10. PURE BUSINESS, PART 1 (20:10)

No one can claim to be righteous (see Proverbs 20:7-12, especially 20:9), unless that person's business dealings are righteous. **Differing weights and differing measures** (20:10) is, literally, "stone and stone, measure and measure," two expressions which appear in Deuteronomy 25:13-16 (with the additional phrase, "great and small"). Dishonest vendors would use stone weights or measuring bowls of differing sizes, one reflecting the actual standard of measurement and another just a shade smaller. Customers thought they were purchasing a certain amount of grain, but, because of the deceptive use of the smaller weight or measure, they received less. That this practice was not uncommon is evident from frequent condemnations (including Proverbs 20:23; 11:1), from the efforts of reforming kings to standardize the system of weights and measures, and from archaeological evidence of "short" weights.

11. RIGHTEOUSNESS HAS NO AGE LIMIT (20:11)

If **even a child is known by his actions** (20:11), parents must take seriously their responsibilities to carefully consider the character of that **child** and work to shape that character while it can still be molded. The use of **even** to begin the proverb implies something more. If even a child's behavior gives him away, how much more an adult's? Some translations change **right** to "bad" or "wicked" in order to created an antithesis with **pure,** but this requires an unnecessary change in the original Hebrew.

12. OUR BASIC EQUIPMENT IS FROM GOD (20:12)

Set at the conclusion of this series of proverbs on righteousness, 20:12 reminds us that God has given us what we need to live righteously—"we get our basic equipment from God!" (THE MESSAGE). Our task is to use our **eyes** and **ears** to become wise and avoid wickedness. Since **eyes** and **ears** do not automatically work this way, we must continue to count on the Giver of this equipment to help us use it wisely. What we must not do, and what would be the height of ingratitude, is to use these gifts to slight their Giver.

13. THE VIRTUE OF LABOR (20:13)

While Proverbs 20:13 stands outside the preceding collection (see 20:7-12) which concerns righteousness, it is linked to 20:12 by reference to proper use of the eyes—**stay awake** being, literally, "open your eyes." The second phrase in line 2—**you will have food to spare**—is also a command and might better be rendered "be satisfied with bread." By stating this as a command, the proverb not only promises bread, but emphasizes the inevitability of satisfaction. Perhaps the sluggard prefers his dream world of great feasts and abundant riches to the real world of hard work and simple bread. The proverb orders him to wake up and "be satisfied with bread."

14. LET THE SELLER BEWARE (20:14)

In and out of the marketplace, let the seller beware. Prices are not usually marked on life's commodities, and, in the bartering, you may be told that what you thought was valuable is not. If you believe whatever you hear, you may find you have sold cheaply a priceless treasure. This warning against dishonest customers provides a needed (although sobering) complement to Proverbs 20:10, 23, which caution against dishonest merchants. From both directions, we find reasons to listen with discernment.

15. A PRICELESS JEWEL (20:15)

While we are in the marketplace, let us consider what is of greatest value. **Gold** and **rubies in abundance** (20:15; literally, "abundance of costly stones") are thought by many commentators to refer to kinds of adornment, rather than units of wealth. The two ideas are not mutually exclusive; even today some Middle Eastern women wear the family wealth as jewelry. The absence of a main verb (except for the verb "there is," which begins the verse) has left the proverb open to several interpretations. According to the New International Version and many other translations, **lips that speak knowledge are a rare jewel** (literally, precious article or vessel) which surpasses **gold** and **rubies** in value. Crawford Toy proposes instead that "wise lips" are being favorably compared to all three: gold, rubies, and "precious vessels."[3] Another possibility refers to the "wise man's lips" which "drink from a more precious cup."[4] By any of these readings, wisdom surpasses all that is precious (see 3:14-15).

16. DON'T COSIGN FOR A STRANGER (20:16)

Although suretyship has already been condemned in Proverbs (see 6:1-5), 20:16 returns to the subject long enough to advise how we should treat the one foolish enough to cosign for **a stranger** and **a wayward woman.** The New International Version has followed ancient precedent in reading the Hebrew as a feminine noun, but the New Jerusalem Bible and others are probably correct to translate the phrase as masculine plural: "persons unknown." The proverb warns against entering blindly into a business arrangement with such a bad risk. Because he was not wise enough to take some kind of collateral, you should. The command to take his **garment** may suggest that the clothes on his back may be all his folly has left him.

17. A MOUTHFUL OF GRAVEL (20:17)

Stolen food was the menu at Lady Folly's party in Proverbs 9:17. That party ended in the grave; this meal ends with **a mouth full of gravel** (20:17). The Hebrew behind this word is used only one other time in the Old Testament, also in the context of God's judgment. Lamentations 3:16 describes God's judgment on the disobedient, whose teeth are broken on the gravel and who have been trampled in the dust and filled with bitter herbs. **Food** gained deceitfully at first **tastes sweet** (Prov. 20:17) because it is flavored with excitement and danger. That flavoring quickly wears off, and the **food** becomes hardened by guilt and fear of apprehension. In the end, this **food** is not only repulsive and hard to digest, but even life threatening.

18. THE IMPORTANCE OF GOOD ADVICE (20:18)

Just as no one would declare **war** without first consulting experts on national security (20:18; see Proverbs 11:14), no one should **make plans** without **seeking advice** (see Luke 14:31-33). Because life is too important and sometimes like a battle, **obtain guidance** (Prov. 20:18). This proverb may have originated as advice to future rulers, but came to represent a principle true in every area of life.

19. AVOID BLABBERMOUTHS (20:19)

From those who are tempted to listen too little (see Proverbs 20:18), we move to one **who talks too much** (20:19; literally, "one who opens his lips"). Gabby people tend to be gossips. Having long since exhausted, due to sheer volume, their stockpile of sensible comments, their only remaining verbal supply must come from the problems of others . . . including those secrets you confided to them.

Hebrew grammar allows for a stronger and milder level of intensity for prohibitions; **avoid** reflects the stronger, more permanent type, found in only one other place in Proverbs (see 24:21). Because association with a blabbermouth seems so innocent, but can be so disastrous, the strikingly stern warning is warranted.

20. HONOR YOUR PARENTS (20:20)

According to Mosaic law,[5] the one who cursed his parent was to be put to death (see Leviticus 20:9). Proverbs 20:20 poetically describes his destruction: **His lamp will be snuffed out.** One's life can be described as a **lamp** (see 13:9); his **will be snuffed out in pitch darkness** (20:20), probably in the middle of the night. When a Hebrew verb is stated in the passive voice, as here, the author often intends for God to be understood as the implied subject; those who destroy such an ungrateful offspring do so as God's agents. The man spoke a curse against his parents, fully intending it to bring them harm, but instead the harm comes on him.

21. EASY COME, EASY GO (20:21)

What a timely proverb for a society like ours which spends billions to satisfy every whim of its children. There is a time for an **inheritance,** but, given too soon, it can evaporate, leaving those we love devoid of the blessing we intended. It is cruelty, not kindness, to give too much to the unprepared. What is gained little by little is blessed in the end (see Proverbs 13:11) because it allows a proper balance between reward and maturity. This principle works in many arenas. Education must be accumulated "line upon line" or else the pupil becomes discouraged. Human relationships need time to develop; spend too much time too soon with a person, and you may quickly learn to dislike each other.

22. LEAVE IT TO THE JUDGE (20:22)

Like other proverbs on revenge (see 17:13; 24:29; 25:21), 20:22 encourages us to take our case to **the LORD,** rather than try to vindicate ourselves. **I'll pay you back for this wrong** is, literally, "I will repay evil." The person is not merely seeking revenge for a specific wrong; he plans to bring about complete and total vindication. This, says the proverb, should be left to God. Wrongs have been most certainly committed, but they are not assumed as my responsibility. Instead, they are placed in God's hands, and His deliverance is awaited. Such is the example set in the Imprecatory Psalms[6] and the book of Revelation. Commentator Derek Kidner sees "an ascending scale" in these four proverbs on revenge: The first describes the results of revenge; this verse advises leaving it with the Lord; Proverbs 24:29 warns against having a vindictive spirit; and Proverbs 25:21 promotes the proper choice when one is wronged.[7]

23. PURE BUSINESS, PART 2 (20:23)

Proverbs 20:23 repeats and thereby emphasizes the message of 20:10: God hates **dishonest** business practices. Here, **[God] detests** is placed first for emphasis, and **dishonest scales** replaces "differing measures" (20:23; 20:10). **Do not please him** is, literally, "are not good." We also meet this phrase in 18:5 (also 17:26 and 19:2) where it means something much more ominous than it sounds.

24. THE ONE WHO KNOWS THE WAY (20:24)

Some see Proverbs 20:24 as merely a variation on the adage, "Man proposes, God disposes," but something more is being said. The proverb encourages trust in Yahweh (**LORD** is emphasized in the

Hebrew[8]) who is capable of seeing everything clearly, even when we cannot (**how then can anyone understand** is also emphatic in the original). We can better understand our **way** by understanding the One who directs our way, since He always orders in line with His character. To see in this verse a note of quiet despair—"We are only pawns on God's chessboard of life"—is to disregard the very clear evidence throughout the rest of Proverbs that God puts a great deal of control into our hands. To say this does not negate 20:24a; God's sovereignty is our best reason to trust Him.

25. NO RASH PROMISES (20:25)

Proverbs 20:25 makes it clear that God is more concerned that His people keep their **vows** than He is that they make them. In other words, He is more interested in integrity than religious fervor. **Vows** were entirely voluntary but, once made, were a solemn obligation. Therefore, "It is better not to vow than to make a vow and not fulfill it" (Ecclesiastes 5:5). The Hebrew term behind **rashly** (Prov. 20:25) is used in Job 6:3 where it refers to impetuous speech prompted by intense suffering. **To dedicate something rashly** and later regret it is to be trapped by one's vow (Prov. 20:25; **trap** is used elsewhere for the snare in which birds were caught). Ironically, vows were often made in times of difficulty in order to win God's deliverance. Liberated from the "frying pan" in response to your vow, you now land in the fire, more ensnared than ever.

26. THE WHEELS OF JUSTICE (20:26)

Like 20:8, this proverb describes the king as the minister of justice. Unlike 20:8, specific mention is made to the king's wisdom, and the device has changed from his "eyes" to his **wheel** (20:26). Instead of sitting on his throne, **he drives the threshing wheel** (literally, he "returns a wheel"; see Isaiah 28:27-28). In Proverbs 20:8 he "winnows out . . . evil," but in 20:26 he crushes **the wicked.** According to Derek Kidner, the emphasis in verse 8 is on the king's powers of discrimination, while here it is on his actions.[9] As with verse 8, the picture of the heavenly Judge lies close to the heart of this proverb. Yahweh,[10] for whom we wait (see 20:22), will one day let His wheel pass over the wicked.

27. SEARCHING HIDDEN CORNERS WITH GOD'S LIGHT (20:27)

Various interpretations exist for Proverbs 20:27. The New International Version text reflects the predominant view which makes Yahweh[11] the searcher and the human spirit the object of His scrutiny. While this view agrees with other passages in Proverbs (see 15:3, 11; 16:2; 21:2), it requires the addition of **searches** in line 1 (20:27). Perhaps the better reading is found in the NIV margin note, which makes the human spirit the searcher, Yahweh's **lamp** the tool that makes searching possible, and the realm searched the **inmost being** ("the deepest self" [NJB]). The verse then confidently asserts that we need not be victims of self-deceit since we have "this inner light" on which we can rely.[12] The two interpretations eventually meet, for if *we* discern what goes on inside and outside us by the Lord's **lamp,** *He* certainly sees this as well.

28. AUTHORITY RESTING ON LOVE (20:28)

Commentator Derek Kidner rightly observes that Proverbs 20:28 provides the crucial counterbalance to the authority of 20:26.[13] The king's throne is once again mentioned (see 20:8), but here it is described as resting upon or upheld (rather than **made secure** [20:28]) by **love.** While the **king** must judge the wicked, a **safe . . . secure** reign requires faithful **love** (emphasized by its repetition in both lines). More than sentiment, such **love** should reveal itself as the motive by which justice is administered, in policies which have at heart only the best interest of the governed, and in people of integrity. **Love** belongs as the foundation of the king's **throne** because it is the foundation of God's throne, and the greatest security is godliness.

29. HONOR EACH OTHER (20:29)

Proverbs 20:29 functions well at several levels of interpretation. As a straightforward statement of fact, it is true that **young** people are generally strong and the elderly are generally experienced (as illustrated by **gray hair**). This statement also becomes a reminder that people should respect the **young** for their **strength** (and enthusiasm, energy, and idealism) rather than wishing they would "grow up." **The old** should be honored for their **gray hair** (that is, their years of experience, accomplishments, wisdom, and stability) instead of being criticized for being "old fashioned." Each one should accept the status of others—whether young, old, or in between—and not be critical. As well, each should accept oneself for who he or she is. Laughable are the young who try to act old; more ridiculous are the old who try to act young. Finally, each should be grateful to God for His wonderful creativity. He equipped each age with the virtues and abilities needed at that age.

30. DESPERATE TIMES, DESPERATE MEASURES (20:30)

For the strength of the young to ripen to the wisdom of the old, discipline is essential. **Blows, wounds,** and **beatings** are severe measures, but so is the difficulty (20:30). **Evil** that lies deep in one's **inmost being** stubbornly resists removal, but God is able, often through desperate measures, to bring cleansing. Faithful, loving rebuke in small doses at a tender age makes these desperate measures unnecessary.

ENDNOTES

[1]Law refers to either the Levitical Code (all God's rules and regulations), the Ten Commandments, or the Pentateuch (the first five books of the Old Testament: Genesis, Exodus, Leviticus, Numbers, and Deuteronomy; also called the Law of Moses or Mosaic law). It is often capitalized when it means the Pentateuch or the Ten Commandments.

[2]This verse should be read as a single sentence, with line 1 as the subject and line 2 as the predicate:

A righteous man who walks in his integrity,
Blessed are his sons after him,

rather than translate it as two independent clauses, as the New International Version does.

[3]Crawford H. Toy, *Proverbs,* The International Critical Commentary (New York: Charles Scribner's Sons, 1899).

[4]R. B. Y. Scott, *Proverbs, Ecclesiastes* in The Anchor Bible, vol. 18, eds. William F. Albright and David Noel Freedman (New York: Doubleday, 1965); see THE MESSAGE.

[5]See endnote 1.

[6]Imprecatory Psalms are those which speak of cursing one's enemies.

[7]Derek Kidner, *Proverbs: An Introduction and Commentary,* Tyndale Old Testament Commentaries, ed. D. J. Wiseman (Downers Grove, Illinois: InterVarsity Press, 1964), p. 139.

[8]The New International Version and other translations use LORD in small capitals following an initial capital *L* to denote "Yahweh" in the original Hebrew.

[9]Kidner, p. 140.

[10]See endnote 8.

[11]Ibid.

[12]William McKane, *Proverbs,* The Old Testament Library (Philadelphia: Westminster Press, 1970), p. 547.

[13]Kidner, p. 140.

PROVERBS 21

21:1-31

This chapter of Proverbs begins and ends with a clear proclamation of God's sovereignty. The one who directs the heart of the king (see 21:1) is also the one who provides **victory** in battle (21:31). But God's sovereignty must also be acknowledged in every other aspect of life—at home (21:9, 12, 20), in court (21:15, 28), in the marketplace (21:6), and in the Temple (21:27)—for there is **no plan that can succeed against the LORD** (21:30).[1]

1. THE KING'S KING (21:1)

To describe the **king's heart** as **a watercourse** (21:1) is an appropriate comparison. As water is a life-giving and life-sustaining commodity, especially in Palestine, so would be the king in God's hands. **Watercourse** refers to an irrigation ditch designed to direct water where most needed. As with other proverbs directed to the king, 21:1 also applies to his subjects. All should remain flexible, willing to do the will of God. When we are placed in His hands, God can accomplish wonderfully refreshing things. This and the next two proverbs specifically mention Yahweh,[2] which is uncommon in Proverbs. This is also the first of four proverbs which call God's people to obedience; appropriately, it is directed to the Divine King's first subject.

2. YOUR HEART IN THE BALANCE (21:2)

This proverb, virtually repeated in 16:2, continues the thought of 21:1 in its theme (obedience), its mention of Yahweh,[3] and the use of the word **heart** (21:2). It furthers the thought of 21:1 by emphasizing that Yahweh knows the true measure of each person's **heart.** The first line reminds us how easily we can rationalize our actions (literally, "right in his own eyes"), while the second shows that God's vision is not limited like ours. He **weighs** all hearts (21:2), from the king's to the commoner's—that is, He "assesses them at their true value."[4]

3. WHAT CARRIES WEIGHT WITH GOD (21:3)

If you want to know what weighs heavily with God, Proverbs 21:3 provides the answer. Not sacrifices, whether animal, vegetable, or mineral (for example, money), but **what is right and just** matters to God. He is not opposed to sacrifices; after all, He commanded that they be offered. Nor is His desire for obedient hearts a new observation, as Deuteronomy 6:5 makes clear. If forced to choose, however, God would prefer righteousness and justice to sacrifices. While we usually associate righteousness with morality ("clean living before God" [THE MESSAGE]), here it probably refers more to how we treat other people ("equity"[5]). "To do righteousness and justice" (literally) means treating them properly and fairly.

4. HOW TO FLUNK YOUR WEIGH-IN (21:4)

Just before a match, wrestlers become very concerned about what they eat. To wrestle at their chosen weight class, they must not be too heavy or too light at their pre-match "weigh-in." This proverb constitutes our weigh-in; it shows what God does not like and, therefore, what His obedient people should avoid (continuing this same theme from 21:3). **Haughty eyes** look down on mere mortals from a self-assumed position of superiority (21:4; see 21:2). The **proud heart** explains the **haughty eyes;** perhaps its owner would be more humble if he realized who was watching (21:4; see 21:2). **Lamp of the wicked** could be a third characteristic (21:4; as NJB) describing the search of **the wicked** for wrongs to commit. Or it could summarize the first two: the life or well-being of **the wicked** (see 13:9b; see also THE MESSAGE). By any reading, **the wicked** person has failed God's weigh-in because of **sin** (21:4).

5. HASTE MAKES WASTE (21:5)

With Proverbs 21:5 we turn to diligence, a quality God admires and one which characterizes the wise. Since **the plans of the diligent** portrays both forethought (**plans**) and careful execution (**diligent**), **haste** probably refers to a lack of planning plus careless execution. Although left untranslated in the New International Version, both lines contain the word "only." When included, it adds an element of finality and overstatement to this proverb well reflected in the New Jerusalem Bible:

> The hardworking is thoughtful, and all is gain;
> too much haste, and all that comes of it is want.

A word play between **lead to profit** *(ach lemotar)* and **leads to poverty** *(ach lemachsor)* powers home the point of this proverb.

6. DECEIVING YOURSELF TO DEATH (21:6)

Proverbs 21:6 continues the theme of profit from 21:5 and may have been placed here to clarify the reference there to "haste." You might gain **a fortune** from **a lying tongue** (21:6) by overselling your product, promising investors what you have no intention to deliver, cheating on your taxes, or any number of other ways. In the end, however, you will find that your **fortune** and your life have vanished like **a fleeting vapor**. **Vapor** translates the same Hebrew word found often in Ecclesiastes where it is usually rendered "meaningless." The translation **Deadly snare** follows the Septuagint,[6] but the word for **snare** might be better translated "seekers." The New Jerusalem Bible makes sense of the difficult expression (literally) "a driven vapor, seekers of death" by translating it as "such is the idle fantasy of those who look for death" (21:6b). Those who pursue their fortune by deceitful means are, in fact, committing "no less than suicide" (CEV).

7. CREATING A MONSTER (21:7)

More bad news for **the wicked** follows in this Proverbs 21:7, which joins the themes of dishonesty (see 21:6) and unrighteousness (see 21:2-5). With every violent act, **the wicked** (21:7) have been creating and training a monster which one day will turn and destroy them. **Will drag them away** is used in Habakkuk 1:15 to picture the reeling in of a fish from the sea. Helpless at the hands of their own creation, the doom of **the wicked** is certain. Do not feel sorry for them as they flop helplessly on the shore, for they have consciously chosen to disobey God (**They refuse to do**

what is right [21:7b]). **Right** translates the same Hebrew word rendered "just" in 21:3; they have refused to treat others justly and to obey God. This proverb may contain bad news for **the wicked,** but it brings good news to the righteous, who are often victims of **the violence,** and is an important reminder to choose God's way (21:7).

8. CROOKED OR STRAIGHT (21:8)

In another effort to encourage righteousness, Proverbs 21:8 contrasts the righteous with the wicked, specifically **the way of the guilty** with **the conduct of the innocent.** The Hebrew word translated **guilty** *(vazar)* is used only here in the Old Testament. It may have been chosen to make a word play with **innocent** *(vezak);* the two words stand alongside one another in the Hebrew. By translating **devious** and **upright,** the New International Version has missed the real contrast in the original, that between the crooked and the straight.[7]

9. PEACE IN A CORNER OF THE ROOF (21:9)

This is the first of two very similar proverbs (see 21:19) in Proverbs 21 which counsel the young man on the importance of choosing the right **wife.** One who is **quarrelsome**—that is, one who nags and stirs up trouble—can make life so miserable you would prefer cramped and uncomfortable quarters to luxury in her company. While stated humorously, the frequent repetition of such warnings betrays the seriousness of the situation (see 25:24 for the same saying, and 21:19; 19:13-14; 27:15-16 for similar ones).

10. A LOOK INSIDE THE SOUL OF THE WICKED (21:10)

Nearly as bad as living with "a quarrelsome wife" (21:9) is living alongside a **wicked** and contentious **neighbor** (21:10). No matter what you try to do, this **neighbor** is never pleased. The Hebrew contains imagery almost beyond translation. **Wicked man** literally refers to the *nephesh* of the wicked; *nephesh* can have the meaning "soul" or "throat." This man **craves evil**—that is, he has a very strong appetite for it, as one might have for meat (see Deuteronomy 12:20) or fruit (see Micah 7:1). Proverbs 21:10 describes one whose throat is open and hungering for **evil** like a man starving for food. Such an appetite leaves no possibility for mercy.

11. THE BENEFITS OF DISCIPLINE (21:11)

Proverbs goes to great lengths to encourage the use of discipline, even to repeating similar proverbs, as with 21:11 and 19:25. There the "scoffer" is flogged, while here a more generic word (**punished**) is employed. The difference between learning prudence (19:25) and gaining **wisdom** (21:11) is slight; **the simple** benefit in either case. The "discerning man" gains "knowledge" from "rebuke" (19:25), while the **wise man** (literally) "takes" **knowledge** from instruction (21:11). Both proverbs teach that while **the simple** learn from discipline, mockers do not. All the **wise man** needs is to be **instructed** (21:11) or, at the most, to receive a word of "rebuke" (19:25).

12. WATCHING EYES (21:12)

Although Proverbs 21:12 is somewhat ambiguous, it clearly continues the theme of punishment for **the wicked** from 21:11. The New International Version may be correct to take the ambiguous phrase **Righteous One** (21:12) as a reference to God. He is *the* only truly righteous being and is elsewhere described as punisher of **the wicked**. However, since nowhere else in Proverbs is God described by this phrase, it could instead refer to the "righteous man" (see NIV margin note) who is given the privilege of seeing the downfall of his enemies. Not only is this grammatically possible, but it allows a closer connection between two uses of the same Hebrew verb, translated "instructed" in 21:11 and **takes note** in 21:12. In other words, 21:12 provides the content of the "instruction" referred to in 21:11. The righteous man lives by the qualities God admires, according to 21:3. That this reading makes the righteous the destroyer of **the wicked** is unusual, but not impossible (21:12; see 21:15, 22[8]).

13. LISTENING EARS (21:13)

In Proverbs 21:3 we noted God's interest in treating others fairly, a theme also implied in 21:12. That teaching continues in 21:13, specifically with reference to **the poor.** The preceding proverb spoke of eyes that see wickedness; this one of **ears** that hear the cries **of the poor.** If one ignores those cries, *his* cries (the Hebrew is emphatic) will be ignored by God (implied). The book of Proverbs makes it clear that wisdom may lead to wealth (see 21:5, 20), but must always lead to concern for those less fortunate (see 24:11-12; 25:21).

14. THE POWER OF MONEY (21:14)

From a proverb which speaks of the proper use of wealth, we move to one which speaks of its improper use and to the first of a pair dealing with justice. As with similar proverbs encountered thus far (see 17:8; 18:16), this is not meant as an endorsement of bribery, but as an observation which sets the stage for the verse to follow.

15. THE JOY OF JUSTICE (21:15)

While money can influence the powerful, God desires **justice** (21:15; see 21:3 where the same Hebrew word occurs). **When justice is done** is probably better than "to do justice"[9] since the latter reading makes the **evildoers** terrified of doing right, an awkward idea. **The righteous** (21:15; see 21:3, 12) rejoice at **justice** because it marks the triumph of God's cause. **Justice** brings **terror** to the wicked because it means certain punishment. The same Hebrew word could be rendered "destruction" (Psalm 89:40) or "ruin" (Proverbs 10:29; Jeremiah 17:17) where it stands as the opposite of refuge. The peace purchased by injustice (see Proverbs 21:14) cannot be compared to the **joy** which **justice . . . brings** (21:15).

16. STAY ON THE PATH (21:16)

Justice may bring **joy** (21:15), but wisdom brings life itself (see 21:16). In Yellowstone National Park, where access to many of the sites is gained by boardwalks, safety is found on the wooden paths; those who stray risk stepping through the mineral crust into danger and possibly death. Safety is found on **the path of understanding** (from the same verb translated "instructed" in 21:11 and "takes note" in 21:12). Those who stray (literally) "rest in the assembly of the ghosts." More than just an alternative for the idea of "death," **rest** (21:16) speaks to the inactivity of those who stray, brought out more emphatically by the use of "ghosts." Often people wander from the path as a sign of independence; how ironic it is that they **rest in the company** of other rebels.[10]

17. ALL THINGS IN MODERATION, PART 1 (21:17)

Even good things like **pleasure . . . wine and oil** (21:17), elsewhere described as rewards for wisdom or righteousness (see 21:20; 3:9-10; 27:9), can become the means of impoverishment if not used in moderation. Love them—that is, make them your goal—and they will destroy your concentration and drain your resources. Although this sage advice would fit in *Poor Richard's Almanac,* the context clarifies it as Yahweh's advice.[11] The same Hebrew word appears in 21:17 (**pleasure**) and in 21:15 ("joy"), suggesting that what brings joy has significant consequences. Positioning this proverb between verses 16 and 18 emphasizes the importance of moderation. A better use for one's resources than self-indulgence was offered only a few verses earlier (see 21:13).

18. A RANSOM FOR THE RIGHTEOUS (21:18)

What does it mean that **the wicked become a ransom for the righteous** (21:18)? Some suggest that because **the righteous** prosper, they can afford to buy cheaply the resources of **the wicked** who have foolishly squandered them. Today's English Version suggests another possibility by translating, "The wicked bring on themselves the suffering they try to cause good people." The interpretation which seems best sees God granting release to **the righteous** at the expense of **the wicked.** This is the meaning of the same Hebrew term in Isaiah 43:3 where God speaks of ransoming one people (Israel) by means of another (Egypt). This interpretation apparently lies behind the following rendering of Proverbs 21:18:

God's people will escape,
but all who are wicked will pay the price (CEV).

19. PEACE IN THE WILDERNESS (21:19)

As with Proverbs 21:9, verse 19 counsels wisdom in marriage by showing the dangers of a foolish marriage. The "corner of the roof" (21:9) has now become the **desert** (21:19; literally, "a wilderness land"), a location more remote and uncomfortable than before, perhaps because the **wife** is now not only **quarrelsome** (same word as in 21:9) but also **ill-tempered** (21:19). This Hebrew word is used to describe provoking and taunting which makes one annoyed, sad, angry, and anxious.

Proverbs 27:3 considers such treatment heavier to bear than stone and sand. No wonder her husband prefers the wilderness.

20. ALL THINGS IN MODERATION, PART 2 (21:20)

Moderation makes **wise** use of the wonderful resources God has put at our disposal (21:20). We are neither to love them unduly (see Proverbs 21:17) nor to use them excessively (see 21:20). **Stores of choice food** (21:20) is, literally, "precious treasure." Comparison with 21:6 where the same Hebrew word is used (there translated "fortune") shows that treasure can be obtained illegally or properly. **The wise** not only know how to make a fortune, but they know how to make it last (21:20). The fool gobbles it up as if there were no tomorrow. Eugene Peterson captures the sense with humor:

Valuables are safe in a wise person's home;
fools put it all out for yard sales (THE MESSAGE).

21. THINGS WORTH CHASING (21:21)

Proverbs 21:21 continues the theme of treasure from 21:20, although it focuses on spiritual, rather than material, wealth, and concerns itself with the acquisition of this treasure rather than its use. We have met **righteousness** (21:21) in 2:3 as one of the things God finds acceptable. **Love** *(chesed)* refers to a committed kindness, a love that lasts because of loyalty. These qualities must be found in all our relationships, both with God and with others. Neither will be easily obtained or maintained, so we must pursue them—**pursues** translates a Hebrew word which can mean "chase" or "hunt." Some see a difficulty with the appearance of **righteousness** (**prosperity**) in both lines, but its double inclusion makes wonderful sense. If we treat God and others properly and with steadfast **love,** God will bless us with **life,** righteousness (we will be treated properly), and **honor.**

22. THE POWER OF ONE WISE PERSON (21:22)

If you want people to make wisdom, not power, their goal, show them the power of wisdom, the apparent goal of Proverbs 21:22. Power secures itself in a fortress (**city of the mighty** is emphasized in the Hebrew), but wisdom's attack overpowers and takes **the city.** Wisdom beats power at its own game, while using fewer resources; note that it is a single wise man who defeats a whole **city** inhabited by powerful people. Joab's clever strategy of attack against Jebusite Jerusalem (see 2 Samuel 5:8; 1 Chronicles 11:6) provides a good illustration of this proverb.

23. SOUL INSURANCE (21:23)

Proverbs 21:23 continues the thought of the preceding verse by showing that wisdom not only brings victory, but can prevent defeat by helping us to watch what we say (see 13:3 for a very similar proverb). The same Hebrew word appears twice, once translated **guards** and then **keeps** (21:23); guard your mouth, and you will guard yourself. This is no easy task, as the mention of both **mouth** and **tongue** implies. **Himself** is, literally, "his soul" or "his throat" (see comments on 21:10), providing a subtle reminder that those who watch their words protect themselves at a crucial and vulnerable spot.

24. MEET THE MOCKER (21:24)

In addition to warning against pride, a frequent theme of Proverbs, 21:24 asserts a more damning truth about arrogance. Pride is a chief quality in the **"Mocker,"** one of this book's arch-villains. Arrogantly assuming superiority, even superiority over God, the "scoffer" sniffs at God's demands. According to F. Delitzsch, he "shows reverence for nothing, scornfully passing sentence against everything."[12] God has the final word, however, and promises to "mock the mockers" (3:34).

25. KILLED BY CRAVING (21:25)

Having described the "Mocker" (21:24), this and the next verse are clearly paired to describe the sluggard and contrast him with "the righteous" (21:26). The sluggard has put himself in a deadly double-bind. Lacking self-discipline, his appetite is insatiable, but, lacking motivation, he is too lazy **to work** for what he craves (21:25). If it were not deadly serious, it would be funny; here is his excuse for not working: **His hands refuse.**

26. ALWAYS WANTING OR ALWAYS GIVING (21:26)

The sluggard (see Proverbs 21:26; the same subject is to be assumed from 21:25) craves voraciously (**craves for more** can be rendered "covets covetously") and continually (**all day long**). By contrast, **the righteous** person gives **without sparing**—that is, without holding back anything. As Today's English Version translates the last line, "A righteous man, however, can give, and give generously."

27. ADDING INSULT TO INJURY (21:27)

The rogues gallery continues in Proverbs 21:27 with mention of **the wicked.** When such a one appears before God to perform a religious ritual, God is grieved. How detestable to carry sacrifices to God in hands stained with guilt! How much more insulting, then, when that **wicked** person brings sacrifices not to please God, but **with evil intent.** Perhaps his **intent** is to wipe the slate clean so he can sin again, or to fool others into imagining him as righteous. Whatever his motives, a grieved and insulted God finds such religion detestable and worse.

28. TRUTH TRIUMPHS (21:28)

Proverbs 21:28 pictures another troublemaker, this time the **false witness.** The first line is clear enough: Such liars will be destroyed. No consensus exists, however, on how to interpret the second line. All options seem to fall into one of two categories: those who see a description of one who **listens to** the **false witness** (NIV) or those who see a contrast between the liar and someone more noble (see NIV margin note). A more literal translation—"But a man who hears forever will speak"—lends support to the second category, but questions remain. Are the words of this man to live forever (as NIV margin note), or is this a promise that a man "who knows how to listen" will never "be silenced" (NJB), will "always speak truth,"[13] or will always be believed (TEV)? Derek Kidner's view may be best: The man who listens is the man worth listening to.[14]

29. AN OUNCE OF PLANNING IS WORTH A POUND OF IMAGE (21:29)

In these days, when image is everything, Proverbs 21:29 provides a helpful corrective. What really matters is not reputation, but something invisible: forethought. **Bold front**—literally, "a firm face"—is used elsewhere to describe the resolution of the disobedient who care nothing for God's rules (see 7:13), but here the context suggests a reliance on image for success. What really succeeds, however, is careful planning (see 21:5). This is why the **upright** (the Hebrew is emphatic here), rather than the **wicked** will succeed. This proverb begins a trilogy which speaks of the power and weakness of human plans.

30. PLANS IN HIS HANDS (21:30)

As important as plans may be (see Proverbs 21:29), plans alone are not enough. To make the point even more clearly, three phrases are heaped up: **no wisdom, no insight, no plan** (21:30), against the terse phrase, "before Yahweh."[15] The combination in the original Hebrew of abundance in line 1 with abruptness in line 2 (the NIV adds **can succeed**) packs a punch. All the best plans in the world cannot compare to the wisdom of God.

31. VICTORY IN HIS HANDS (21:31)

Just as no human "plan . . . can succeed" against God (21:30), so no amount of force can wrench victory from His grasp. Make **ready** (the verb is the same as what the "upright" are instructed to do in 21:29) the chariots and cavalry, **but victory rests with the LORD**[16] (21:31). Verses 29 through 31 make it clear that, while we can and should plan, we should not depend on our plans for success. Instead, we must trust in God for **victory.**

ENDNOTES

[1]The New International Version and other translations use LORD in small capitals following an initial capital *L* to denote "Yahweh" in the original Hebrew.

[2]See endnote 1.

[3]Ibid.

[4]R. N. Whybray, *Proverbs,* The New Century Bible Commentary (Grand Rapids, Michigan: Wm. B. Eerdmans Publishing Co., 1994), p. 240.

[5]Crawford H. Toy, *Proverbs,* The International Critical Commentary (New York: Charles Scribner's Sons, 1899).

[6]The Septuagint is the Greek version of the Old Testament, translated from the original Hebrew scrolls, and written in the second and third centuries B.C. It is often indicated by the Roman numerals LXX in accordance with the legend that it was translated by seventy scribes.

[7]Toy.

[8]See also *Proverbs, Ecclesiastes* in The Anchor Bible, vol. 18, by R. B. Y. Scott, eds. William F. Albright and David Noel Freedman (New York: Doubleday, 1965), p. 36.

[9]F. Delitzsch, *Proverbs, Ecclesiastes, Song of Solomon,* Commentary on the Old Testament, by C. F. Keil and F. Delitzsch, vol. 10 (Grand Rapids, Michigan: Wm. B. Eerdmans Publishing Co., 1978 [1872]), p. 78.

[10]Derek Kidner, *Proverbs: An Introduction and Commentary,* Tyndale Old Testament Commentaries, ed. D. J. Wiseman (Downers Grove, Illinois: InterVarsity Press, 1964), p. 144.

[11]See endnote 1.

[12]Delitzsch, p. 78.

[13]Ibid.

[14]Kidner, p. 141.

[15]See endnote 1.

[16]Ibid.

PROVERBS 22

22:1-29

The first sixteen verses of Proverbs 22 continue the themes found frequently in the book: the benefits of wisdom, the importance of discipline and the fear of the Lord, the need to avoid immorality and folly. The new section which begins in verse 17 and extends through chapter 23 presents similar themes, but in a slightly different style.

1. CHOOSE A NAME (22:1)

Choosing a baby's name is a delightful and important exercise. You want it to be a name that reflects the (yet unknown) personality of the baby, but will be easy for the child to spell. Bullies should not be able to twist it into a nasty nickname. Choosing your own name is even more important. This proverb places that **name** above wealth in value. The original Hebrew does not specifically mention **a good name,** only a **name,** although the context makes clear that the New International Version is right to add **good.** As it stands in the Hebrew, the choice is between choosing to leave one's mark (**to be esteemed**) and passing unnoticed from this life.

The memory of the righteous will be a blessing,
but the name of the wicked will rot (10:7).

2. OUR COMMON MAKER (22:2)

The theme of wealth and its absence continues from 22:1 (the same Hebrew word translated "riches" in verse 1 is here rendered **rich** [22:2]). There we saw that riches could not compare with a good reputation; here we see another limitation to wealth: It cannot make us what we are not. The **poor** can take comfort in knowing that their poverty does not diminish their human worth. They, too, are part of God's handiwork. The **rich** should remember that they come from the same workbench as the **poor;** their riches do not make them superior to their brothers. This proverb should guide our social interactions, for everyone we meet is a divine creation and deserves appropriate respect on that basis alone (see 14:31; 29:13).

3. READ THE ROAD SIGNS (22:3)

Two cars travel down the expressway; the first driver pays careful attention to road conditions, speed limits, and other signs, while the second is too busy. Between adjusting the radio, talking on his cellular phone, and admiring the scenery, he fails to notice that he has just raced into a construction zone where the fines are doubled. The first driver, the **prudent man** (22:3), has alertly seen the **danger** and slowed down. The second, **the simple,** has not, and he will **suffer for it.** The Hebrew behind **suffer** refers to a punishment or fine (see Exodus 21:22), and what a fine this will be! It is instructive that **takes refuge** is in the *active voice* (meaning the person takes the initiative to act), while **suffer** is (in the original) in the *passive voice* (meaning that events happen to a person); prudence allows us more control of our own destiny, while **the simple** are more subject to consequences from outside (Proverbs 22:3). The humor of the scene (unless you are the simpleton) is accentuated by the word play between **sees** and **danger,** which are nearly identical in the original Hebrew.

4. AGAIN, "BLESSED ARE THE POOR IN SPIRIT"[1] (22:4)

While Proverbs 22:1 compared honor to wealth, this verse shows how to obtain both. According to the New International Version, **wealth and honor and life** come from both **humility and the fear of the LORD,**[2] a somewhat surprising formula since reverence for Yahweh already implies **humility.** Other translations[3] take **fear of the LORD** as the most significant of several benefits the humble receive, benefits which include those found in line 2. Although the second reading is probably preferred, both make **humility** essential. **Wealth** is the same word found in 22:1, while 21:21 contains the same words here translated **honor** and **life.** In these we see something of the kingdom of heaven (see Matthew 5:3) which Jesus promised to those who were "poor in spirit"—that is, to the humble.

5. THE GUARDED SOUL (22:5)

It may not always appear this way, but **the wicked** have a tougher path to walk than the righteous (22:5). Beset with **thorns and snares** (these two words rhyme in Hebrew), progress is difficult. A closer look at **the wicked** shows why. **Wicked** might better be translated "perverse or crooked man." Deceitful, twisted, and devious all describe his actions, motives, and words (see Proverbs 2:15; 8:8; 11:20; 17:20; 19:1; 22:5; 28:6; Deuteronomy 32:5; Psalm 101:4). His paths are blocked with **thorns** and filled with **snares** because he has taken the crooked, narrow footpaths tailored to trickery rather than the high moral road (Prov. 22:5). The one **who guards his soul**[4] avoids these paths and, therefore, the **thorns and snares** found there.

6. OFF ON THE RIGHT FOOT (22:6)

Psalm 127:4 compares children to "arrows in the hands of a warrior." Proverbs 22:6 tells how we can help those arrows to fly straight. The most crucial time is at the beginning; this is suggested by **train** or "start" (see NIV margin note). Elsewhere this verb conveys the meaning "to dedicate," as in the dedication of the Temple by Solomon (see 1 Kings 8:63). What do raising a child and dedicating the Temple have in common? Both occur early to establish the direction for the future, and both acknowledge God's full control over what goes on inside. To educate **a child** is to consecrate that child to God's purposes (Prov. 22:6). Rooted in this verb is the idea of cultivating, at an early age, an appetite for God. According to some scholars, the term suggests the action of midwives who dipped their fingers in date syrup and placed them in the mouths of infants to stimulate the sucking reflex. This must take place very early and, as the tense of the verb makes clear, is not optional but imperative.

An early beginning is also implied in a literal translation of **in the way he should go**—"upon the mouth of his way." It is from this point onward that the child must be shown what is right and how to decide. Also, the training must be "suitable to his character" (NJB)—that is, respectful of the child's needs and individuality. It may be impossible to spend an hour each week with each child, as Susanna Wesley, John's mother, is reported to have done with each of her nineteen children. But time is essential. As discussed in the commentary introduction, some have misinterpreted this proverb as a promise. Instead it should be read as a most comforting principle: If children are raised this way, the effects will continue to be felt even into **old** age. This kind of training leaves too deep an impression and is too valuable and too winsome, and God's spirit is too faithful for early lessons to be easily forgotten.

7. PURSUE WEALTH (22:7)

More than a mere observation, the placement of Proverbs 22:7 makes clear that proper upbringing in wisdom and righteousness is crucial if a child is to avoid the bondage and poverty indicated in this verse. The larger context (particularly 22:1-3, 16, 22-23) warns the reader against taking the reference to riches too positively. The proverb has its own literary richness; there is a play on words between **is servant** *(loveh)* and **lender** *(malveh)*.

8. THE HARVEST WILL COME (22:8)

As Proverbs 22:7 constituted a law in the real world, so does 22:8. The righteous are encouraged to continue in their righteousness, even if they are being oppressed, because the harvest is coming. Two different metaphors appear to be employed: sowing and reaping in line 1, and hunting or warfare in line 2. In fact, both metaphors are from the agricultural world. The wicked man's **rod** is his means of oppressing the poor. At God's harvest time, what the wicked sowed they will reap, and they will no longer tyrannize others. The verb translated **will be destroyed** can also be rendered "will fail" or "will vanish"; divine judgment is implied. The proverb promises the wicked a harvest which combines both the fruits of their own labor and of divine anger.

9. HOW GOOD IS YOUR EYE? (22:9)

This question, often asked of hunters or birdwatchers, should really be asked of everyone. **A generous man** translates the Hebrew idiom, "a good eye" (22:9). This phrase puts the emphasis where it belongs—not just on generous words, but on the eye that is willing to look and see the needs of others. The eye was also thought to provide a window into a person's character. An evil eye describes the envious, critical, devious person, while a "good eye" describes the generous, kind, and forgiving one. This man not only sees, but he gives even the **food** from his own table to **the poor.** He will most certainly be doubly **blessed** (the Hebrew grammar emphasizes this fact); **the poor** will bless him for his kindness, and God will bless him, too.

10. A SABBATH REST FROM STRIFE (22:10)

Proverbs 22:10 serves several purposes. It provides a clear picture of the source of many conflicts and what kind of people produce them. More directly, it warns against associating with such individuals (see 22:24-25 for a similar warning against another type of troublemaker). Why do mockers cause so much **strife** (22:10)? Since God's laws[5] were meant to produce a harmonious society, deliberate and reckless violation of those laws—what **the mocker** does naturally—brings disharmony and conflict. Get rid of such a person, and your conflicts **are ended.** The original verb behind this phrase is closely related to the Hebrew word *Sabbath.* Seek a Sabbath rest from strife.

11. BOTH PURE AND PLEASANT (22:11)

Contrast "the mocker" of Proverbs 22:10 with the person of 22:11. No one wants to be free of his company; in fact, his **pure heart** and gracious **speech** are so winsome that even **the king** desires his friendship.[6] Commentator Derek Kidner comments on this striking combination of integrity and charm.[7] Each can be found separately—the abrasive legalist, the charming conniver—but put the two together, and you have something rare, something both beautiful and powerful. As with so many "royal" proverbs, what **the king** admires, so, too, does God (see 22:12).

12. HE WATCHES OUT FOR KNOWLEDGE (22:12)

If we are correct in seeing God's approval implied in Proverbs 22:11, 22:12 continues that theme. What does it mean that God keeps **watch over knowledge?** Some solve the problem by translating **knowledge** as those who possess knowledge. A better solution is to translate **keep watch** as "protect" or "preserve."[8] Not only people who know, but **knowledge** itself—that God-endowed wisdom reflecting the reality beneath and behind the universe—matters to God. "Where knowledge of the true and good exists, there does it stand under the protection of God."[9] Therefore, **He frustrates** those who, by their faithless **words,** seek to undermine its influence. They speak, they rail, they plot against His knowledge, but He "contradicts"[10] their every word.

13. EXCUSES: EASIER THAN WORKING (22:13)

Humor has long been used to produce insight and insure good behavior; Proverbs 22:13 provides a good example. Because **the sluggard** would rather remain at home, comfortable and idle, he must excuse his inactivity. The New International Version suggests two excuses: danger from **a lion** or danger from a murderer (**or** must be added). More likely the danger is single, that of being killed by **a lion.** Lions were present in Israel in biblical times, but preferred thickets to city streets. **Murdered** or "killed" is a strong word, but may have been chosen to make the sluggard's case more ridiculous. For other feeble excuses by **the sluggard,** see 21:25 and 26:13.

14. BEWARE: OPEN PIT (22:14)

Several longer passages in Proverbs warn against the dangers of adultery (see 2:16-19; 5:1-23; 6:20-35; 7:1-27). This proverb compares the **adulteress** to **a deep pit** into which some unsuspecting young man may **fall** (22:14). Why focus on her **mouth?**[11] Because her words are where the adultery begins by smoothly seducing the simple (see 5:3; 7:14-21). Counselors agree that adultery starts on the emotional level, with words that offer longed-for acceptance. God does not push the young man into the **pit;** his **fall** reveals that he was **under the LORD's wrath** (22:14).[12]

15. BENDING THE TWIG (22:15)

This proverb could almost be considered the pessimist's version of 22:6. Both proverbs encourage raising wise children, but 22:15 reminds us that children do not need to be taught to be foolish. It does not teach that children are fools by nature, but that they will tend toward **folly** if they are not corrected. Correction may be physical, but never harsh, lest the parent violate the spirit of 22:6. Look closely, and you will see the positive tone to this proverb since it allows for the possibility, albeit painful, that children can grow to be wise men and women. Together, 22:6 and 22:15 provide a holistic portrayal of the important task of parents.

16. GREED LEADS TO POVERTY (22:16)

The last of the proverbs in this long section which began in 10:1 concerns greed, a reminder how much of the proverbs' wisdom is social. Although the general sense of 22:16 is clear, the specifics—whether it warns against two different expressions of greed or one, and whether it threatens two separate consequences or one—are not so clear. The New International Version prohibits both oppressing **the poor** and trying to buy one's way to favor, warning that the result will be **poverty.** Only one action is in view, according to R. B. Y. Scott, with two consequences:

> One who oppresses the poor to aggrandize himself,
> Will have to yield to the rich and will end in poverty,

but his translation loses the symmetry of the original. Still another possibility is offered by the New Jerusalem Bible:

> Harsh treatment enriches the poor,
> but a gift impoverishes the rich.

This translation is right to envision God as the One who can reverse fortunes, but it only loosely follows the Hebrew. A very literal translation reveals the awkwardness which produces such a variety of renderings:

> One who oppresses the poor to increase (himself or his own wealth)
> one who gives to the rich only to want.

Perhaps the proverb warns that while someone might oppress **the poor** and thereby become rich, the end result of such "pocket lining" is only **poverty,** because God will intervene on behalf of the oppressed. Scott's summary comment cuts through the maze of possibilities, "The general sense is that greed is self-defeating, whatever may be the precise point of the proverb."[13]

17. SAYINGS OF THE WISE (22:17-21)

A new section clearly begins with Proverbs 22:17. Not only do we have several verses of introduction (see 22:17-21), but these are identified as **Sayings of the Wise.** They continue, however, to be offered, as with 10:1 through 22:16, as the advice of a father to a son (see 22:19; 23:15, 19-26; 24:13, 21). Further, the proverbs which follow differ from those in 10:1 through 22:16. They tend to be longer, utilize more rhetorical questions, and are more directive than those which preceded them; they more closely resemble the material in Proverbs 1 through 9. As discussed in the commentary introduction, 22:17 through 24:22 appear to reflect a dependence on earlier Egyptian wisdom. If so, they have been modified for Israel's religion (see references to Yahweh[14] in 22:19, 23; 23:17; 24:18, 21). A second, shorter collection of similar sayings follows in 24:23-34.

In the introduction to these sayings (22:17-21), the father commands his son's attention (verse 17) and explains why this is necessary. His wisdom must be taken to **heart** (literally, "belly"), employed on the **lips,** and passed on to others (verse 18) with the result that his **trust may be in the LORD** (verse 19). **Even you** (verse 19) reveals the father's deep desire that his wisdom be heard.

Verses 20 and 21 describe the nature of this wisdom. The reading chosen by the New International Version—**thirty sayings**—has become popular, especially since the discovery of the Wisdom of Amenemope which has 30 chapters. **Sayings** is not in the original Hebrew, however, and must be supplied. Other possible translations for **thirty** include "formerly" or "excellent things" (see NIV margin note), "triply" (Septuagint),[16] or as the name of the person receiving the wisdom.[17] The **written** material will provide **counsel and knowledge** for guiding decisions, and **true and reliable words** so that the son might know what is right and soundly answer **him who sent you.** This phrase, quite similar to one found in Amenemope, could refer to the youth's role as messenger, to the youth's ability to answer the questions of those who would test his wisdom, or to enlighten those who come to him for answers.

18. THE PROTECTOR OF THE POOR (22:22-23)

The advice begins in Proverbs 22:22 with a warning against oppressing the **poor,** the topic with which the previous section concluded. As with the counsel given in 22:24-28, this section begins with a prohibition. The setting of these verses is the courtroom; **in court** is, literally, "in the gate" where such cases would be tried. God serves as both defense counsel and the judge who punishes. Note how the punishment precisely fits the crime.

19. BEWARE THE HOTHEAD (22:24-25)

Proverbs 22:24 prohibits befriending or even associating with **a hot-tempered man.** Although lost in translation, the verse issues this warning (literally) in a chiasm (see commentary introduction):

Make no friendship with a man given to anger,
with a wrathful man do not go.

If you do, you will become just like him **and get yourself ensnared** (literally, "and take in a snare your soul"). The proverb does not focus on the immorality of anger (which it assumes), but on its consequences. Anger is a trap that snares your soul. Angry words, once spoken, can never be taken back. Angry deeds, once done, cannot be undone. A lifetime of sorrow cannot erase the effects of one moment of anger.

20. BE CAREFUL WHAT YOU PROMISE (22:26-27)

Surety, warned against in Proverbs 6:1-5 and elsewhere (see 11:15; 17:18; 20:16; 27:13) could bring serious financial consequences. The process of pledging surety is described in the two phrases of 22:26. **Strikes hands in pledge** is equivalent to shaking hands on a deal; **puts up security for debts** means guaranteeing repayment of a loan not your own. Verse 27 explains why such action is foolish. When that loan comes due, you will have to pay, even if it means having the **bed** you are sleeping on **snatched from under you.**

21. LEAVE THAT ANCIENT STONE ALONE (22:28)

Moving a **boundary stone** constituted a serious breach of law in Israelite society (22:28; see Proverbs 23:10-11; Deuteronomy 19:14; 27:17). Such a theft, easily executed, deprived the owner of income from the stolen land. Still more serious, the land belonged to God, and its allotment represented God's blessing. To move **boundary** stones reflected disregard for this allotment and, thus, for God's sovereignty. This verse adds yet another reason: The **boundary** lines are of long standing, **set up by your forefathers** (Prov. 22:28) and "rendered sacred by its antiquity."[18]

22. STRIVE FOR EXCELLENCE (22:29)

The final proverb in chapter 22 encourages the acquisition of skill with the promise of prestige. The one who is "expert in his calling"[19] gains the privilege of standing **before kings** rather than ordinary people (22:29; see 22:11 and 27:18 for others who stand before kings). The last two lines of verse 29 are arranged chiastically (see commentary introduction):

Before kings he will stand;
he will not stand before obscure men.

Commentator Derek Kidner draws a connection between this verse and those preceding: "Anyone who puts his workmanship before his prospects towers above the thrusters and climbers of the adjacent paragraphs."[20] The **skilled** person (22:29) stands as a good alternative to those who would get ahead dishonestly (22:22-23), foolishly (22:26-28), or harshly (22:24-25).

ENDNOTES

[1]Matthew 5:3a (NIV).

[2]The New International Version and other translations use LORD in small capitals following an initial capital *L* to denote "Yahweh" in the original Hebrew.

[3]NJB; NJPS; F. Delitzsch, *Proverbs, Ecclesiastes, Song of Solomon,* Commentary on the Old Testament, by C. F. Keil and F. Delitzsch, vol. 10 (Grand Rapids, Michigan: Wm. B. Eerdmans Publishing Co., 1978 [1872]).

[4]Or should we see a double meaning here, since another translation of this Hebrew word, *nephesh,* can be "throat," just what a robber, lurking on such a road, would hold his knife to?

[5]Law refers to either the Levitical Code (all God's rules and regulations), the Ten Commandments, or the Pentateuch (the first five books of the Old Testament: Genesis, Exodus, Leviticus, Numbers, and Deuteronomy; also called the Law of Moses or the Mosaic law). It is often capitalized when it means the Pentateuch or the Ten Commandments.

[6]For others admired by the king, see verse 29 and 14:35.

[7]Derek Kidner, *Proverbs: An Introduction and Commentary,* Tyndale Old Testament Commentaries, ed. D. J. Wiseman (Downers Grove, Illinois: InterVarsity Press, 1964), p. 148.

[8]NJB; Delitzsch.

[9]Delitzsch, p. 91.

[10]R. B. Y. Scott, *Proverbs, Ecclesiastes,* The Anchor Bible, vol. 18, eds. William F. Albright and David Noel Freedman (New York: Doubleday, 1965).

[11]A similar proverb (23:27) sees the prostitute herself as the pit.

[12]See endnote 2.

[13]Scott, p. 129, note 16.

[14]See endnote 2.

[15]The Septuagint is the Greek version of the Old Testament, translated from the original Hebrew scrolls, and written in the second and third centuries B.C. It is often indicated by the Roman numerals LXX in accordance with the legend that it was translated by seventy scribes.

[16]From this reading, Origen, the early church father, took it that all Scripture has three levels of meaning.

[17]Thierry Maire, "Proverbs XXII 17ss.: Enseignment a Shalishom?" *Vetus Testamentum,* vol. 45, no. 2 (1995), pp. 227–38, citing parallels in earlier literature from Ugarit.

[18]Delitzsch, p. 102.

[19]Ibid.

[20]Kidner, p. 150.

PROVERBS 23

23:1-35

The previous chapter of Proverbs concluded with a word about who will gain entry into the presence of the king; this chapter begins with advice for those so privileged.

1. SWALLOWED UP (23:1-3)

When invited **to dine with a ruler,** show self-control in what you eat (23:1). **Gluttony** in this setting puts you under obligation to your host whose motive for inviting you may have been self-serving; perhaps this is what is meant when it is said that his **food is deceptive** (23:3). Even in ancient Israel there was no such thing as a free lunch. Your lack of self-discipline at the table probably reveals a similar lack of discipline in other areas of your life, something which can be used against you. Unable to control your appetite, you swallow yourself whole.

In a clever example of word play, the author has employed quite similar Hebrew words (translated **to your throat** and **if you are given** [23:2]) nearly side by side. The latter phrase is more literally rendered "if a man of appetite you are" with "appetite" translating the word *nephesh*. By choosing this Hebrew word, which is elsewhere rendered "throat," the author reinforced his point about putting **a knife** to the **throat** of the one with the gluttonous appetite. **Note well** (23:1) should be underlined, given the special emphasis it receives from the grammatical construction of the Hebrew. The question of whether 23:1 should read **what is before you** or "who is before you" (see NIV margin note) may represent deliberate ambiguity. You must consider well what is on your plate because of who is before you, watching. **Delicacies** means **food** which is savory or tastes good, not necessarily to food which is rare (23:3; see Genesis 27:4, 7, 9, 14, 17, 31, where this same word is translated "tasty food" and refers to food which Isaac loved).

2. ON EAGLES' WINGS (23:4-5)

Proverbs 23:4-5 continue the theme of self-discipline, particularly as it concerns wealth. If money becomes your goal, you will always be disappointed. Just when you thought it was yours, wealth soars out of reach as on the strong wings of **an eagle** (23:5). Some see contradiction between this more neutral attitude toward wealth and the more positive view of 10:1 through 22:16, but no disagreement exists. Proverbs 23:4-5 does not oppose money, but opposes the folly of setting it as one's goal, a view with which the rest of Proverbs agrees. The New Testament also agrees with this view, as Luke 12:20 and 1 Timothy 6:7-10 demonstrate. As with the previous section of Proverbs, the verses are carefully crafted to bring out his point. The same verb which begins 23:5 appears again as the second to last word in that verse. Perhaps even its placement as second to last, rather than last, suggests the frustration of which the verse speaks. The words for **glance** (23:5; literally, "your eyes") and **they are gone** are homonyms. **For they will surely sprout wings** (23:5) employs a strong grammatical construction in Hebrew for emphasis (the same construction occurs in 23:1 for "note well").

3. A WASTED MEAL (23:6-8)

We return to the table (see 23:1-3) for another set of proverbs on self-control (see 23:1-5). This time we are guests of a **stingy man** (23:6). Literally, he is "evil of eye," but, given the use of this phrase elsewhere (see 28:22), the use of its opposite in 22:9, and the context here, the New International Version has correctly translated. Although the setting is different, the counsel is similar. The similarity is reinforced by the repetition of several words from 23:1-3: "to dine" (23:1) reflects the same Hebrew word as **eat** (23:6); **do not crave his delicacies** is identical in the original Hebrew to this phrase in 23:3. Although the first line of 23:7 is difficult (the NIV margin note reading represents only two of several proposals), the overall sense of the verse is clear. Eating the food of the **stingy** is a **wasted** meal. He begrudges all you eat, only tolerating your presence because he has some ulterior motive. Your compliments will be **wasted** for two reasons: First, you will realize, too late, that you have been "had"; second, **you will vomit up the little you have eaten** (23:8)—your body will not profit from the meal.

4. SAVE YOUR WORDS (23:9)

Although Proverbs 23:9 differs from what precedes it in length and style, it continues the theme of self-discipline in words. As the compliments to the "stingy" host were "wasted" (23:6, 8), so is wise counsel to a fool. **Do not speak to a fool** is, literally, "in the ears of a fool, do not speak." Commentator R. N. Whybray suggests that speaking in someone's ear elsewhere refers to a serious or urgent conversation.[1] Concentrate instead on instructing the wise who will profit from your counsel (see 9:7-8; 17:10). Proverbs 23:9 also implies that those who refuse to listen to advice deserve this unwelcome label.

5. DEFENDER OF THE DEFENSELESS (23:10-11)

The repetition of this warning so soon after Proverbs 22:28 (where the same phrase for **ancient boundary stone** appears [23:10]) suggests its importance to God. Although two actions are described, both speak of oppressing the defenseless; the second line singles out one group who have no earthly defense against fraud. The helpless do have a helper—a "mighty kinsman"—who will argue **their case** in court (23:11). **Defender** comes from the Hebrew word *gaal*, elsewhere translated "redeemer." God designed Israel's society so that in the absence of a husband or father, someone else—a kinsman redeemer—would fill the missing role (see Ruth 4 for an example of how this works). Standing behind this human figure was the divine Kinsman Redeemer, who assumed this role for those without any other recourse. **Take up** *(yareev)* and **their case** *(reevam)* come from the same Hebrew verb (23:10-11); the word play strengthens the impact of the proverb.

6. A HEART TUNED TO WISDOM (23:12)

Proverbs 23:12 introduces the two sections which follow—23:13-14 and 23:15-16—with a summons to assume the learner's posture. By mentioning the **heart** first, and then the **ears,** the author has reminded us that wisdom begins within. Only when the **heart** wants to listen can one's **ears** hear the truth.

7. DON'T SPARE THE ROD (23:13-14)

Not only children, but parents also must assume the learner's posture. Against the impulse to **withhold discipline** and avoid the accompanying unpleasantness, parents must punish their children (23:13). The New International Version is correct to render the opening Hebrew word of 23:13 as a command—**Do not withhold discipline**— since this reflects the emphasis given to this phrase in the original Hebrew. Children may respond to punishment as if you had inflicted a mortal wound, but they **will not die.** In fact, punishment actually spares your child **from death** (literally, "Sheol"); it is clearly the more loving choice. These verses portray careful crafting: The very similar Hebrew words for **withhold** (*timna*) and **from a child** (*minaar*) are placed side by side. The Hebrew word for "instruction" which appeared in 23:12 is found again in 23:13. Both **rod** and **punish him** appear in 23:13 and 23:14.

Past abuses and the present trend toward toleration create a climate of resistance to such a call for corporal punishment. While a treatise on discipline lies outside the scope of this commentary, Proverbs cannot be legitimately used as a safe haven for child abusers. The book counsels moderation in everything and is designed to produce wisdom, not cowering, fearful servitude, in our children. The context of these verses makes it clear that a child's will must be shaped, not broken, so that joy, not sorrow, becomes the result (see 23:15-16).

8. A PARENT'S JOY (23:15-16)

As the previous verses addressed parents, Proverbs 23:15-16 speak to the child from the perspective of the parents. The parents appeal to the **son** to become **wise** (23:15) so that they may experience joy. **Heart** appears twice in 23:15; if a son's **heart** is wise, a parent's **heart ... will rejoice** (23:16). This connection is strengthened by the addition of the phrase "also I" in 23:15b (omitted by the NIV). In 23:12 we noted the development from "heart" to "ears"; in 23:15-16 the movement is from **heart** to **lips.** The chiastic arrangement (see commentary introduction) of these two verses is clear, even in the English. Notice how verses 15a and 16b refer to the son's wisdom and right words, while verses 15b and 16a speak of the parents' response. **Inmost being**—literally, "kidneys"—appears here as synonymous with **heart.**

9. JEALOUS OR ZEALOUS (23:17-18)

Parental advice continues with an appeal to **be zealous** for Yahweh (23:17).[2] The question, rightly, is not whether the youth will **be zealous,** but what he will **be zealous for.** The parent counsels, **Do not let your heart envy sinners**—that is, do not **be zealous** for unrighteousness, jealous of those who can sin with impunity. By issuing this prohibition, the parent reminds the son that **envy** is a choice, something he need not choose. Reference to the **heart** properly locates jealousy's domain; it must be dealt with as a **heart** condition. Derek Kidner observes that the remedy to envying the wicked "is to look up (17b) and look ahead (18)."[3] Future reward, although it means delayed gratification, is much better than being **cut off** (23:18). Do not doubt God's way or sovereignty for one moment, but **always**—literally, "all the day"—**be zealous** for Him (23:17).

10. AVOID THE PATH TO POVERTY (23:19-21)

Few things bring more pain to a parent than to watch a child squander time, resources, talent, and life itself in profligate living. Proverbs 23:19-21 counsel wisdom by warning against association with **drunkards and gluttons** (23:21). **Listen** (23:19) is reminiscent of Deuteronomy 6:3-4,[4] which begins with the same Hebrew verb. The addition of a personal pronoun in the Hebrew (not translated in the NIV) makes the command here in Proverbs even more emphatic. **Keep** translates a less common Hebrew word; it is probably chosen because it closely resembles the word for "happy." **The right path,** the author suggests, is the path to happiness. Verse 20 cautions against taking the wrong path, the path traveled by those who eat and **drink** to excess. So excessive is their behavior that they can be characterized as **drunkards and gluttons** (23:21). The problem is not **wine** or **meat,** but those who make these their goal (23:20). Note that the parent warns the son against associating with drunks and gluttons, rather than against drunkenness and gluttony. Although these behaviors bring poverty (see 23:21), the temptation to drunkenness and gluttony would be greatly minimized without the companionship of drunks and gluttons.

The reason for avoiding such people, thereby falling victim to their bad behavior, is provided in 23:21. Drinking too much **wine** and eating too much **meat** (23:20) leads to drowsiness which makes you less inclined to work and, thereby, **poor** (23:21). Ironically, those who go looking for a good time deprive themselves of the resources to afford it. Also, those who choose this path for the companionship are too sleepy to enjoy it.

11. A WISE PURCHASE (23:22-25)

In advice reminiscent of Proverbs 1 through 9, the parents encourage their son to acquire **wisdom** (23:23). He is commanded to **listen** to his **father** and **mother** who stand to gain or lose based upon what he does with their counsel (23:22; see 23:24-25). To strengthen the reasons to obey, the parents are described. The father is the one **who gave you life**—literally, "this one, he begot you." **Mother** is presented as aged and thereby deserving of respect.[5] Proverbs 23:23 provides the essence of the parents' wishes: **Buy ... truth** (**the** is not in the Hebrew). **Truth** should be underlined because it is given special emphasis in the Hebrew. The New International Version has supplied **get;** a better rendering for this verse might be,

Purchase truth—never sell it—
wisdom, discipline, and discernment (NJB),

or perhaps this version:

Buy truth, and do not sell
wisdom, instruction, and understanding.[6]

The son who buys and retains **wisdom** brings **joy** and delight to his father (23:24). **Great joy** translates a very strong Hebrew expression; "rejoices joyously," while cumbersome, comes closer to a literal rendering. This restatement of the essence of 23:15 reveals a direct connection between wisdom and righteousness. This section concludes with a final invitation to **wisdom** in 23:25, this time stated indirectly. **May** they **be glad** implies that the source of their **joy**—their son's **wisdom**—has become reality (23:23-25). The verbs from 23:24a and 23:24b are repeated here in reverse order. The final line focuses on the mother's reaction (as 23:24 focused on the father's), but describes her as **she who gave you birth,** using essentially the same phrase applied to the **father** in 23:22a and 23:24b.

12. SECOND-GENERATION PURITY (23:26-28)

As the title implies, this series of verses not only summons the young man to purity, but to follow the path of purity traveled by his father (see Proverbs 23:26; ". . . let my life be your example" [TEV]). **Let your eyes keep to my ways** renders the Hebrew literally and is the choice of other versions (see RSV; NJPS). Others[7] believe a better reading follows the inversion of two letters (reversing an assumed copying error), which produces the translation, "Let your eyes delight in my ways."[8] The latter rendering lacks the expected Hebrew preposition ("in"), but both translations bring us to nearly the same place. The **prostitute** and adulteress are dangerous, according to 23:27, because they are like **a deep pit** and **a narrow well.** Those who fall in find themselves too far down or too tightly caught to be rescued. Another description follows in 23:28, this one more serious: "Moreover, she will rob you like a bandit"[9]—more aggressive and ruthless than a passive pit. The last line of 23:28 describes the social consequences of immorality: She drags many with her into infamy. Loose morals harm not only individuals (for example, through sexually transmitted diseases), but all of society. May God give us parents who can say to their children, "Follow my example of sexual purity."

13. THE RIDDLE OF DRUNKENNESS (23:29-35)

Proverbs 23 concludes with an extended warning against intemperate drinking. A riddle-like series of rhetorical questions (see 23:29), uncommon in Proverbs, introduces the warning. This litany of suffering belongs to whom? Verse 30 provides the answer: "those whom wine keeps till the small hours" (23:30a NJPS) and who are "ever on the look-out for the blended liquors" (23:30b NJB). As in 23:20-21, the problem lies not in the use, but the abuse of **wine** (23:30). "Don't believe the ads" could be written as the caption for 23:31. Beer, liquor, and wine advertisers spend millions making their products look attractive: "They will bring you acceptance, women (or men), sophistication, and happiness." Don't believe the ads. Instead go to the detoxification unit of your hospital, to a rescue mission, to a homeless shelter, or to nearly any downtown alley if you want to see what drunkenness is really like (see 23:32-35).

Verse 32 compares drunkenness to a snakebite, which is painful at best, deadly (**viper**) at worst. The drunken **see strange sights** (23:33)—

things which are not there—which can refer both to hallucinations (like pink elephants) or to the deceptiveness of 23:31 ("eyes" appears in both verses 31 and 33). Drink makes you think and say what does not make sense (see 23:33b) and endangers you (see 23:34). Some see 23:34 as comparing drunkenness to seasickness (see CEV); others put the sleeper of 23:34 on board a ship. Given a more literal rendering—"You will be like one who lies down in the heart of the sea"—something more dangerous may be in view. Even trying to sleep on the **rigging** of a ship, far above the rolling, churning sea, is a foolish thing to do (23:34). Adding an ominous tone to the whole verse is Israel's dread of the sea. The inability to feel pain (see 23:35a) seems, at first, like something good. But it is not, since the blows are unnecessary (**needless bruises** [23:29]), and the pain will remain after the drunkenness has gone. In spite of the sorry picture presented in 23:32-35a, the sleeping drunk can only think of one thing: how to make the cycle begin again (see 23:35b).

ENDNOTES

[1]R. N. Whybray, *Proverbs,* The New Century Bible Commentary (Grand Rapids, Michigan: Wm. B. Eerdmans Publishing Co., 1994), p. 334.

[2]The New International Version and other translations use LORD in small capitals following an initial capital *L* to denote "Yahweh" in the original Hebrew.

[3]Derek Kidner, *Proverbs: An Introduction and Commentary,* Tyndale Old Testament Commentaries, ed. D. J. Wiseman (Downers Grove, Illinois: InterVarsity Press, 1964), p. 152.

[4]Deuteronomy 6:4 begins the Shema—the confession of faith for the Jews, comprised of Deuteronomy 6:4-9; 11:13-21; and Numbers 15:37-41.

[5]The Hebrew translated **when** could also be rendered "for."

[6]R. B. Y. Scott, *Proverbs, Ecclesiastes,* The Anchor Bible, vol. 18, eds. William F. Albright and David Noel Freedman (New York: Doubleday, 1965).

[7]See CEV; NJB; F. Delitzsch, *Proverbs, Ecclesiastes, Song of Solomon,* Commentary on the Old Testament, by C. F. Keil and F. Delitzsch, vol. 10 (Grand Rapids, Michigan: Wm. B. Eerdmans Publishing Co., 1978 [1872]).

[8]John Joseph Owens, *Ezra–Song of Solomon,* Analytical Key to the Old Testament, vol. 3 (Grand Rapids, Michigan: Baker Book House, 1991).

[9]Scott (NIV omits "moveover").

PROVERBS 24

24:1-34

The first part of this section of Proverbs ("Sayings of the Wise" [22:17–24:22]) concludes with an important paternal reminder to **fear the LORD and the king** (24:21-22).[1] Another smaller collection (see 24:23-34) concludes this chapter.

1. AVOID THE OBSESSED (24:1-2)

Although righteousness is always the better road to travel, one's vision can be clouded by **envy** (24:1; see Proverbs 23:17-18; Psalm 73). Why do the **wicked** prosper, while the righteous suffer (Prov. 24:1)? With evil **hearts** prompting evil words, **the wicked** are "obsessed with all that is negative,"[2] and yet nothing seems to happen to them. At first glance, the reason provided in 24:2 appears obvious and unable to bring needed clarity: Do not envy the wicked because they are wicked. On more careful reflection, however, is this not precisely what we often need to hear? It is easy to be blinded by the happiness, possessions, and acceptance by others that the **wicked** enjoy. We need to be reminded that **violence** and **trouble** are wrong; such people must be avoided, however blessed they might appear. Actually, 24:2 represents a higher level of motivation, one that rises above the fear of punishment and promise of reward. It calls to us through the fog of **envy** (24:1) to choose holiness because this is God's command.

2. THE HOUSE THAT WISDOM BUILT (24:3-4)

Having cleared the ground in Proverbs 24:1-2 with a call to righteousness for God's sake, the next five verses speak of the blessing of wisdom. Throughout the book of Proverbs, wisdom and righteousness coexist, each requiring and making a place for the other. Verses 3 and 4

promise the security and comfort which **wisdom** and her sisters—
understanding and **knowledge**—can bring. The progressive
construction from **built** to **established** to **rooms . . . filled with . . .
treasures** "shows up well against the nihilism of verse 2,"[3] which seems
intent on destruction.

These two verses are true on several levels. To build a residence
requires a certain level of skill (one definition for Old Testament wisdom).
Wisdom can fill the **rooms** of that **house** with material wealth. The
Hebrew word translated **house** *(beth)* can also refer to one's family; it takes
understanding and **knowledge** to have a good marriage and raise children
well. **House** can also refer to one's descendants (see 2 Samuel 7:11).
Wisdom can build a noble heritage that will continue long after our earthly
tent is destroyed (Prov. 24:3). Still another layer of meaning emerges
when we compare this house with the one Lady Wisdom built, according
to 9:1-12, and the one managed by her embodiment in 31:10-31.

3. THE WAR THAT WISDOM WON (24:5-6)

Wisdom not only provides security and comfort, but strength for
victory as well (24:6). The Hebrew of Proverbs 24:5 is difficult,[4] both
for its abruptness and because it makes **strength** a by-product of wisdom.
Because of the difficulties, the Septuagint[5] altered the Hebrew and
rendered it as a comparison. Other translations followed, such as the
Revised Standard Version's,

> A wise man is mightier than a strong man,
> and a man of knowledge than he who has strength.

Although other passages contrast wisdom and strength (see 21:22), the New
International Version is correct to retain the Hebrew and treat 24:5 as a
description of wisdom's **strength,** especially if one reads this verse together
with the next, which speaks of **victory.** Wisdom has a **strength** which out-
muscles brute force, but by brains, not brawn. Wisdom opens your eyes to
see who is your real enemy. Wisdom reveals the extent of your resources
and those of your enemy and helps you to know how to maximize yours and
minimize theirs. Wisdom provides a "strategy" ("guidance" [24:6 NJB])
that shows when and how to deploy those resources to bring about **victory.**
One of those resources, without which you cannot expect **victory,** is the
counsel of others (**many advisers** [24:6]; see 11:14). One is only truly
wise who knows enough to take advice (24:5).

4. THE HEIGHTS OF WISDOM (24:7)

The theme of **wisdom** continues (24:7), although we return to the two-line pattern (in Hebrew; see commentary introduction) which has been uncommon since Proverbs 22:17. The New International Version reading **too high** (*ramot;* 24:7) requires a slight change in the Hebrew from what would otherwise be rendered "coral." If the latter reading is maintained, the verse may mean that the **fool** considers **wisdom** too costly to buy, but then finds himself speechless in public without it. While most versions join the NIV in making the change, the result is still somewhat unclear. What does it mean that **wisdom is** so **high** that the **fool,** otherwise known for his talkativity, must keep silent? The New Jerusalem Bible proposes,

> For a fool wisdom is an inaccessible fortress:
> at the city gate he does not open his mouth.

The **fool** cannot gain entry into this city, and even if he could, he would be struck speechless as the large gates swung open to admit him. As appealing as this suggestion is, it requires less common interpretations for *ramot* and for the activity at the city **gate.** Some suggest that **wisdom** is too lofty for the **fool** to understand, leaving him speechless at public discussions ("Wise sayings are beyond the understanding of the fool"[6]). But this interpretation flounders on the fool's gabbiness (see 10:14; 12:23; 20:3; 29:9). He is never at a loss for words, even empty ones (but see 17:28). Proverbs 24:7 probably speaks of wisdom's moral loftiness. **Wisdom** cannot be proven wrong or ineffective, and no amount of foolish words can change that. Wisdom's finger of accusation, pointed in the face of the fool, leaves him speechless, unable to explain his foolishness. This proverb serves as a transition between 24:3-6, which speak of wisdom, and 24:8-9, which describe other examples of foolishness. Choose wisdom, not folly, and you will be blessed with comfort, security, and victory. Choose folly, and you will be publicly silenced and despised (see 24:8-9).

5. WATCH YOUR REPUTATION (24:8-9)

These verses continue the rogues' registry begun in Proverbs 24:7. There the fool was publicly humiliated; here both deed and punishment are worse. The **schemer** (24:8) plots evil against others, contrary to

God's law.[7] The New International Version brings out the word play between **schemer** (*baal mezimmot;* 24:8) and **schemes** (*zimmat;* 24:9). Worse still is the **mocker** who scorns God's law. These three characters—"fool" (24:7), **schemer** (24:8), and **mocker** (24:9)—are known by others for what they are (**will be known as**), are disliked by others (**detest**), and come under the judgment of God who punishes **sin** (24:8-9). Avoid these evildoers, and you will avoid the scorn they bring on themselves.

6. ARE YOU READY? (24:10)

As Proverbs 24:7 provided a transition between 24:3-6 and 24:8-9, 24:10 does the same for 24:3-9 and 24:11-12. Do you have sufficient strength to pursue the wisdom which brings comfort and strength (verses 3-6)? Do you have the strength to resist the crowd described in verses 7-9? You will need it to rescue and sustain those in trouble (verses 11-12).[8] **If you falter** (24:10) is found in this verb pattern in only two other places in the Old Testament. Joshua uses it to ask the Israelites how much more time they would waste before taking possession of the land of Canaan (see Joshua 18:3). In Proverbs 18:9 it describes the lazy person. Here (24:10) the term refers to weakness, but not that of the child or infirm. This is self-induced weakness caused by lack of faith or motivation. The impact of the proverb is helped along by a word play between **trouble** (*zarah*) and **strength** (*zar*), virtually identical words placed side by side in the original Hebrew.

7. RESCUE THE PERISHING (24:11-12)

Proverbs 24:11-12 is striking for its crusader-like tone and explicit reference to God's omniscience (always implied in Proverbs, but rarely stated). An important key to understanding 24:11-12 is knowing who are **those being led away to death** and **those staggering toward slaughter.** Since these verses follow the rogues' registry (see 24:7-9), those led to their death may be the fools, schemers, and mockers who lead themselves **to death** by their behavior. Verses 11 and 12 probably do not speak of rescuing criminals on their way to be stoned to death for their crimes (if they do, there is an important balance in 28:17). They supplement the advice given earlier: Do not merely resist the temptation to join such people (see 24:10), but go out of your way to help them. They are more like animals being led to **slaughter**[9] than criminals being executed. No excuse will do for doing nothing (see 24:12).

We cannot deny knowing about this, because the book of Proverbs is full of warnings concerning coming destruction for the fool. God, unnamed but strongly emphasized in 24:12, knows what we are thinking: thoughts of revenge ("That schemer deserves to be punished for deceiving me"); self-righteous indignation ("Anyone who mocks God in that way deserves death"); or pride ("What a fool! He is getting what he deserves" [see 24:17-18]). As God watches over us (**guards your life** [24:12]) in spite of our shortcomings, we should watch over others.

8. LIKE HONEY FROM THE COMB (24:13-14)

Eat honey seems like strange advice (24:13), even for a book like Proverbs, which has so much to say about the very practical aspects of life (see 5:3 and 16:24 for other references to honey). This command is meant to illustrate the second and more important command, found in 24:14. **Eat honey, and you will find it good** and **sweet to your taste** (24:13). **Wisdom** also **is sweet,** but to **your soul** (24:14). Even more than the enjoyment of obtaining **wisdom** are the benefits it brings. The **taste** and sweetness of **honey** do not last long, but **wisdom** provides a lasting, permanent **hope. If you find it** suggests that finding **wisdom** may take a little more effort than finding **honey.**

9. DOWN, BUT NOT OUT (24:15-16)

The son receiving this advice has not suddenly turned into a vicious criminal. The prohibition of violence in Proverbs 24:15 is given to show the futility of such behavior, not because the son plans to raid the **righteous.** Taken together, 24:15-16 encourage righteousness by contrasting the security of the **righteous** with the insecurity of the **wicked;** they provide a fuller description of the promise given in 24:14. Righteousness does not protect you from falling, even falling repeatedly. It does assure you that you will be given the power to get up and be standing in the end (see Ephesians 6:10-13). **The wicked** have no such assurance, for they **are brought down by calamity** (Prov. 24:16). This phrase reveals the double whammy of disobedience. **Calamity** translates the same Hebrew word elsewhere translated "evil." **The wicked** destroy themselves by their evil actions, falling into the traps they have dug for others (see 1:18). **Brought down** suggests that their destruction comes from God, as ultimately it does. He who designed evil to be self-defeating can take credit for punishing **the wicked** who have no one to blame but themselves. Although not explicitly stated, when **the wicked are brought down,** it is final.

10. WIPE THAT SMILE OFF YOUR FACE (24:17-18)

When the wicked are punished (see Proverbs 24:15-16), the righteous are not to **rejoice** (**gloat** [24:17]).[10] After 24:11-12, such a prohibition should come as no surprise. Israel was being told to "turn the other cheek" hundreds of years before the Sermon on the Mount. Being forbidden to **rejoice** (Prov. 24:17) at the punishment of the wicked may seem to contradict other passages where God laughs at the wicked (see Psalm 2:4; 37:13; 59:8). There is a difference, however, between joy which comes from righteous indignation—that is, joy at the triumph of righteousness—and joy that arises from a personal sense of vindication. God's joy is in seeing righteousness prevail; He could not be God and feel otherwise. Because it is almost impossible for us to keep from slipping from righteous to self-righteous indignation, God forbids us to rejoice at all in such cases.

Ironically, by not gloating, the suffering of the wicked continues; when we rejoice in their suffering, it ceases. Although God's disapproval of our gloating should be enough to stop us, something more ominous may be implied. **Disapprove** (24:18) is, literally, "evil in his eyes," evil coming from the same root word as "calamity" in 24:16. Perhaps God turns away **his wrath from** the wicked (24:18) because He considers our "evil" gloating sufficient punishment for them. As well, if "evil" brings punishment to the wicked, perhaps our "evil" will mean God turns **his wrath away from** the wicked in order to direct it at us.

11. A CANDLE SNUFFED OUT (24:19-20)

Although we must try to preserve fools from the consequence of their folly (Proverbs 24:11-12) and must not rejoice when the wicked are punished (24:17-18), the fact remains that the wicked will be punished (24:1-2, 15-16). The message of 24:19 has been heard before; **be envious** translates the same Hebrew verb found in 24:1 and in 23:17. Proverbs 24:20 explains that we should not envy **the wicked** because such a person **has no future hope** (24:20), unlike the wise person in

24:14 where the same Hebrew term appears. **The wicked** will be extinguished, **snuffed out** like a **lamp** in divine judgment (24:20; see 13:9; 20:20).

12. FEAR THE LORD AND THE KING (24:21-22)

Here we find an injunction to fear Yahweh[11] and the king. The source of the punishment alluded to in Proverbs 24:19-20 is here revealed. Verse 21 outlines the proper attitude for a young person who seeks God's blessing: **Fear** God **and the king,** and avoid those who do not. Note the order—**fear the LORD** first, then honor **the king.** Israel's king was to be God's visible representative. He was to carry out God's will in every detail and, for this reason, was to be very familiar with it (see Deuteronomy 17:18-20). The reason for the proper attitude is given in Proverbs 24:22. Yahweh and **the king** will bring punishment; most often, but not always, the king was the instrument of discipline.[12] This judgment will come suddenly and to an extent known only to God. The remainder of Proverbs 24 contains a second set of "Sayings of the Wise" (24:23-34) dealing with justice (24:23-25), honesty (24:26), self-control (24:27), forgiveness (24:28-29), and diligence (24:30-34).

13. PROFIT FROM IMPARTIALITY (24:23-25)

The strongly interpersonal flavor of the additional **sayings** (24:23) is conveyed in Proverbs 24:23-25, which call for impartial judgment by pointing out consequences of injustice. Following the straightforward condemnation of **partiality** in 24:23b is a statement illustrating the attitude being condemned (see 24:24a). The rest of verse 24 and verse 25 present the consequences of partiality: first negative, then positive. Those who show **partiality** are cursed by peoples and abhorred by **nations** (24:23-24). Not only is justice necessary for equity and honesty within relationships (see 24:26), but it is an essential element in national affairs. Impartiality is not easy; no one who has served on a jury and been faced with the responsibility of judging another human being would imagine it so. But those who convict **the guilty** become the recipient of delight (**it will go well with those**) and **rich blessing** (24:24-25). Ironically, people are usually partial for a profit, but these verses promise profit instead to the impartial.

14. A KISS ON THE LIPS (24:26)

A proverb calling for honesty is appropriately placed after verses encouraging impartial judgment. There is a simple beauty in 24:26 that enables it to stand alone. The **kiss** of a lover is one of the greatest delights known to humans. That same level of delight results from **an honest answer** (literally, "right words"). R. B. Y. Scott's rendering of the verse is closer to the Hebrew and more profound: "He kisses the lips who answers honestly."[13]

15. DO EVERYTHING IN PROPER ORDER (24:27)

Although Proverbs 24:27 is directed toward the farmer, the principle applies to any situation: Complete what is essential before doing what is only important. A **house** would be of little use to a farmer with no crops in the field. The command to **build your house** may refer not merely to one's residence, but to starting a family. Wisdom is capable of helping us discern between the essential and the important.

16. "VENGEANCE IS MINE . . . , SAITH THE LORD"[14] (24:28-29)

Proverbs 24:28-29 suggests the evil of dishonesty, but its chief aim is to discourage revenge. Verse 28 does forbid giving false testimony **against your neighbor** and using **your lips to deceive** (literally, "and make wide your lips"), but the reason for such dishonesty is given in verse 29: revenge. No attempt is made to say that a wrong was never committed against you, only that you are not permitted to retaliate. **I'll pay that man back for what he did** sounds as if you are usurping God's role, of whom 24:12 asks, "Will he not repay each person according to what he has done?" Proverbs 20:22 counsels what to do with unavenged wrongs.

17. PARABLE OF THE SLUGGARD (24:30-34)

Proverbs 24:30-34 reads like a story parable meant to elaborate on 24:27 and encourage diligent labor. Verses 30 and 31 picture the sluggard's dilapidated **field** and **vineyard.**[15] **Thorns . . . everywhere** make it difficult to walk around. **The ground** is **covered with weeds,** not crops. **The stone wall** has fallen into disrepair, leaving the **field** and **vineyard** without any protection. Verses 32 through 34 provide the application of this picture. The abundance of verbs (four) in verse 32 makes it clear that the onlooker is a person of action, unlike **the sluggard** (verse 30). His problem seems innocent enough; he only wants a little more of something harmless, even essential. But too much idleness allows serious consequences. **Poverty** comes either **like a bandit** ("vagrant" [24:34 NJB]) or "marching"[16]; the Hebrew is unclear. There is no question about the hostile attack in the last line where **scarcity** comes **like an armed man.** While **the sluggard** (24:30) will be surprised, he really should have known they were coming. After all, they are described (in the original Hebrew) as "your poverty" and "your scarcity" (6:10-11 is virtually identical to 24:33-34).

ENDNOTES

[1]The New International Version and other translations use LORD in small capitals following an initial capital *L* to denote "Yahweh" in the original Hebrew.

[2]Derek Kidner, *Proverbs: An Introduction and Commentary,* Tyndale Old Testament Commentaries, ed. D. J. Wiseman (Downers Grove, Illinois: InterVarsity Press, 1964), p. 153.

[3]Ibid.

[4]Literally, "A wise man is in strength."

[5]The Septuagint is the Greek version of the Old Testament, translated from the original Hebrew scrolls, and written in the second and third centuries B.C. It is often indicated by the Roman numerals LXX in accordance with the legend that it was translated by seventy scribes.

[6]R. B. Y. Scott, *Proverbs, Ecclesiastes,* The Anchor Bible, vol. 18, eds. William F. Albright and David Noel Freedman (New York: Doubleday, 1965).

[7]God's Law refers to either the Levitical Code (all God's rules and regulations), the Ten Commandments, or the Pentateuch (the first five books of the Old Testament: Genesis, Exodus, Leviticus, Numbers, and Deuteronomy). Law is often capitalized when it means the Pentateuch or the Ten Commandments.

[8]One translation makes the connection stronger with verses 11 and 12 by translating these verses as a series of "if" clauses (see NJPS).

[9]R. N. Whybray (*Proverbs,* The New Century Bible Commentary [Grand Rapids, Michigan: Wm. B. Eerdmans Publishing Co., 1994], p. 348) points out that the Hebrew noun translated **slaughter** is never used for judicial executions.

[10]The connection between verses 15 and 16 and verses 17 and 18 is not only thematic (**calamity of the wicked**), but verbal. **Falls** translates the same Hebrew word in both verses 16 and 17; **stumbles** in verse 17 and **brought down** in verse 16 reflect the same original, while **calamity** (verse 16) and **disapprove** (verse 18) are both derived from the same Hebrew root.

[11]See endnote 1.

[12]The relationship between God and the governing authorities is taken up by various New Testament authors (see 1 Peter 2:17; Romans 13:1-7).

[13]Scott.

[14]Romans 12:19b (KJV).

[15]**Sluggard** and **man who lacks judgment** are meant to describe the same person.

[16]John Joseph Owens, *Ezra–Song of Solomon,* Analytical Key to the Old Testament, vol. 3 (Grand Rapids, Michigan: Baker Book House, 1991).

PROVERBS 25

25:1-28

As Proverbs 25:1 indicates, a new section begins here and
continues through 29:27. These proverbs resume the style of
those found in 10:1 through 22:16.

1. PROLOGUE (25:1)

Chapter 25 begins another section of Proverbs attributed to
Solomon and is identified as having been **copied by the men of
Hezekiah king of Judah** (25:1). This editorial note employs a verb
which refers to the passing on of material from an earlier time—in this
case, about two centuries earlier. Reference to **Hezekiah,** king of
Judah from 715 to 686 B.C., suggests that there was, at this time,
increased interest in wisdom. Such an interest is not surprising for at
least three reasons: first, Hezekiah's reign was fairly stable and
prosperous, an environment in which wisdom could flourish; second,
we know of Hezekiah's interest in restoring the worship designed by
David (see 2 Chronicles 29:30), so a parallel interest in the wisdom
written by David's son makes sense; third, Hezekiah ruled over a
reunited nation, the Northern Kingdom having fallen to Assyria in 722
B.C. It would be to his political advantage to associate his reign with
David's and Solomon's, the only other kings of a united Israel.

This collection of Solomonic proverbs differs from the earlier
collection. Those were mostly two-line sayings, but a sizable minority
of these are longer than two lines. Because chapters 25 through 27
differ in style (more proverbs of comparison) from chapters 28 and 29,
some have suggested that this was originally two collections.

2. INQUIRING MINDS WANT TO KNOW (25:2)

Not surprisingly, a collection of proverbs celebrating the wisdom of King Solomon begins with a series of verses (25:2-7) which celebrate wise **kings** (25:2). In verse 2, that wisdom is exemplified in the king's ability to search out what **God** (*Elohim,* uncommon in Proverbs where Yahweh is the more frequently used name for God[1]) has hidden. What does it mean **to search out a matter?** While it may refer to the wise king's ability to provide right judgment in legal matters (see 1 Kings 3:16-28) or to efficiently administer the kingdom, it cannot be limited to these. The king searches out what **God** has hidden; it seems odd to speak of **God** as hiding right legal decisions or the secret to wise administration. **To search out a matter** (literally, "a thing") probably refers to the ability to understand nature, history, human behavior, and the ways of God. These are the spheres in which God hides His design—in the instincts of an ant, in a turn of events, in the way of a mother with her child, in the certain but invisible tread of God across the scenes of our lives—all these are spheres Solomon explored (see Proverbs 1:1–22:16; 1 Kings 4:29-34).

Proverbs 25:2 raises the question, Why does God conceal things from us? Would it not be easier if He made everything plain and undeniable? Some things might be easier, but life would be less rich. We would miss the true nature of God who, while He became man, continues to be God—invisible both to sight and incomprehensible to understanding. And we would miss the true glory of being human. We most fully live out the image of God and our role as stewards of God's creation as we discover what He has concealed there.

3. VAST SUPPLIES OF UNDERSTANDING (25:3)

Not only do wise kings have inquiring minds, but their thoughts are **deep** and **unsearchable** (25:3; this translates the same Hebrew verb, only in its negative form, as that translated "search out" in 25:2). The phrase "unsearchable hearts" is used only a few times in the Old Testament. In one passage it describes what we might call "soul-searching" (see Judges 5:16). Other references use the phrase to refer to hidden thoughts of an improper nature. Here the meaning is that the king's heart contains so much knowledge that it cannot be fully explored. Other references make it clear that the king's heart, "unfathomable" to all others, is an open book to God (see Psalm 44:21; Jeremiah 17:10).

4. A PURIFIED THRONE (25:4-5)

The king must not only be an explorer and philosopher, but he must also be a righteous judge. As **the silversmith** improves the quality and value of his material by smelting, so the worth of **the king's** reign is **established** ("firmly founded") by removing **wicked** people (25:4-5), possibly by force (as suggested by the comparison with purification by fire). Some question remains whether the second line of 25:4 refers to the **material** with which **the silversmith** can work (see NIV) or the finished product (see NIV margin note). The New International Version rendering makes more sense of the process, since putting **silver** into the fire does not, in itself, produce a **silver** object. However, because the verse does not promise a step-by-step guide to silver making, and because the reading in the NIV margin note is closer to the Hebrew, it should be preferred. The second line of 25:5, repeated in 16:12b, suggests that righteousness is not only the means to establishing **the king's** reign, but its chief characteristic ("on uprightness his throne is founded" [25:5b NJB]). We see an extended word play between the Hebrew terms for **material** (25:4; *keli*), **his throne** (25:5; *kiso*), and **silver** (25:4; *kaseph*).

5. TAKE A BACKSEAT (25:6-7)

If Proverbs 25:6-7, which counsels humility in the presence of the king, sounds familiar, it is probably because Jesus alludes to these verses in a parable in which He makes social etiquette into a principle for living (see Luke 14:7-11). Those who insist on placing themselves where they do not belong, in hopes of being recognized for what they are not, will find themselves royally humiliated. The final phrase, **What you have seen with your eyes** (Prov. 25:7), could fit either with this verse (as in the NIV margin note) or with verse 8 (see NIV; Septuagint[2]). F. Delitzsch's translation reveals how the line emphasizes the humiliation of the scene:

Display not thyself before the king,
and approach not to the place of the great.
For better that one say to thee, "Come up hither,"
than that they humble thee before a prince,
whom thine eyes had seen.

He explains, "Thine eyes have seen him in the company, and thou canst say to thyself, this place belongs to him, according to his rank, and not to thee—the humiliation which thou endurest is thus well deserved, because, with eyes to see, thou wert so blind."[3]

6. EMBARRASSMENT (25:8)

Proverbs 25:8 continues to advise the young man on how to maintain his reputation and avoid embarrassment in social settings (see Proverbs 25:6-7), specifically in **court.** Because this theme predominates through 25:10, we can presume that young people in ancient Israel, as in our own society, wrestled with the temptation to climb the social ladder at the expense of others. The New International Version is probably correct in reading verse 7c with verse 8. To do so creates two lines (in Hebrew) of approximately equal length which balance the two lines of Hebrew represented in verses 9 and 10. As well, it creates a balance between what one sees and hastily reports (see verse 7c) and what one hears and carelessly speaks about (see verses 9-10).

Those who hurry to **court** against their **neighbor** (25:8) with charges based upon what they "have seen" (25:7) may learn the hard way that appearances can be deceiving. The Hebrew phrase translated **puts you to shame** covers a wide range of humiliation (25:8). It is used to refer to mild embarrassment (Jeremiah 6:15), disgrace (Psalm 44:9; Proverbs 28:7) and the shame of nearly being publicly murdered by your own father (1 Samuel 20:34). It is also used for those things which might cause shame, such as reproach (Job 19:3), harassment (Ruth 2:15; 1 Samuel 25:7) and impoverishment (Judges 18:7). Perhaps the proverb has in view both the cause and the result; a lost **court** case might produce both a fine for slandering **your neighbor** and your own **shame** for dragging him recklessly to **court** (Prov. 25:8).

7. MORE EMBARRASSMENT (25:9-10)

Although Proverbs 25:9-10 continues to speak of a dispute with a **neighbor** (25:9), some argue that they represent a preferred way to handle conflict than that found in 25:8. There the dispute was taken to "court," while here it appears to be taken up directly with one's **neighbor** (25:9). While this may be the case, these verses suggest more strongly that disputes of any kind increase the chance of humiliation. As noted above, verse 8 refers to what one sees; verses 9 and 10 to what one hears.

Verses 9 and 10 encourage the young man to maintain confidences by showing the negative consequences of disclosure: more humiliation (see 25:6-8). Note how the level of humiliation increases from public embarrassment (25:6-7), to legal defeat and possibly a fine (25:8), to permanent loss of **reputation** (25:9-10). Taken together, verses 6 through 10 display how trying to succeed at the expense of others may, in fact, mark one as a permanent failure.

8. A FITTING WORD: A THING OF BEAUTY (25:11)

From a series of inappropriate actions and words (see Proverbs 25:6-10), we move happily to **a word aptly spoken** (25:11). **Aptly** (used only here in the Old Testament) means more than "an idea well-expressed" (TEV); it comes much closer to "the right word at the right time" (CEV). The Hebrew word translated **apples** refers to some type of fruit, but probably not the apple, which was not found in Israel at this time. More important than identifying the fruit is appreciating the beautiful craftsmanship the picture suggests and recognizing the skill required to speak the appropriate word. This is the first of a series of comparisons on the theme of speech (see 25:11-14); verses 11, 12, and 14 are metaphors (NIV adds **like**), while verse 13 is a simile.

9. HOW BEAUTIFUL IS THE WISE REBUKE (25:12)

Rebukes are never easy to take, but **a wise man's rebuke**—one sure to be on target—**to a listening ear** is a beautiful thing (25:12). This verse provides an example of "a word aptly spoken" (25:11) and describes the proper response to such a word. This combination is again compared to the fine work of the **gold** craftsman (25:12). **Ornament** might be better rendered "necklace" or "jewels" (25:11; see Song of Songs 7:1). Referring to the beauty of this picture Derek Kidner notes, "reproof is one of the few things more blessed to receive than to give."[4]

10. HOW REFRESHING! (25:13)

Reliable friends who do what they say
are like cool drinks in sweltering heat—refreshing (THE MESSAGE).

Eugene Peterson's translation captures the meaning of this proverb, which encourages **trustworthy** speech by comparing it to something refreshing. The reference here is probably not to snowfall, unlikely **at harvest time.**[5] **The coolness of snow** (something cold) would bring welcome relief from the heat of the day, whether in the form of a cooling breeze or an ice cold drink. The author has strengthened the impact of the proverb by employing a play on words between **messenger** *(zir)* and **harvest** *(qazir)*. Although the additional line is unusual among these proverbs, it further explains the comparison.

11. DON'T BELIEVE THE WINDBAG (25:14)

In yet another proverb dealing with proper speech (see Proverbs 25:11-14) and employing a comparison from the weather (see 25:13), 25:14 promotes promise keeping by describing those who break promises. Such empty boasters are **like clouds and wind** which produce no **rain.** These conditions normally brought Israel the **rain** it needed; **like** the **clouds and wind,** the one who promised gifts raised expectations. Disappointment and frustration accompanied both empty clouds and broken promises. **Gifts** *(matat)* sounds very much like one of the Hebrew words for "rain" *(matar),* although a different word for **rain** is used in 25:14. Jude 12 may borrow this imagery to describe the false teachers troubling the early church.

12. QUIET GENTLENESS WORKS WONDERS (25:15)

Both lines of Proverbs 25:15 make the same point: "Quiet, composed, thoughtful behavior . . . in the end secures a decision in our favour."[6] Such behavior can persuade even a high official of the rightness of our cause. The first line refers to the power of **patience,** while the second, more specifically, to patience in speech. **A gentle tongue** contrasts with the "passionate, sharp, coarse one, which only the more increases the resistance which it seeks to overcome."[7] The "soft tongue"[8] **can break a bone,** another way of saying that **gentle** words can make a powerful impression.

13. THE NAUSEATING NEIGHBOR (25:16-17)

While Proverbs 25:16 could stand alone as good advice against gluttony, it is probably meant to illustrate the truth of 25:17. Visiting your neighbor, like eating **honey,** is fine in moderation (25:16; see 24:13-14 where honey symbolized wisdom). But **too much of you** (25:17), like

too much of it (25:16)—both phrases come from the same Hebrew verb—can make your neighbor sick (see 25:27 where honey is compared to seeking one's honor). **If you find honey** implies wild honey found accidentally (25:16). Such a discovery would bring great joy, not unlike the serendipitous joy of meeting a new friend. How tragic when, by lack of discipline, that friendship becomes an object of revulsion.

14. OUCH! THAT HURTS! (25:18)

Using language virtually identical to the phrase as it occurs in the Ten Commandments (see Exodus 20:16), Proverbs 25:18 warns against being a **man who gives false testimony against his neighbor.** This counsel refers specifically to testimony in court and emphasizes how highly God values justice. To show how serious—even deadly— deceit can be, the writer compares it to three weapons, each capable of delivering a mortal blow. The Hebrew word translated **club** refers to an object ("hammer"; "mace"[9]) or a person ("scatterer"[10]) which can smash something. Modifying **arrow** with the adjective **sharp** conveys, even more pointedly, the deadliness of such speech. Although any one of these weapons would have served as a suitable point of comparison, three are chosen. The verse seems to say not that deceitful **testimony** is as deadly as one of these, but that it is as deadly as all three employed together.

15. DON'T PUT CONFIDENCE IN A CON MAN (25:19)

A bad tooth (25:19) brings pain and usually means that area of your mouth is off limits for biting or chewing. **A lame foot** (literally, "a foot that slips") may bring pain and may cause you to stumble, but it certainly limits your activity. This verse encourages faithfulness by showing how **reliance** on the unreliable can be painful and confining. The original Hebrew allows that **the unfaithful** person could refer either to one who was trusted ("I was counting on you, and you let me down") or to one who trusted someone else ("You were supposed to trust me, but you lost faith"; "fickle" [NJB]). Since the comparison is with that which limits and produces pain, the former is probably to be preferred (as the NIV). Do not put your confidence in a "double-crosser" (THE MESSAGE) or you will find yourself unable to pursue your goals. Some take the first line of verse 20 with verse 19:

> Decaying tooth, lame foot,
> such is the fickle when trusted in time of trouble:
> as well take off your coat in bitter weather (25:19-20a NJB).

The last line fits awkwardly with verse 19, but admittedly, it does not fit much better with the following verse.

16. A TIME TO REFRAIN FROM SINGING (25:20)

While there are things about Proverbs 25:20 which are difficult to understand—whether to take the last line of verse 19 with verse 20, what is the point of adding **vinegar** to **soda**—the general sense is clear enough. There is a time to refrain from singing (see Ecclesiastes 3:1-8). F. Delitzsch notes that all three of these actions are wrong and ill advised.[11] One should not take someone's coat **on a cold day** (Prov. 25:20; if this line belongs here rather than with 20:19). Pouring **vinegar . . . on soda** (lye or nitre) produces great effervescence, but destroys the usefulness of the **soda.** The point of the proverb is that as these actions are wrong, so it is wrong to try to cheer up the grieving with a song. God apparently leaves room for appropriate grief.

17. HAVE ANOTHER HELPING OF COALS (25:21-22)

Paul quotes these verses (all but the last line) in Romans 12:20 to support his warning against "repaying evil with evil." Mercy did not originate with the New Testament; these verses in Proverbs have the same purpose as Paul's: to discourage revenge. If you have been wronged by another, you know how difficult mercy can be. Mistreatment leaves you feeling helpless and victimized, paralyzed by anger. These verses propose a better path, one more emotionally healthy; you can show mercy to **your enemy** (25:21)—"I have already been wronged. Why should I spend my hard earned money to feed the person who wronged me?" Your mercy **will heap burning coals on** the **head** of **your enemy** (25:21-22; literally, "one who hates you"). This metaphor, used nowhere else in the Old Testament, could refer to an act of punishment, although it seems strange to describe judgment coming from us rather than God. More likely, this refers to an Egyptian ritual of atonement in which the guilty demonstrates repentance by carrying hot coals on his head for a short distance.[12] Such a ritual not only punishes the offender, but more importantly demonstrates his contrition. It is your kindness which may turn an **enemy** into a friend.

However difficult and expensive mercy might be, give generously in the confidence that God **will reward you.**

18. DARK WORDS, DARK LOOKS (25:23)

The problem with Proverbs 25:23 as it appears in the New International Version is that the **north wind** does not bring **rain** to Israel; the west wind does. Some commentators read northwest for **north;** while geographically possible, this seems to read too much into the passage. Among those who retain a translation like **a north wind brings rain,** some consider the proverb to have been borrowed from a location, like Egypt, where this is geographically true. It is difficult, however, to imagine a proverb's having much impact or durability when it is continually contradicted by reality. For either view, the emphasis in line 1 is on the certainty that certain weather conditions will bring **rain;** rain is not viewed as something negative. Just as surely as the north(west) wind brings rain, so will **angry looks** result from **a sly tongue** (literally, "tongue of secrecy")—that is, one which engages in backbiting, sinister whisperings, and slander.

Given the geographical reality, ancient versions and Jewish commentators translated the verb in line 1 as "drives away." Although meteorologically accurate, this view assumes an unusual rendering for a verb which more often has the meaning of "produces," "dances," or "writhes." Further, since this verb must serve both lines, we are left with the surprising observation that **a sly tongue** "drives away" **angry looks.** While no clear solution has emerged, the proverb's call for honest and kind speech is clear in any weather.

19. AGAIN, PEACE IN A CORNER OF THE ROOF (25:24)

Proverbs 25:24 is virtually identical with 21:9; its placement here provides another example of the wrong type of speech (see 25:23), prepares us for a good example (see 25:25) and reinforces to the son the need to choose his mate very carefully.

20. WELCOME WORDS (25:25)

Proverbs 25:25 makes the obvious point that **good news** is welcome, especially when it comes from far away where a loved one or a source of help is located, by comparing that news to the refreshment of a **cold** drink to a parched throat (see 25:13). It also encourages the young man to bring **good news**—that is, to make himself the source of words and deeds that are unexpected yet welcome. Its placement alongside 25:26 may have been coincidental, but the two proverbs join to make an even stronger point. Your ability to refresh depends on keeping yourself fresh, not "muddied" or "polluted" (25:26).

21. KEEP THE PURE WATER FLOWING (25:26)

Because water was so highly prized in ancient (and modern) Israel, it becomes a fitting symbol for what is highly valued, such as righteousness. When **a righteous man,** wavering in the stiff breeze of temptation or persecution, **gives way to the wicked** and succumbs, the source of that water is **muddied** and **polluted** (25:26), no longer able to provide refreshment (see 25:25) and life. Some take **gives way** (25:26) as involuntary; **the wicked,** by force, overwhelm the **righteous.** This proverb then pronounces the sad result.

22. AN OVERDOSE OF PRAISE (25:27)

Earlier, "honey" was used as a metaphor for association with a neighbor (see Proverbs 25:16-17) and for wisdom (see 24:13-14). Here it symbolizes seeking **one's own honor** (25:27). The first line is similar in meaning to 25:16. The second is very awkward, but could be translated "seeking after glory upon glory." The two lines are intended to revolve around the phrase **it is not good** (25:27), which appears in the middle of the verse in the Hebrew and functions as the verb clause for both. Eating **too much honey** is **not good,** nor is seeking after **one's own** glory. The former makes you sick; the latter makes you sickening. **Too much honey** and you hate the sight of it; too much boasting and others hate the sight of you.

23. KEPT SAFE BY SELF-CONTROL (25:28)

An example of one **who lacks self-control** (25:28; see 25:27) is followed by a proverb which describes the consequences of such a lack. Many translations refer specifically to anger, but the phrase is more general, including the absence of **self-control** of any kind (25:28). Those without self-discipline dissipate their physical, emotional, and spiritual energies. In the end, they lie open and vulnerable as **a city whose walls are broken down,** into which the enemy can come and take control.

ENDNOTES

[1]The New International Version and other translations use LORD in small capitals following an initial capital *L* to denote "Yahweh" in the original Hebrew.

[2]The Septuagint is the Greek version of the Old Testament, translated from the original Hebrew scrolls, and written in the second and third centuries B.C. It is often indicated by the Roman numerals LXX in accordance with the legend that it was translated by seventy scribes.

[3]F. Delitzsch, *Proverbs, Ecclesiastes, Song of Solomon,* Commentary on the Old Testament, by C. F. Keil and F. Delitzsch, vol. 10 (Grand Rapids, Michigan: Wm. B. Eerdmans Publishing Co., 1978 [1872]), p. 153.

[4]Derek Kidner, *Proverbs: An Introduction and Commentary,* Tyndale Old Testament Commentaries, ed. D. J. Wiseman (Downers Grove, Illinois: InterVarsity Press, 1964), p. 158.

[5]Barley was harvested in April or May, wheat in May or June, and fruit and olives in late summer or fall.

[6]Delitzsch, p. 161.

[7]Ibid., pp. 161–62.

[8]R. B. Y. Scott, *Proverbs, Ecclesiastes,* The Anchor Bible, vol. 18, eds. William F. Albright and David Noel Freedman (New York: Doubleday, 1965).

[9]Delitzsch; NJB.

[10]John Joseph Owens, *Ezra–Song of Solomon,* Analytical Key to the Old Testament, vol. 3 (Grand Rapids, Michigan: Baker Book House, 1991).

[11]Delitzsch.

[12]Scott, p. 156, note 22.

PROVERBS 26

26:1-28

This chapter contains more of Solomon's proverbs as passed along by Hezekiah's scribes. These proverbs revolve mainly around three themes which describe three examples of wrong behavior: the fool (26:1-12), the sluggard (26:13-16), and malicious talk (26:17-28).

1. OUT OF SEASON (26:1)

Whether Proverbs 26:1 was included to warn the young man against becoming **a fool** or against giving **honor** to one, the point is clear: "Fool praising" is never in season. Like snowfall **in summer or rain in harvest,** such **honor** does not belong. The Hebrew behind **fitting** can describe an action which is appropriate and whose effects are seen in pleasant consequences (see Psalm 33:1; 147:1). In Song of Songs it refers to what is lovely and attractive (see 1:5; 2:14; 4:3; 6:4). The phrase is used three times in Proverbs, and each time with the negative, **not** (Prov. 26:1; see 17:7; 19:10). Proverbs 17:7 contends that excellent speech is out of place in the fool's mouth; do not look for it there. While **a fool** may become wealthy, this, too, **is not fitting** (26:1; see 19:10). Too foolish to know the right way to spend it, he will surely waste his wealth or worse.

According to this verse, giving **honor** to **a fool** is inappropriate since he does not behave in an honorable fashion. When **a fool** is honored, something is wrong with the value system of that society. As **rain** during **harvest** (late spring through the summer) may damage the crops, honoring **a fool** could even have harmful consequences (see 26:8; 25:27).

2. LIKE A FLUTTERING BIRD (26:2)

One of my parishioners complained to me that he was being falsely accused at work. A look at this proverb helped put that problem in perspective. Criticism is never pleasant, and false accusations are always frustrating. But, like harmless birds which flutter and swoop but never stay around long, those criticisms will fly away to trouble no more. Actually, the proverb speaks of curses, which in the ancient world were more serious than criticisms.[1] The curse was seen to have real power for harm. If **undeserved** curses were not to be feared, **undeserved** criticisms gave even less cause for alarm. Do not waste time trying to catch those birds; they will fly away soon enough.

3. JUST ANOTHER STUBBORN ANIMAL (26:3)

The source for the comparison in Proverbs 26:3, as with 26:1-2, is the natural world. As the **whip** is needed to motivate a stubborn **horse** and the **halter** is required to restrain **the donkey,** so the **rod** is essential if the fool is to be prompted and controlled (26:3). He is too stupid and too stubborn to learn by milder means. **Fools** are beaten not only because they lack motivation and restraint, but also because they lack the ability to say what they should (see 14:3).

4. TO ANSWER OR NOT TO ANSWER (26:4-5)

These two contradictory proverbs were deliberately placed side by side (the same Hebrew words lie behind **answer** and **according to his folly;** 26:4-5). Taken together, they reveal the frustration of dealing with **a fool.** If you **answer** him, he may make you look foolish. Without your corrective answer, he will go on to greater heights of **folly.** When should you **answer,** and when should you be silent? A clue lies hidden in the phrase **according to his folly,** used with slightly altered meanings in the two verses. According to verse 4, silence is preferred to arguing with the **fool according to his folly**—that is, by taking his foolish questions as deserving of discussion. One should **answer a fool according to his folly** (verse 5) when it is necessary to reveal him as the **fool** he is.

5. A FOOL'S ERRAND (26:6)

Send a messenger, and you add a pair of **feet** to your own (26:6). Send a foolish messenger, however, and you might as well cut off your own **feet.**[2] A messenger is supposed to lighten your load. The foolish messenger—by failing to communicate accurately or at all—will burden your life. You will be left "to swallow nothing but damage."[3] Find a "trustworthy messenger" instead (25:13) and you will find the consequences much more refreshing.

6. WHAT A WASTE! (26:7)

Using **a fool** left one lame in 26:6, while in 26:7 it is the fool's use of a proverb that is **lame. Legs that hang limp** cannot do what they were made to do. They cannot walk, run, work, or kneel. Proverbs are anything but **limp.** Ounce for ounce, these short, memorable, and meaningful sayings can outperform the loftiest arguments. But put one **in the mouth of a fool,** and the **proverb** hangs as **limp** as a wet noodle. The proverb is powerless; it can do nothing for the **fool** because he will not apply the wisdom it contains, nor will he help others with this knowledge. Verse 9 offers another picture of what fools can (and cannot) do with a proverb.

7. THE HONORED FOOL (26:8)

In Proverbs 26:1 we suggested that honoring a fool was not only inappropriate, but dangerous. Here that danger is compared to the foolish and potentially harmful action of **tying a stone in a sling** (26:8). This defeats the purpose of the **sling,** which is to propel that **stone** to a target. In the same way, honoring **a fool** defeats the purpose of **giving . . . honor.** When all the other recipients of your praise have been fools, who but **a fool** would want to join them? Tying **a stone** the size of a tennis ball **in a sling** means that that **sling** may come around to hit me solidly and painfully on the head. The **honor** we give **a fool** may return to haunt us. Finally, as **a sling** with **a stone** tied inside is ridiculous, so is an honored **fool.** "The procedure is nonsensical, for the stone is there to be slung out. So is the fool."[4]

8. STAND CLEAR OF THE FOOL (26:9)

Not only is the **fool** ill equipped to employ **a proverb** (26:9; see 26:7), but he might use it to do outright damage. Put **a thornbush** (26:9) in the hand of a sober man, and he will put it down, quickly. Put it into the hand of a drunken man whose ability to feel pain may have been diminished by the alcohol he consumed (see 23:35), and he will hold onto it. Provoke the drunkard, and expect to see that **thornbush** used against you. He may be too drunk to hit you, but if he does, you will know it.

Wisdom in the hands of the **fool,** like a **thornbush** in the hand of a drunk (26:9), may miss by a mile or may do great harm through misuse. The irony of this picture is that as the drunkard cannot feel the thorn and, even if he could feel it, could not remove it, so the **fool** cannot see how the **proverb** in his **mouth** actually condemns him.

9. CHECK HIS REFERENCES (26:10)

The very difficult Hebrew text in Proverbs 26:10 has given rise to several different translations, none completely satisfactory. One rendering of the verse is rather literal, but has little clarity:

A master can produce anything,
but he who hires a dullard is as one who hires transients (NJPS).

According to most modern translations (including the NIV), the verse suggests that when hiring workers, choose carefully, or you will regret it. This proverb, continuing the theme of 26:1-12, compares the person who hires the **fool** or **passer-by** to **an archer** who shoots without aiming. The employer who does not check references (or the person who is careless in choosing a friend) wastes his shots at success. Instead, he should carefully take aim and make every arrow count.

10. THAT'S DISGUSTING! (26:11)

This is not a good proverb to read if you have a queasy stomach, but it is just the thing if you are tempted to see the fool's life as glamorous. **A dog** vomits to fix a problem in its digestive system (26:11). **Folly** is moral illness, not just an alternative lifestyle; it deserves to be compared with vomit. The **dog returns to its vomit**—that is, returns to eat it, out of instinct. The **fool,** possessing the power of choice, returns to **his folly** freely, which makes it even more disgusting. Peter uses the first line of this proverb to describe the false teachers troubling his church (see 2 Peter 2:22).

11. WORSE THAN A FOOL (26:12)

These proverbs dealing with the fool (see 26:1-12) have provided several humorous comparisons. The temptation would be to laugh so hard at the **fool** that we cannot see the folly in ourselves (26:12). We might become proud of not being **a fool,** a pride which makes us worse than **a fool. A fool** may look up from his vomit and be so disgusted by himself that he returns to his father (see Luke 15:17-20). The proud man can never make this step of repentance because he is blind to the one essential ingredient: a sense of need.

12. IT'S TOO DANGEROUS OUT THERE (26:13)

Proverbs 26:13 is the first of several (see 26:13-16) on the theme of the lazy person, a close cousin to the fool. These descriptions, both sobering and comical, are not intended to warn **the sluggard,** but to warn others against laziness. **The sluggard** can read these and laugh, but he never sees himself. He has become proficient at making excuses, but he will be the last to know he is laughing at himself.[5] This proverb provides the lazy person's excuse for remaining at home rather than heading off to work. He fears that a **lion** (26:13), a **fierce** one, may be **roaming the streets,** seeking someone to devour. There were lions in ancient Israel, but since they preferred thickets to towns (see 22:13), the only threat they posed to **the sluggard** was as a convenient excuse for not working.

13. JUST ANOTHER FEW MINUTES (26:14)

The snooze alarm is the sluggard's best friend. One push and he has a few more minutes of glorious sleep. It is neither sleep nor snooze alarms that are the problem, but the sluggard's addiction to sleep (see Proverbs 6:6-11). He is as attached to the **bed** as **a door** (26:14) to a doorframe, and all he can do is swing from side to side like **a door** swaying in the breeze. According to 6:11, the twin burglars of "poverty" and "scarcity" will enter through that open door to pilfer the sluggard's possessions.

14. TOO LAZY TO EAT (26:15)

This proverb is virtually identical to 19:24. Its placement here in a series of proverbs on **the sluggard** reveals that he is not only **lazy** (26:15; see 26:13-14) but foolish. All the preparations have been made (although probably not by him), and he has somehow managed to drag himself to dinner. But because it is too much trouble to lift his hand from the table **to his mouth,** he will starve (26:15). He will die because it is too much trouble to live.

15. THE LAST TO KNOW (26:16)

The series of verses on the fool (see 26:1-12) ended with a warning against pride, a worse sin than folly. This series on **the sluggard** also ends by addressing pride not as a warning, but as a summary evaluation (26:16). While we have laughed at the sluggard's ridiculous excuses and behavior, he has been comparing himself favorably to the wisest of the wise. Find the perfect number of **men who** "give good advice" (NJPS) and he considers himself **wiser** than all of these together. His ego may be the only part of **the sluggard** that gets any exercise.

16. A BITE FOR THE BUSYBODY (26:17)

The remaining proverbs in chapter 26 address malicious talk: its dangers (26:17-19, 28), sources (26:20-21), appeal (26:22), subtlety (26:23-26), and eventual destiny (26:27). The busybody who must meddle in the problems of others will get into trouble. Having spoken out, he has grabbed a dog's **ears** and now must hang on, or, without a doubt, he will be bitten (26:17). The Hebrew words for **passer-by** and **meddles** look alike, but have different meanings, an example of word play which makes the proverb even more pointed. Some commentators take **passer-by** to refer to the **dog.** If so, the passing **dog,** unlike the meddler, had enough sense to mind its own business.[6]

17. DEADLY DECEPTION (26:18-19)

The consequence of malicious talk in the mouth of the meddler will be painful (see Proverbs 26:17); deception is dangerous, and deception denied is **deadly** (26:18). Verse 19 describes the deceiver who lies to **his neighbor** and then denies it—**I was only joking**—as being deceptive to the end. **Firebrands or deadly arrows** (26:18; "firebrands, arrows and death" [NJB]) are serious enough. Put these weapons in the hand of a **madman,** whose actions are irrational, and they become still worse.

18. DON'T FEED THE FLAMES (26:20-21)

Proverbs 26:20-21, while continuing the theme of malicious talk, belong together; both compare quarrels to fires, offer advice on how not to feed the flames, and employ the same Hebrew terms for **wood** and

fire.[7] According to this proverb, **gossip** fuels **a quarrel** like **wood** fuels **a fire.** As commentator Derek Kidner explains, "It is the whisperer or quarreler himself, not (as he would claim) the truth, that feeds the fires; for his mind refashions facts into fuel."[8]

The connections between verses 20 and 21 are strong; they share a common theme, a common metaphor, and the terms for **wood** and **fire.** Verse 20 speaks of the cause of quarrels (**gossip**) and verse 21 the results of quarrels (**strife**). The Hebrew verb translated **kindling** appears to have the same double meaning in the original as "kindle" does in English; it can be used to describe the starting of a fire and the instigation of a quarrel.

19. DON'T SPOIL YOUR APPETITE (26:22)

The particular type of unwholesome talk in view here is **gossip** (26:22), the theme of 26:20 (where the same Hebrew term is used). The author of this proverb, which appears exactly the same in 18:8, adopts the strategy that to be forewarned is to be forearmed. By warning of gossip's tremendous seductive power, the young man will be better able to resist the temptation to swallow the **choice morsels** greedily. The author strengthens his point by a play on words between **they go down** and **inmost parts.**

20. LISTEN TO THE HEART (26:23)

From here to the end of Proverbs 26, the writer progressively develops the theme of the subtlety (26:23-26), destiny (26:27), and danger (26:28) of malicious speech. Verse 23 specifically addresses the fact that "not all that glitters is gold." **Fervent lips** (literally, "burning lips," resuming the metaphor of fire from 26:18-21) are those filled with passionate claims of friendship. Such speech can hide **an evil heart** as **glaze** or "silver dross" (see NIV margin note) hides the dull, red appearance of earthenware pottery. The alternate reading in the New International Version margin note is to be preferred here since it follows the Hebrew more closely and makes good sense. "Silver dross," left over from purifying silver, can improve the appearance of clay so that, from a distance, the **earthenware** looks valuable. The same is true with **lips** which burn with friendship. Closer inspection will reveal the poor quality of the silver and the baseness at the heart of the matter.

21. WHY YOU SHOULD LISTEN TO THE HEART (26:24-26)

Proverbs 26:23 reveals how some claims of friendship are insincere, like silver-coated clay; 26:24-26 helps explain that metaphor. These verses describe the kind of person who makes such claims, and they reveal the insincerity behind the claims. The **malicious man** (literally, "he who hates") hides his hatred behind **charming** speech which flows from a poisoned source (26:24-25). **Seven abominations fill his heart** (26:25), indicating the utter depths of **his wickedness** (26:26). Note that this **man,** who seeks to hide the **evil** of **his heart** behind deceptive words, will be publicly revealed as **malicious** (see 26:24-26).

22. SELF-DESTRUCTION (26:27)

If it were standing alone, Proverbs 26:27 would make sense as a warning against the effects of evil, a point made frequently in the book. In the context of these verses which describe the danger of malicious words, perhaps we should see this verse describing the deceiver's punishment. He intends to harm others with his deceptive words, but will himself be harmed, perhaps when "his wickedness" is "exposed in the assembly" (see 26:26).

23. LYING IS NO JOKE (26:28)

Early in this series of proverbs which deal with malicious speech, someone tried to excuse his deceit by saying, "I was only joking!" (26:19). Lying, however, is no joking matter. Those who lie hate those they hurt; do not listen to the excuse that they lied to protect you. The specific type of lie known as flattery is no better; those who flatter bring **ruin** on the heads of those they compliment (26:28). The truth may hurt and must be administered "in love" (Ephesians 4:15), but it is ultimately the kindest thing you can say. Reference to how deceit damages one's victim balances the reference in Proverbs 26:27 to what deceit does to the deceiver.

ENDNOTES

[1]Although verse 2 is the only one in verses 1 through 12 which does not directly address the fool, it follows naturally after a proverb on honor by addressing honor's counterpart, the curse.

In the Old Testament, God's power was invoked through power-laden words (blessings and curses) often spoken in prayer form. Through these blessings or curses, God's people would call upon Him to provide or care for them by affecting them in a positive way or those around them in a positive or negative way. In Judaism, some blessings were reserved for the priests, but others were a regular part of the synagogue services. Curses were much less prominent and were forbidden

[2]R. B. Y. Scott, *Proverbs, Ecclesiastes,* The Anchor Bible, vol. 18, eds. William F. Albright and David Noel Freedman (New York: Doubleday, 1965), p. 159.

[3]F. Delitzsch, *Proverbs, Ecclesiastes, Song of Solomon,* Commentary on the Old Testament, by C. F. Keil and F. Delitzsch, vol. 10 (Grand Rapids, Michigan: Wm. B. Eerdmans Publishing Co., 1978 [1872]), p. 177.

[4]Derek Kidner, *Proverbs: An Introduction and Commentary,* Tyndale Old Testament Commentaries, ed. D. J. Wiseman (Downers Grove, Illinois: InterVarsity Press, 1964), p. 162.

[5]Ibid., p. 163.

[6]William McKane, *Proverbs,* The Old Testament Library (Philadelphia: Westminster Press, 1970), p. 601.

[7]Connections also exist between verse 20 and verses 18 and 19. Both refer to fire and employ words which sound similar: **joking** (*sacheq* [verse 19]) and **dies down** (*shataq* [verse 20]).

[8]Kidner, p. 164.

27

PROVERBS 27

27:1-27

M ost of the proverbs in this chapter stand alone as isolated, two-
line sayings. There are a few brief units: verses 1 and 2 deal
with boasting; verses 3 and 4 forbid strong negative emotions
like anger and jealousy; and verses 5 and 6, 9 and 10 concern friendship.
The proverbs' counseling for contentment (see 27:7) and prudence (see
27:12) helps to balance and elaborate on other advice which stands
nearby. Commentator R. N. Whybray sees in verses 12 through 22 a
"kind of compendium of educational material," beginning with a parental
call to wisdom in verse 11.[1] The closing verses (verses 23-27) offer
extended counsel on prudent stewardship.

1. "IN ALL YOUR WAYS ACKNOWLEDGE HIM"[2] (27:1)

The book of Proverbs makes much of life's certainties. Righteousness
brings reward, and wickedness brings punishment; these are divinely
ordained principles on which one can depend. The book also makes it
clear, in proverbs like this, that life, while orderly, is not predictable. We
cannot presume to know just what the future holds. Elsewhere in the Old
Testament, the Hebrew term translated **bring forth** (Prov. 27:1) is used
almost exclusively for giving birth. Just as humans cannot completely
control the womb, so they cannot control the future. James 4:13-16
elaborates on this advice in the spirit of Proverbs 3:5-6: **Do not boast
about tomorrow** (Prov. 27:1a); trust God today (see Psalm 37:3-4).

2. LET SOMEONE ELSE WRITE YOUR OBITUARY (27:2)

Proverbs 27:1 warned against boasting about future accomplishments;
27:2 warns against boasting about those of the past (**praise** in verse 2 and
"boast" in verse 1 translate closely related Hebrew verbs). Unlike the

previous proverb and most other proverbial prohibitions, no reason is given. No reason is needed when you realize that self-praise defeats the purpose of **praise** (27:2); **praise** makes the one praised more attractive, while self-praise makes him less. **Another** should be translated "stranger" (see 27:13 where the same Hebrew word appears) and **someone else** as "foreigner." Proverbs often uses the latter term in the feminine gender negatively, as in 27:13 where it is translated "wayward woman." Our good reputations must precede us to such an extent that even strangers and foreigners will hear about us and "toot our horns."

3. A TON OF TROUBLE (27:3)

If you thought hauling stones was hard work, try spending time with **a fool** (27:3). **Heavy** stones cannot compare to the **burden** of **provocation by a fool.** Some take this phrase to refer to what **a fool** does to another.[3] More likely, it speaks of the fool's anger ("grudge" [NJB]). To be the companion of an angry **fool** means you bear the **burden** of that anger. When he foolishly says and does what he should not, you must carry the embarrassment. When he loses his temper and breaks something, you must share the blame and cost of repair. When he turns sullen and quiet, you will have to breathe that atmosphere, so thick you could cut it with a knife. The Hebrew term for **provocation** refers especially to the anger which results from the sense of being abused. Part of the **burden** of accompanying an angry **fool** is having to listen to him blame everyone but himself for the problems he created with his own hands.

4. THE IRRESISTIBLE EMOTION (27:4)

Experiencing someone's **anger is cruel** (27:4) because, as 27:3 shows, it places a heavy burden on you. **Fury, anger** out of control, is even harder to endure (27:4). **Fury overwhelming** is, literally, "a flood of anger." But most difficult to bear is **jealousy.** "Jealous" is usually used in the Old Testament to describe a morally neutral (normal; see Proverbs 6:34) or even positive emotion (see Song of Songs 8:6-7). The point of Proverbs 27:4 is not that the jealous person has sinned, since he or she may be justified in their **jealousy.** This verse warns against arousing the jealousy of another (see 6:34-35) because this creates a reaction before which it is difficult to **stand** (27:4).

5. HOW TO BE A GOOD FRIEND (27:5-6)

Proverbs 27:5-6 suggests ingredients for good friendships. Both speak of the value of **a friend** who will **love** you enough to criticize you. Given the danger of pride (see 27:1-2) and anger (see 27:3-4), such **a friend** would be of tremendous benefit (27:6). **Open rebuke** could be as mild as a complaint about your behavior (27:5; see Habakkuk 2:1) to a strong condemnation, even punishing you for it (see Psalm 39:11; 73:14; Proverbs 5:12; 6:23; Isaiah 37:3; Ezekiel 5:15). Derek Kidner calls **hidden love** "morally useless"[4]; however genuine it may be, it cannot benefit the beloved until expressed (Prov. 27:5). It is "like a fire which, when it burns secretly, neither lightens nor warms."[5] Some translations see this phrase as something malevolent ("feigned love" [NJB]). This reading, while it fits 27:6, is not necessary here. In two other passages in Proverbs (see 11:13; 25:9), the contrast between **hidden** and **open** refers to a confidence, concealed in the bosom of **a friend,** which that **friend** should not reveal. This verse reverses these so that to reveal something is now good, and hiding is bad; this reversal emphasizes the author's point.

To prepare us to accept correction, 27:6 expands upon 27:5. **Open rebuke** (27:5) is described as **wounds from a friend** (27:6). Unlike the enemy's **kisses,** such **wounds . . . can be trusted.** The enemy's **kisses,** although many and pleasant, conceal hatred (**enemy** is, literally, "one who hates"), while **wounds from a friend,** although painful, express love (**friend** is, literally, "one who loves"). **Multiplies** is not the word we expect here; something like "faithless" or "treacherous" would provide a better contrast to **can be trusted.** For this reason, and because this Hebrew verb is very rare, several alternative translations have been offered,[6] but none deserve preference over that found in the New International Version.

6. ARE YOU HUNGRY? (27:7)

While this proverb is certainly a true statement about physical appetite, it is probably better seen as a "parable about possessions."[7] Standing here it provides a foundation on which the attitude of 27:5-6 can be built and that of 27:8 can be avoided. The Hebrew word *nephesh* appears twice in 27:7: **he who is full** (literally, *"nephesh* is full") and **the hungry** (literally, *"nephesh* is hungry"). The choice of this term, which can also be translated "soul" or "person," prompted commentator F. Delitzsch to propose that "the Hebrew is so formed that it is easily transferred to the sphere of the soul."[8] Are you content with what you have, or do you only long for more?

7. KNOW YOUR PLACE AND STAY THERE (27:8)

Proverbs 27:8, with its emphasis on our responsibilities, flies in the face of our individualistic society which is so focused on our rights and privileges. Although the general sense is clear enough, the precise meaning depends on whether the **bird** is a baby or mother. If the former, the child has prematurely abandoned the role of learner. Without proper parental training, a person is unprepared to face the real world. More likely, the **bird** is a mother bird which has deserted her brood. Her work undone, she has forsaken her responsibilities; the result for her brood will be certain death. Lending support to this view is a more literal translation of **his home** as "his place." My "place" includes my responsibilities, my commitments, my purposes, my obligations. When Adam and Eve rejected their "place" in God's plan as obedient stewards and disobeyed, they lost their place in God's garden.

8. FRAGRANT COUNSEL (27:9)

A comparison of Proverbs 27:7 and 27:9 in the original Hebrew provides several links between these two verses: **pleasantness** (27:9) and "sweet" (27:7) translate the same word, and **earnest** renders *nephesh*. One must always maintain an appetite for honest **counsel,** even when it hurts (27:9; see 27:5-6).[9] What takes the pain out of "wounds from a friend" (27:6) is the fragrant, pleasing benefit they bring. **Perfume** (literally, "oil") and **incense** (literally, "perfume") were frequent companions at joyous festivals and feasts (27:9; see Psalm 23:5).

9. THE FRIEND WHO LIVES CLOSER THAN A BROTHER (27:10)

Although composed of three lines rather than two, Proverbs 27:10 continues the theme of friendship. Friendships should be cultivated, not to the exclusion of family members, but in addition to them. **Friend** is modified by **friend of your father**—that is, an old family friend. If such friendships are developed, you will have ready assistance **when** trouble comes (not "if it comes"). Of course, if we are to cultivate such friendships, we must also make ourselves available to others, so they can call on us in trouble.

10. AN ANSWER FOR MY CRITICS (27:11)

Whatever challenge to family relationships is fostered by 27:10, this proverb answers. It speaks of the son's responsibility to be concerned for his father's reputation, and of the parents' responsibility to raise their son to be wise (see 10:1). To some degree, the **contempt** will be justified unless the **son** shows himself **wise** (27:11). Verses 12 through 22 provide admonitions that will help the **son** live wisely. The first (verse 12) sets out a principle illustrated in several of these verses.

11. READ THE ROAD SIGNS (27:12)

Although this proverb is almost identical to 22:3, its placement here describes an important ingredient in the wisdom which the father seeks to impart (see 27:11) and provides a foundation on which other admonitions can be built. **The prudent,** their eyes on the road signs, **see danger** (the author expressed this phrase with two nearly identical words) and **take refuge** (27:12). The alternative to prudence is foolishness; the consequences are disastrous.

12. AGAIN, DON'T COSIGN FOR A STRANGER (27:13)

Prudence will keep you from cosigning a loan and will remind you how to treat one who does. This subject has been addressed several times in Proverbs (especially 6:1-5), but its presence in this brief compendium of instruction emphasizes its importance. As noted in the commentary on 20:16 where this verse appears in virtually identical form, the proverb advises not the cosigner, but the one loaning money to a cosigner. The cosigner was not wise enough to take some kind of collateral, so be sure you do. **Take the garment** (27:13) implies all that this fool has left is his clothing.

13. KEEP YOUR VOICE DOWN (27:14)

Prudence will help you better relate to your neighbor. Here the problem is not the greeting, nor the hour, nor the volume, but the combination of a greeting too early and too loud. Something good at the wrong time becomes something bad. How do you know how early is too early and how loud is too loud? Prudence! How can you be sure your well-intentioned greeting will be properly received? Prudence!

14. CHOOSE HER CAREFULLY (27:15-16)

Prudence will help you choose the right **wife** and avoid the disaster here described (27:15). Other passages warn against marrying the **quarrelsome** woman (27:15; see 21:9, 19; 25:24), and another compares her to **constant dripping** (see 19:13b). Both are combined here; not only must you listen to the "drip-drip-drip" (TEV), but you are confined to the house by the rain. Do not imagine you can stop her from being contentious, because you cannot. You might as well try to contain **the wind** or grasp an object with an oil-soaked hand (27:16).

15. THE GOOD RESULTS OF CONFLICT (27:17)

The problem presented in Proverbs 27:15-16 is not the presence of conflict, but the wrong kind of conflict. There is a kind, according to 27:17, which actually improves the combatants by sharpening them. I become sharper when my bad habits and improper thoughts are challenged, my logical inconsistencies are pointed out, and my blind spots are brought to my attention.

16. "WELL DONE, GOOD AND FAITHFUL SERVANT"[10] (27:18)

Faithful service has its rewards. The rewards for one **who tends a fig tree** (27:18) include more than one crop of the very sweet fruit each year and highly prized shade from its large leaves. The servant **who looks after his master** can also expect rewards; the one specifically mentioned here is honor. The promise of reward may be needed to sustain one's motivation to serve. Tending **fig** trees can be demanding work, especially when, in the absence of the small wasp which fertilizes the fruit, that process must be done by hand.[11] So, too, service to one's **master** may bring challenges, as implied in **looks after,** which translates a Hebrew verb which could also be rendered "guard." Jesus also taught that the path to honor was through service (see Matthew 25:14-30; Luke 12:42-46; 17:7-10), for this principle is true for every master/servant relationship, including that with God himself.

17. A MIRROR FOR CHARACTER (27:19)

In Hebrew, Proverbs 27:19 lacks any verbs and reads, literally,

As the water, the faces to the faces
thus the heart of the man to the man.

Naturally, interpretations of this enigmatic proverb differ. Most agree that the first line refers to a **man** who sees his reflection in **water.** The second line could be saying that I can see my character reflected in others. "Just as a mirror confronts you with your public shape," writes Derek Kidner, "so your fellow man confronts you with the shape in which the thoughts and habits like your own have grouped themselves into a character."[12] More likely, given the switch from plural "faces" to singular **the man,** the second line is saying that **as water reflects** my **face,** my **heart reflects** my character (NIV). I must look within to find out who I am.

18. CONTROL YOUR APPETITE (27:20)

You cannot be truly wise until you are content with what you have. The writer makes this point by comparing the insatiability of human desire with **Death and Destruction** (27:20; literally, "Sheol and Abaddon"), places renowned for their appetite. **Death** is among those "things that **are never satisfied"** in 30:15-16; that insatiability is here extended to **Destruction** as well (see 15:11 where they appear together as places hidden to humanity, but open to God). Their appetite is obvious to anyone who sees how every living creature ends up in their hands. The realization that what you are acquiring will one day be swallowed up by **Death and Destruction** (27:20) would serve as a powerful appetite suppressant.

19. THE CRUCIBLE OF A COMPLIMENT (27:21)

Compliments reveal my character as much as they applaud it. Put **silver** in **the crucible** and **gold** in **the furnace** (27:21); the result will be a metal revealed for what it is and refined of what it is not (27:21a appears in 17:3a). Put a person under the scrutiny of public opinion, and you will see who that person really is. Public opinion is **the crucible**

(27:21), and not the infallible result. When it assigns worth to the worthless, be patient. Eventually the true character of that person will emerge. Compliments to the undeserving will "go to his head," lead to overconfidence, and then lead to choices which reveal his true colors. Compliments to the deserving will be justified by his ability to remain unspoiled by success.

20. INGRAINED FOLLY (27:22)

Grinding . . . grain (27:22) in ancient Israel was often done with small hand mills of various design. The one in view here was likely made of two hard stones, a flat or slightly concave base onto which the **grain** would be spread, and a smaller **grinding** stone about the size of a small loaf of bread which was pressed and rolled onto the grain. Imagine **a fool** as a small pebble (an appropriate comparison, given his character). Grind that **fool** between **mortar** and **pestle,** and you will emerge, after all your efforts, with a pebble; that is his nature through and through. No one would knowingly mix anything with grain, the staple of Israel's diet, for fear of ruining the final product. Such mixing has taken place, however; **grinding him like grain** is, literally, "in the midst of crushed grain." Trying to change **a fool** is not only time consuming and pointless, but it may even be harmful when you bite down on that pebble.

21. BE A GOOD STEWARD (27:23-27)

The final five verses of Proverbs 27 encourage careful stewardship of one's possessions by pointing out the benefits gained thereby. The command, issued in 27:23, encourages one to **know** well (the Hebrew puts emphasis on **know**) the condition of one's **flocks** and **herds.** The reasons for this careful attention follow in 27:24-27. One must be continually vigilant, because past success is no guarantee of future performance (see 27:24). **Riches** and **crown** picture wealth in exaggerated terms; the latter term suggests that the writer was thinking of how this principle applies beyond the farm. Good stewardship will produce good living, including **new growth** (27:25), a bountiful harvest (27:26-27b), and enough income to hire maidservants (27:27c).

ENDNOTES

[1]R. N. Whybray, *Proverbs,* The New Century Bible Commentary (Grand Rapids, Michigan: Wm. B. Eerdmans Publishing Co., 1994), p. 382.

[2]Proverbs 3:6a (NIV).

[3]Whybray.

[4]Derek Kidner, *Proverbs: An Introduction and Commentary,* Tyndale Old Testament Commentaries, ed. D. J. Wiseman (Downers Grove, Illinois: InterVarsity Press, 1964), p. 165.

[5]F. Delitzsch, *Proverbs, Ecclesiastes, Song of Solomon,* Commentary on the Old Testament, by C. F. Keil and F. Delitzsch, vol. 10 (Grand Rapids, Michigan: Wm. B. Eerdmans Publishing Co., 1978 [1872]), p. 201.

[6]For example, "knives" (R. B. Y. Scott, *Proverbs, Ecclesiastes,* The Anchor Bible, vol. 18, eds. William F. Albright and David Noel Freedman [New York: Doubleday, 1965]) and "deceitful" (NJB).

[7]Kidner (p. 165) goes on to assert that the proverb "bears on the disposition we acquire by the level of comfort we choose. A bilious outlook is a poor prize."

[8]Delitzsch, p. 202. This term can be translated "throat" (as in NJB), but this seems unlikely.

[9]Assuming the New International Version is correct in its rendering of the difficult Hebrew of verse 9b. Other translations arrive at about the same meaning.

[10]Matthew 25:21a (NIV).

[11]Patricia L. Crawford, "Fig," *Harper's Bible Dictionary,* gen. ed. Paul J. Achtemeier (San Francisco: Harper Collins—Society of Biblical Literature, 1985), p. 308.

[12]Kidner, p. 167.

PROVERBS 28

28:1-28

The opening verse in Proverbs 28 sounds its dominant theme: the benefits of righteousness, a theme which recurs in well over half of its 28 verses. While the Mosaic law makes few appearances in Proverbs, several are found in this chapter, especially in verses 4, 7, and 9.[1]

1. FAITHFUL AND FEARLESS (28:1)

One of the benefits of being **righteous,** and a benefit sure to appeal to a young man, is courage. For all the bravado characteristic of **the wicked,** it is really **the righteous** who **are as bold as a lion** (28:1). How does righteousness bring courage? It brings a clear conscience which enables you to stand up for your beliefs without fear of being revealed as a hypocrite. With a clear conscience, you can have confidence before God; this brings confidence before men. As Paul put it, "If God is for us, who can be against us?" (Romans 8:31b). **The wicked,** frightened by the thought that everyone is as they are, run away at the sound of rustling leaves. Perhaps King Hezekiah had this proverb included because of his experience with Assyria (see Isaiah 36–37; 2 Kings 18–19; 2 Chronicles 32). **The wicked man** fits Sennacherib, and **the righteous** would refer to the residents of Judea and Jerusalem.

2. FAITHFUL AND FIRM (28:2)

Assuming the New International Version's translation of the difficult Hebrew of Proverbs 28:2, this verse is a telling commentary on the fate of the Northern Kingdom of Israel. From its beginnings it rebelled against God by erecting rival sanctuaries to the Temple in Jerusalem. Its continued wickedness fostered a tumultuous history with nine dynasties in two hundred years; nearly all ended by assassination (**many rulers**). In contrast, the more righteous Southern Kingdom of Judah retained the same dynasty for its entire existence (**a man**). Hezekiah, the king responsible for including this section of material (see 25:1), was a descendant of David whose reign was long and prosperous. While 28:1 promises courage to the righteous, 28:2 offers peace.

3. LIKE A DRIVING RAIN (28:3)

Although **ruler** fits the context (28:3; see 28:1-2), the Hebrew term should probably be translated "poor man" (see NIV margin note) as in 28:6. This verse encourages justice, a particular type of righteousness (see 28:1-2), by describing its opposite—oppression. **Rain,** essential in Palestine, must fall at the proper times (28:3). In the fall it is needed to soften the ground to enable planting, and in late spring it brings the moisture needed to ripen the **crops.** If the **rain** comes too late, however, it can destroy the **crops** awaiting harvest. The "poor man," who should understand the plight of his fellowman and bring relief, instead brings destruction (see Matthew 18:23-30 for an example).

4. A RIGHTEOUS STANDARD (28:4)

In earlier appearances in Proverbs, *torah* has been used in a general sense, to describe parental instruction (see 1:8; 3:1; 4:2; 6:20, 23; 7:2; 13:14). Here it refers to the Law given by God to Moses on Mount Sinai.[2] This Law brings order to society; when it is forsaken, wrong becomes right, and society suffers, examples of which are seen in 28:2-3. In spite of the pressure to conform, the righteous continue to **keep the law,** even finding courage to **resist** the **wicked** (28:4; see 28:1). Romans 1:18-32 expands this scenario.

5. KNOW GOD, KNOW JUSTICE (28:5)

Proverbs 28:5 continues the theme of righteousness (see 28:1-4), particularly as expressed through justice, by contrasting **evil men** with **those who seek the LORD** (28:5). The former **do not understand justice;** it is not in their vocabulary. The latter **understand it fully** because they **seek the LORD,** the author and executor of **justice.** The second line might be better translated "[they] understand everything" (NJB); righteousness helps to explain more than justice (see 28:1-2).

6. WORTH MORE THAN WEALTH (28:6)

"Those who seek the LORD" (28:5)[3] gain a righteousness that surpasses wealth in value. If you had to choose, it would be better to be **poor** and righteous than **rich** and wicked (28:6; 19:1a is identical to verse 6a). Proverbs 28:6, and the book in general, does not devalue wealth; the Hebrew grammar emphasizes that the **rich** man's problem is his corruption, not his cash. Nor does Proverbs glorify poverty; 28:3 provides an example of a wicked poor man (see commentary above). The opposite of a **walk** that **is blameless** (28:6) is a "double-going deceiver."[4] The Hebrew word translated **ways** literally speaks of two ways, emphasizing the hypocrisy of the dishonest.

7. A RIGHTEOUS STANDARD DEMONSTRATED (28:7)

One reason why righteousness is more valuable than wealth is because the righteous bring honor to their families. Honor and shame matter less in our society than they did in ancient Israel where dishonoring your family was one of the most serious crimes you could commit (see the serious punishment on the son who cursed his parents in Deuteronomy 21:18-21). The best way to insure the honor of the family was to teach the Mosaic law (see Proverbs 28:4, 9) to one's children (see Deuteronomy 6:4-8).[5] In contrast to the **discerning son** (Prov. 28:7) who obeyed the Law, we would expect to meet a foolish son who does not obey the Law. Instead, a particular example of folly is described, that of the wastrel who squanders the family's resources and reputation in the company of other **gluttons.** A longer version on this theme is found in 23:19-25.

8. USE IT OR LOSE IT (28:8)

Although Mosaic law is not specifically mentioned in Proverbs 28:8, what this proverb condemns is repeatedly prohibited by that Law (see Deuteronomy 23:19-20; Exodus 22:25; Leviticus 25:35-37).[6] The wicked person who grows rich and impoverishes others by charging **exorbitant interest** will lose that wealth to the righteous person who, because he is righteous, **will be kind to the poor** (Prov. 28:8). The author drives home his point with a word play between **wealth** and **kind.** As in 28:5, this proverb reveals righteousness and justice as inseparable companions.

9. LISTEN OR BE IGNORED (28:9)

Proverbs 28:9 adds another pearl to the strand of blessings which righteousness brings: God's listening ear. Those who do not practice that righteousness as required by God's law[7]—that is, those who do not listen to God—will find that He does not listen to them when they pray (see Proverbs 15:8-9). He hates their prayers as much as He hates the murder of the innocent (see 6:17). Listen to Him, and you will find that He listens to you.

10. ENTRAPPED OR ENRICHED (28:10)

In addition to its other blessings (see Proverbs 28:1-9), righteousness keeps one safe. The wicked person who tries to take **the upright along an evil path** (28:10)—that is, either into disobedience or to their harm—will fall victim to his own schemes. Jesus gives added weight to this idea in His version in Matthew 18:6. Either the fate of **the upright** is left unclear or, as is more likely, their fate should be identified with that of the **blameless** who are not only rescued from danger, but are led to **a good inheritance** (Prov. 28:10).

11. WHAT MONEY CANNOT BUY (28:11)

Although righteousness is not specifically in view, one of its companions is. **Discernment,** the ability to see people and things as they really are, is described here as superior to wealth (28:11). The **rich** person without it is poorer than the **poor** person with it. Without it, the **rich** man is left to his own wisdom and may be condemned by those riches to perpetual ignorance. Because wealth tends to make one more susceptible to pride, the **rich** person may come to believe the lie, "I must be wise if I'm rich." Others will not be quick to reveal the **rich** man's ignorance and lose access to his wealth. Convinced that he is **wise,** he will have little interest in offers of wisdom. The **man** with **discernment,** even though **poor,** will have the advantage. His vision will be sharp enough to see **through** the rich man (literally, "will search him") and understand that "all that glitters is not gold."

12. RIGHTEOUSNESS EXALTS AND EXULTS A NATION (28:12)

Righteousness not only "exalts a nation" (14:34), but exults it. When righteousness reigns supreme, it blesses that society with tranquility, harmony, justice, equity, honor, prosperity, and much more. Imagine a place where the Sermon on the Mount has become reality: Humility, mercy, purity, and peace are most important, people live by the spirit of the Law,[8] worship God, love their enemies, care for the poor, and trust God for all their needs. Who would not rejoice with **great elation** to live in such a place (28:12; see 11:10; 28:28; 29:2)? That the reality has not caught up with the ideal (see Amos 5:13) is no cause for cynicism. We should continue to pray, "Thy kingdom come" (Matthew 6:10 KJV), and anticipate that day when righteousness will triumph once and forever.

13. CONCEAL OR CONFESS (28:13)

For all the emphasis that repentance and sacrifice receive in other parts of the Old Testament, the relative scarcity of references to such matters in Proverbs makes 28:13 stand out. Sin and, by extension, folly are not permanent. God rewards with **mercy** those who are quick to admit a fault and renounce it, as David discovered (see Psalm 32, 51). Those who proudly conceal their **sins** lose out in the end (Prov. 28:13). Righteousness, the theme throughout much of Proverbs 28, is worth the humility and effort it requires.

14. KEPT SOFT BY AWE (28:14)

Although **the Lord** does not appear in the original Hebrew,[9] the New International Version and others are right to understand Him as the object of **fears** (28:14). Those who do not fear God harden their **heart,** a good description of the unbelieving (28:14; see Psalm 95:8; Hebrews 3:8). Those who are quick to confess and renounce their sins find mercy (see Proverbs 28:13). **Fear** (28:14), a stronger term than the one used in 1:7, refers to a sense of dread or awe, and this dread for God should be continual (**always**). By leaving the object undefined, the author has not only emphasized the magnitude and duration of that **fear,** but has reminded us that this reverent, humble attitude should be our perspective for all of life, sacred and secular.

15. THE TERROR OF TYRANNY (28:15)

A righteous society will not be governed by the kind of **wicked** rulers described in Proverbs 28:15-16 (see 28:12). Like wild, dangerous animals, they tolerate injustice, oppress the poor, and feed themselves at the expense of their subjects. This is the opposite of how God treats the poor and how He instructs His people to treat them, but it is especially contrary to His instructions for Israel's kings (see Deuteronomy 17:14-20). **Helpless** might better be rendered "poor" (Prov. 28:15). This is the meaning of the same Hebrew word in 28:8. The rest of the verse implies oppression, and **helpless** would be implied in "poor."[10] The theme of the terrible tyrant continues in 28:16.

16. THE TEMPORARY TYRANT (28:16)

Life under the tyrant encountered in Proverbs 28:15 is terrible because that ruler **lacks judgment** (28:16). While he "is rich in rapacity" (NJB)—that is, in excessive greed or covetousness—he is poor in understanding. This verse clearly suggests that he is also temporary. The righteous one **who hates ill-gotten gain** will not oppress the poor and "helpless" (28:15) like the terrible, though temporary, tyrant, but will **enjoy a long life.** In this proverb lies both a warning for the **ruler** (28:16) and a hope for the "helpless" (28:15).

17. THE SANCTITY OF LIFE (28:17)

While this proverb does not specifically mention the Law (as do 28:4, 7, 9),[11] it builds on the prohibition against murder in the Ten Commandments. The one who murders will be hunted by his own conscience (**tormented** [28:17]; literally, "burdened"), by the victim's next of kin who is to avenge his blood (see Deuteronomy 19:11-13), and by God himself (see Genesis 9:4-6). The last line of Proverbs 28:17 warns, **Let no one support him,** but no person could ever lift his load of guilt. A biblical example of this restless, guilt-ridden murderer is Cain (see Genesis 4). Few examples outside of the Bible are more compelling than William Shakespeare's Lady Macbeth (Macbeth, Act V, Scene 1).

18. SAFE AND SECURE (28:18)

There is something comforting in the placement of 28:18 immediately following a proverb dealing with murder. Life may be painful, but at least the righteous have the security of God's care in which to take refuge. Compare the permanent stain of guilt (see Proverbs 28:17) with the safety that accompanies the **blameless** (28:18), and the path of righteousness looks better than ever. As in 28:6, the **ways** of the **perverse** are, more precisely, two ways (28:18). The **perverse** person is a hypocrite; his public life is on one path, but his private life takes an altogether different route. He can only travel two routes simultaneously for so long until he **will suddenly fall.** A literal rendering of the phrase "fall into one" raises the question, "One what?" Perhaps it suggests that he falls in one blow,[12] falls into one of the two ways he is trying to combine,[13] or falls all at once.[14]

19. FULL OF BREAD OR POVERTY (28:19)

The hardworking and the lazy have at least two things in common: They will both work hard, and their work will **fill** them (28:19). This comes out clearer in a more literal translation:

One who works his land will be full of bread;
but one who pursues unprofitable things will be full of poverty.

Both work hard; the one plants, cultivates, and harvests, while the other spends himself in "frivolous pursuits."[15] Both are filled, the one with bread and the other with **poverty.** If you are going to work hard anyway, the writer says, you might as well work for what truly satisfies. Proverbs 12:11 contains a very similar though simpler version of this same thought.

20. THE SUREST ROUTE TO BLESSING (28:20)

The "abundant food" of Proverbs 28:19 should not be sought for its own sake, for **one eager to get rich will not go unpunished** (28:20). The **faithful** person, on the other hand, is promised rich blessings, material blessings not excluded. Why does the greedy person get nothing, while the **faithful** one is blessed? The latter has the qualities

God admires: commitment, integrity, patience and, especially, a greater concern for the needs of others than for his own. **Richly blessed** might better be translated "overwhelmed with blessings" (NJB); the **faithful** has chosen the surest route to the greatest blessings, although not necessarily the quickest.

21. GOD-LIKE JUSTICE (28:21)

Although Proverbs 28:21 has broader application, it specifically warns against giving false testimony in a trial, evident by the reference in line 2 to a bribe. The first line condemns the practice—**partiality is not good.** The second describes how easily a false witness can be bribed. Not even a loaf **of bread,** but only **a piece** is enough to buy some witnesses. God, who cannot be bribed for any price, will not tolerate this perversion of justice. According to R. B. Y. Scott, the second line refers instead to the seriousness of even minor infractions ("A man may be at fault [even] over a morsel of food"[16]).

22. THE EYE THAT DOES NOT SEE (28:22)

Like 28:20, this proverb concerns the person **eager to get rich** (28:22). While the previous verse threatened punishment, this one makes the punishment explicit. The **stingy** will be punished with **poverty,** an appropriate punishment for the greedy. The **stingy man** is, literally, "a man of evil eye" (28:22; see 23:6 and its opposite, "the good eye" [22:9]). Ironically, the **stingy man** has an eye, but cannot see the **poverty** that lies ahead of him.

23. NO ONE LIKES A REBUKE, AT FIRST (28:23)

Rebukes are unpleasant both for the rebuked and the rebuker (28:23). We would much rather give and receive flattery because this wins the **favor** of others. **Flattering tongue** translates the same Hebrew phrase (literally, "one who makes smooth his tongue") used to describe the "wayward wife with her seductive words" (7:5; 2:16). While it is more difficult, honor comes through honest rebuke, not flattery. Proverbs 28:23 does not specify the source of the honor. The one censured may or may not come to appreciate your rebuke. Others will honor you for your forthrightness and courage. The verse does say that honor, although it might be long in coming (**in the end** or "afterward"), will come.

24. REMEMBER THE FIFTH COMMANDMENT (28:24)

As with Proverbs 28:17, this proverb is based upon one of the Ten Commandments. Instead of honoring one's parents, this son **robs** them and, worst of all, denies any wrongdoing (28:24). Even when robbery is legal and socially acceptable, it is still robbery (see Mark 7:11). The writer compares this son to a destroyer. He **destroys** one of the most sacred human bonds, that joining parent and child (Prov. 28:24; see 1 Timothy 5:4, 8), and he **destroys** the bonds which connect one to God. God hates such behavior and condemns it (see Proverbs 6:19; 20:20), even if the destructive son never admits it.

25. "SEEK FIRST HIS KINGDOM"[17] (28:25)

One reason God hates greed is because it leads to dissension, one of the things God hates most (see Proverbs 6:12-19). **A greedy man** (28:25; literally, "wide of appetite") is never satisfied with what he has. His "evil eye" (see comments on 28:22) scans the possessions of others until he finds what he is hungry for, and then, thinking only of himself, he takes it. Whether it be a mild form of greed, like the person who is always pushing to the front of the line[18] and demanding something better, or a more serious version (see 28:24), **dissension** results (28:25). Matthew 6:19-34 expands upon the second line; "But seek first his kingdom and his righteousness, and all these things will be given to you as well" (Matt. 6:33).

26. "TRUST IN THE LORD WITH ALL YOUR HEART"[19] (28:26)

If "he who trusts in the LORD will prosper" (28:25),[20] **he who trusts** in anyone or anything else, including himself, **is a fool** (28:26). "He who trusts in the LORD" with all his heart will find straight paths (see 3:5-6) and **safe** travel (28:26). The one **who trusts in himself** is not an individualist or a "free-thinker," but **a fool,** and he will lead himself down the road to disaster. The parallel lines of this verse reinforce the close connection between reverence for God and **wisdom,** a connection seen throughout Proverbs.

27. "IT IS MORE BLESSED TO GIVE THAN TO RECEIVE"[21] (28:27)

Proverbs 28:27 continues the theme of trusting God by providing a specific example of how. When you give **to the poor,** you spend your resources on those incapable of repaying you. Thus you demonstrate your trust that God will repay your kindness (see Proverbs 11:24-26; 22:9). Those who do not give **to the poor** prove they doubt God's promise that those who do so **will lack nothing** (28:27). **He who closes his eyes** to the poor blocks them from sight, but cannot block out the sound of their cursing (28:27; see 11:26).

28. WHERE DID EVERYONE GO? (28:28)

The second line of Proverbs 28:12 warned what happened **when the wicked rise to power** (28:28). Verse 28 picks up this theme (using the identical phrase) and expands on it. **People** hide during the reign of **the wicked** to protect themselves since justice and security are neglected by their leaders. They sometimes need to protect themselves from their leaders (see 28:15-16). **When the wicked perish** (28:28) indicates the certainty that God has not gone **into hiding,** but remains to eventually punish wrongdoing. When this takes place, **the righteous,** now vindicated, will **thrive.** The Hebrew behind this term can be translated more specifically as "multiply" or "grow in power."[22] However, since one would necessarily bring about the other, a more general translation (for example, **thrive,** "flourish," or "increase"[23]) is preferred.

ENDNOTES

[1]Law refers to either the Levitical Code (all God's rules and regulations), the Ten Commandments, or the Pentateuch (the first five books of the Old Testament: Genesis, Exodus, Leviticus, Numbers, and Deuteronomy; also called the Law of Moses or the Mosaic law). It is often capitalized when it means the Pentateuch or the Ten Commandments.

[2]Torah is another name for the Pentateuch (see endnote 1). The Hebrew word which *Torah* comes from is translated *law* and refers to divine instruction and guidance. The Torah was the instructions and directions given to Israel by God.

[3]The New International Version and other translations use LORD in small capitals following an initial capital *L* to denote "Yahweh" in the original Hebrew.

[4]F. Delitzsch, *Proverbs, Ecclesiastes, Song of Solomon,* Commentary on the Old Testament, by C. F. Keil and F. Delitzsch, vol. 10 (Grand Rapids, Michigan: Wm. B. Eerdmans Publishing Co., 1978 [1872]).

[5]See endnote 1.

[6]Ibid.

[7]Ibid.

[8]Ibid.

[9]See endnote 3.

[10]R. B. Y. Scott, *Proverbs, Ecclesiastes,* The Anchor Bible, vol. 18, eds. William F. Albright and David Noel Freedman (New York: Doubleday, 1965); CEV; TEV.

[11]See endnote 1.

[12]Derek Kidner, *Proverbs: An Introduction and Commentary,* Tyndale Old Testament Commentaries, ed. D. J. Wiseman (Downers Grove, Illinois: InterVarsity Press, 1964), p. 171.

[13]Ibid.; NJB.

[14]Delitzsch, p. 234.

[15]Scott.

[16]Ibid., pp. 165, 167.

[17]Matthew 6:33a (NIV).

[18]"He is the person who will always barge to the front of the queue, standing on the toes of others and jabbing them with his elbows in the process" (William McKane, *Proverbs,* The Old Testament Library [Philadelphia: Westminster Press, 1970], p. 627).

[19]Proverbs 3:5 (NIV).

[20]See endnote 3.

[21]Acts 20:35 (NIV).

[22]NJB; R. N. Whybray, *Proverbs,* The New Century Bible Commentary (Grand Rapids, Michigan: Wm. B. Eerdmans Publishing Co., 1994).

[23]NIV; Scott; NJPS.

PROVERBS 29

29:1-27

The final chapter of Proverbs that is attributed to Solomon (chapter 29; see 25:1) continues the theme of righteousness from chapter 28 (see especially 29:2, 6-7, 10, 16). Several proverbs speak of the importance of justice (29:2, 4, 7, 12-14) and provide guidance for the king and other rulers (29:2, 4, 12, 14, 26); 29:18 specifically mentions the Law (see introduction to Proverbs 28).[1] Three other themes which receive renewed attention in chapter 29 are the contrast between the wise person and the fool (verses 3, 8-9, 11), discipline (verses 15, 17, 19, 21), and anger (verses 8-9, 11, 22). Commentator R. N. Whybray notes that chapter 29 (see verses 25-27) and the extended section (chapters 25–29) conclude with a reference to Yahweh[2] and kings and a call to righteousness, much as the section began (see 25:1-5).[3]

1. STIFFENED TO THE BREAKING POINT (29:1)

In an effort to cultivate a teachable spirit, Proverbs 29:1 warns what happens to the one who cannot take correction. By refusing, repeatedly, to bend his neck in submission to God, he becomes **stiff-necked.** Like clay allowed to harden, any attempt to shape him finally results in destruction. Line 2 describes this destruction (see 6:15b) as sudden and **without remedy.** The latter expression—literally, "without healing"— indicates that destruction is complete. As with Humpty Dumpty after his fall, no one can put the pieces together again. **Suddenly** could suggest the work of God's hand; more likely it refers to the inevitable outcome of the unteachable spirit. You can only stiffen your neck so long before it breaks, and that is the end.

2. RIGHTEOUSNESS EXULTS A CITY (29:2)

Proverbs 29:2 picks up a theme treated twice in the preceding chapter, the second time only two verses before this (see 28:12, 28). **Thrive** (29:2) translates the same Hebrew verb found in 28:28b where it had a general meaning (see commentary on 28:28). Because it stands, in 29:2, parallel to **rule** in the second line, perhaps **thrive** might be better rendered "are in authority."[4] **People groan** under the oppressive **rule** of **the wicked;** they know that **when the wicked thrive,** "so does sin" (see 29:16). They **rejoice** when **the righteous** govern, because they know justice will prevail and God will be pleased.

3. HOW TO MAKE YOUR FATHER HAPPY (29:3)

Righteousness not only causes a city to "rejoice" (29:2), but also **brings joy** to a family (29:3; the same Hebrew verb is used in both verses). The reason is also the same, except on an individual scale. The **father** knows that his wise son will honor God and his family with wise choices. Instead of a direct parallel ("a fool brings grief to his father"), line 2 provides a specific example of folly which makes it easier to spot a fool and to show (by a mirror image) what wise behavior looks like (see 28:7). This particular example also makes clear that folly brings not only grief to the parents, but a host of problems to others (poverty, illness, and illegitimate children, for example).

4. JUSTICE: A SOLID FOUNDATION (29:4)

Our focus has shifted from society in Proverbs 29:2 to the family (29:3), and now back to society (29:4). **A country** is stabilized **by justice;** this point is made again and illustrated in 29:14. **One who is greedy for bribes** is, literally, a "man of offerings." These "offerings" might be **bribes** concealed as gifts to the **king;** some might consider these the ancient equivalent to the contributions of political action committees to our elected officials. Because "offering" translates a Hebrew term used elsewhere to describe religious gifts, the offering could also be a tax, supposedly intended to support Temple worship, but pocketed by the **king.** Note, however, that the **king,** by his actions, has forfeited the right to his title and is referred to only as "a man."

5. WHEN YOUR EARS TICKLE, LOOK DOWN (29:5)

When you are being flattered, instead of enjoying that ticklish feeling in your ears, look down, and you will probably see yourself walking into a trap. Learn to take compliments carefully; accept what is true, but do not depend on flattery for your feelings of self-worth. Also, learn to give compliments genuinely; never intend to trap others with your words (see Proverbs 28:23). Some take 29:5 as predicting the entrapment of the flatterer, not the flattered. Both the flatterer and the flattered, in fact, are trapped by such words, as 29:6 makes clear.

6. RIGHTEOUSNESS: THE PATH OF LEAST RESISTANCE (29:6)

To describe righteousness as the path of least resistance may sound contradictory, but it is true. God has designed this world in such a way that **evil** leads, inevitably and by its own hand, to destruction, while righteousness, by the same universal law, leads to blessing (29:6). While the **evil** are trapped in the snares set for others, the **righteous . . . can sing and be glad.** The imagery may be that of a bird, free of the traps set for its capture, which sings jubilantly. Commentator Derek Kidner suggests the reading, "runs and rejoices."[5] By either translation, this verse contradicts the commonly held notion that righteousness is restrictive and wickedness is freedom.

7. RIGHTEOUSNESS: THE PATH OF GREATEST COMPASSION (29:7)

Righteousness is not only the path God prefers and, therefore, the path of least resistance (see Proverbs 29:6), but it is also the path of greatest compassion. This might require us to rethink our definition of righteousness. Whatever that word connotes of right actions and right belief, something is wrong if righteousness does not also contain a healthy dose of compassion **for the poor** (29:7). After all, God, who wrote the book on righteousness, repeatedly reveals himself as a friend of **the poor** and the helpless. Those who claim to be **righteous** must do the same. **The wicked have no such concern**—literally, they do not "understand knowledge." They will see our compassion as a bad investment—just "coddling the lazy"—so far are their hearts from God's.

303

8. "BLESSED ARE THE PEACEMAKERS"[6] (29:8)

Contrasted in Proverbs 29:8 are two types of citizens (or parishioners, or family members). The **mockers,** by their disdain for society, their defiance of social conventions and, ultimately, their defiance of God— the foundation of society—**stir up a city.** The metaphor suggests the crowd as dry kindling with these characters holding a can of kerosene and a match. The **wise,** on the other hand, **turn away anger.** They douse inflammatory words with common sense and prayer, seeking the good of others rather than their own. Verses 8 through 10 seem to have been combined both on stylistic and thematic grounds. All three begin with the Hebrew word for "men" (verses 8, 10) or "man" (verse 9), and all provide insight on how to deal with conflict.

9. DON'T ARGUE WITH A FOOL (29:9)

Rather than prohibiting the **wise man** from litigation with the **fool** (as NIV), Proverbs 29:9 explains that any attempt to resolve controversy (see 29:8-10) **with a fool** will prove pointless. He only **rages and scoffs** (29:9); you will get no satisfaction for your trouble (**there is no peace**). The New International Version adds **the fool** in line 2; these words might refer to the extreme but futile efforts of the **wise man** to convince **the fool.**

Let someone wise argue with a fool,
anger and good humour alike will be wasted (NJB).

10. RIGHTEOUSNESS: THE PATH OF PERSECUTION (29:10)

If righteousness is the path of least resistance (see Proverbs 29:6), and the path of greatest compassion (29:7), it is also the path of persecution (29:10). Peter wrote of the inevitability of persecution for the righteous when he counseled his readers, "Do not be surprised at the painful trial you are suffering, as though something strange were happening to you" (1 Pet. 4:12). The **bloodthirsty** (Prov. 29:10), offended that their wickedness is revealed by the purity of the righteous, seek to obliterate the source of that light. The second line of this proverb is very difficult to understand because the original Hebrew has **the upright** seeking **to kill** the **man of integrity** (literally, "and the upright seek his soul").

Various proposals have been offered. The New International Version makes **the upright** the object, rather than the subject, of the verb—**the bloodthirsty . . . seek to kill the upright**—but this forces an awkward translation onto the Hebrew. Some render "seek his soul" as a positive action or modify it slightly to give it this meaning:

> The bloodthirsty hate the honest,
> but the upright seek them out (NJB).

Elsewhere, however, this phrase always refers to harmful treatment, and none of the modifications are without difficulty.[7] The Revised Standard Version seeks to eliminate the difficulty by altering the Hebrew word translated **upright** to the word for "wicked." Perhaps the best solution leaves the Hebrew text as it is, but reads the first word (in Hebrew) of the second line with the first line:

> Men of blood hate the guiltless
> And the upright; they attempt the life of such.[8]

Lines of uneven length, not unheard of in Hebrew poetry, have the effect of emphasizing the shorter line.

11. BLOWING OFF STEAM (29:11)

When the **fool** is angry, you will know it, for he **gives full vent to his anger**—literally, "all his breath he lets out" (29:11). A literal rendering of the **wise** man's response—"He holds it [anger] back"—is not entirely clear. Is it the **wise** man's own anger he restrains, or that of the **fool**? If the former, does he hold back his anger like a dam holds back water, or does he calm his anger like Christ calmed storms on the Sea of Galilee? Should the Hebrew preposition *(beachor)* be translated (which the NIV does not do) and, if so, how? The proposals include "in the background of his soul," "finally," and "quietly,"[9] among others. In spite of the uncertainties, the New International Version rendering gives a good sense of the passage.

12. HONESTY BREEDS HONESTY (29:12)

Only the **ruler** who stands to gain by the deception **listens to lies** (29:12). Perhaps his ego enjoys hearing others falsely flatter him. More likely, the **lies** are told him in his role as judge. He tolerates them because he has been bribed to do so. Injustice practiced at the highest level will spread so that **all his officials** also **become wicked.** There seems to be a connection between this verse and the two which follow. The unjust **ruler** will create a climate of injustice (29:12) which contrasts with God's watchful eye (29:13) and with the reign of the just ruler (29:14).[10]

13. LIGHT TO THE EYES OF BOTH (29:13)

Even while the wicked rule and oppression is the business of the day, **the poor** and **the oppressor** should remember that Yahweh[11] gave **sight** to **both** (29:13). Both should remember that the God who granted to each the ability to see must himself have that ability; this should bring hope to **the poor** and sober **the oppressor. The poor** man who remembers that God gave him **sight** will be encouraged by that reminder of God's love. **The oppressor** who remembers that God gave him **sight** may realize that with awareness comes responsibility. He may also understand that if God gave **sight** to **both,** then **both** have value in God's sight. For a similar proverb, see 22:2.

14. LONG MAY HE REIGN (29:14)

The trio of verses dealing with oppression and justice (see Proverbs 29:12-14) concludes here with the reminder that the reign which is just will **be secure** (29:14). No reason for that security is given in this verse, but the surrounding verses suggest several possibilities: injustice poisons integrity, (29:12), and results in dissatisfied subjects (29:2) and destructive leaders (29:4). Most importantly, the God who is the source of "justice" (29:26) will reward justice.

15. SPARE THE ROD AND EMBARRASS THE PARENTS (29:15)

Proverbs 29:15 begins a cluster of verses (see 29:15-22) on the theme of discipline and its effects. Wisdom, the essential commodity which brings joy to parents and blessings to the child, cannot come without discipline. **Rod of correction** is, literally, "rod and reproof" (29:15; see 29:1 where the same word is translated "rebukes"). **Rod** refers to physical punishment, while reproof involves spoken correction; both can be effective tools for discipline. The common element to both is an interest and involvement in the life of the child so he is not **left to himself**

(29:15). Although your son may never grow up to be king, discipline will help to make him a just person (see 29:14) and one who avoids the wickedness spoken about in 29:16.

16. THE CERTAIN TRIUMPH OF RIGHTEOUSNESS (29:16)

Without discipline, wickedness is permitted to **thrive** (29:16), and where it thrives, **so does sin. Thrive,** the same verb used in 29:2 and 28:28, appears twice in the original Hebrew (only one of which is represented in the NIV). Some translate them with the same meaning—"When the wicked are on the increase, sin multiplies" (29:16a NJB); others with two different meanings—"When the wicked are in power, wrong increases."[12] Either rendering reminds us that wickedness might attain great heights for a time, but that time is limited. Eventually, **the righteous** will watch in triumph as **the wicked** fall from those heights.

17. DISCIPLINE NOW, DELIGHT LATER (29:17)

Discipline is just as unpleasant for the parent as for the child (29:17). However, if parents will **discipline** themselves to **discipline,** the rewards are wonderful. Not only do they avoid the disgrace described in Proverbs 29:15, but they will experience **peace** and **delight** (29:17). The first term could also be rendered "rest" or, better, "peace of mind" (NJB). **Delight to your soul** suggests rich foods which appeal to our appetites.[13] Used here metaphorically, the disciplined child "will gratify you with dainties" (NJPS).

18. BLIND ABANDON (29:18)

Proverbs 29:18 reads like a commentary on the actions of the Israelites in Exodus 32 when, in Moses' absence, they had Aaron make them a golden calf. Without their prophet, Moses, they lost their source of **revelation** from God and **cast off restraint** (Prov. 29:18). The same Hebrew verb is used twice in Exodus 32:25 to describe the wild and idolatrous behavior which accompanied the worship of the calf. How much more blessed to have waited patiently for the Law which Moses was receiving from God at that very time (see Proverbs 28:4, 7, 9 for other references to the Mosaic law).[14] Israel, at its better moments, recognized what a wonderful thing the Law represented and the great blessings it brought to the obedient (see Psalm 119). The common

307

elements of joy and discipline may have prompted Hezekiah's men to place this proverb after 29:17.

19. APPROPRIATE DISCIPLINE (29:19)

The theme of discipline continues in Proverbs 29:19, which focuses specifically on the discipline of servants (**be corrected** uses the same Hebrew verb translated "discipline" in 29:17). Correction must always take motivation into account. Because he was not an heir, the **servant** lacked the internal motivation of the son. **Though he understands** could be translated "though he claims to understand." Recognizing this, the wise master provided external motivators, either positive (for example, rewards to better assignments), or negative (for example, harder tasks, physical discipline). The same principle applies to other relationships. Discipline works best when appropriately applied.

20. THINK BEFORE YOU SPEAK (29:20)

One could hardly have a section of proverbs on the subject of discipline without including one on self-disciplined speech. Proverbs 29:20 may have been placed alongside 29:19 because both refer to "words." **Who speaks in haste** is, literally, "a man who is hasty in his words" (29:20). The **man** without control over his words is worse than **a fool** (see a similar proverb in 26:12). He will probably say something he will later regret, like Jephthah in Judges 11:29-39 or the cosigner of Proverbs 6:1-5.

21. START YOUNG (29:21)

If you want to shape the direction of something or someone, start early says Proverbs 29:21. The **servant** who is pampered rather than disciplined will not amount to much. You will end up waiting on him, rather than having him wait on you (see Luke 17:7-10). This much is clear enough without a clear sense of the Hebrew word translated **grief** (Prov. 29:21). Other possible translations for this baffling word include "ungrateful" and "heir."[15] If this last suggestion is correct, the proverb predicts that a pampered **servant** will one day inherit your estate.

22. THE TROUBLE WITH ANGER (29:22)

The unit of proverbs on the topic of discipline and its effects concludes with 29:22, which describes what happens when self-control is lacking (see 29:11). This is not a man who becomes angry, but **an angry man** (29:22): one characterized by anger. Note the serious consequences of his fiery temper. He **stirs up dissension,** which is number one on the top seven things God hates (see 6:16-19); this is just one of **many sins** one commits in anger.

23. LOWER YOURSELF OR BE LOWERED (29:23)

When Jesus pronounced in Matthew that "whoever exalts himself will be humbled, and whoever humbles himself will be exalted" (23:12), He might well have been alluding to this proverb. One difference, however, between Jesus' words and this proverb involves who does the humbling and exalting. By using the passive voice ("be humbled"; "be exalted"), Jesus implied that God would carry out the action; this is known in Greek grammar as the Divine passive. In Proverbs 29:23, both verbs are in the active voice. The stress is put not on what God will do in response to your **pride** or humility, but on the consequences of your own choices. Either your **pride** will humiliate you or your humility will **honor** you. The New International Version reflects a word play between the original Hebrew for **brings him low** and **lowly;** both words are formed from the same Hebrew root.

24. HONESTY IS ITS OWN REWARD (29:24)

When you disobey, you place yourself in a no-win situation, as illustrated by the thief's **accomplice** (29:24). When caught, he is forced to choose between testifying against his partner or telling a lie. If he chooses the former, he might suffer physically; if he chooses the latter, he runs afoul of God. **Put under oath**—literally, "curse he hears"—refers to the **oath** sworn by witnesses and described in Leviticus 5:1 where essentially the same Hebrew phrase is used. The witness called down a curse on his own head if he did not tell the truth (see Numbers 5:11-31; 1 Kings 8:31-32). The one who, through disobedience, puts himself in such a bind, discovers what it means to become **his own enemy** (Prov. 29:24; literally, "hater of his soul"). Honesty is definitely the best strategy.

25. SAFELY OUT OF REACH (29:25)

Proverbs 29 and extended section (see Proverbs 25–29) conclude on a royal note and one which emphasizes the importance of choosing righteousness over wickedness. To **fear** others is to imprison yourself (29:25). You force yourself into decisions you will later regret, such as cosigning loans or telling lies. **Snare** translates the same word used in 29:6. **Whoever trusts in the LORD is kept safe** (29:25).[16] **Kept safe** carries the idea of being set on high, out of reach of those who would try to control us. In 1 Corinthians 4:1-5, Paul shows how this principle can be put into practice in pastoral leadership.

26. SEEK AN AUDIENCE WITH THE KING (29:26)

Proverbs 29:26 shows why it is better to trust Yahweh than people.[17] Seeking redress for grievances from the government is not wrong, only inadequate. God alone can be depended upon to bring **justice** in every situation. If the temptation to hobnob with bigwigs is nothing new, neither is the antidote: a clear sense of where real power lies.

27. MUTUALLY ABHORRENT SOCIETY (29:27)

Throughout Proverbs, righteousness has been proposed as the path which brings the greatest blessings to us and the greatest glory to God. Chapter 29 concludes with the reminder that righteousness, while it is the right choice, is not always the most popular path; it may even be the most painful one (see 29:10). Verse 27 also points out that **the righteous** should **detest the dishonest** since wickedness has a corrupting influence (see 29:12) and yields socially destructive consequences (see 29:2, 4, 8, 16).

ENDNOTES

[1]Law refers to either the Levitical Code (all God's rules and regulations), the Ten Commandments, or the Pentateuch (the first five books of the Old Testament: Genesis, Exodus, Leviticus, Numbers, and Deuteronomy; also called the Law of Moses or the Mosaic law). It is often capitalized when it means the Pentateuch or the Ten Commandments.

[2]The New International Version and other translations use LORD in small capitals following an initial capital *L* to denote "Yahweh" in the original Hebrew.

[3]R. N. Whybray, *Proverbs,* The New Century Bible Commentary (Grand Rapids, Michigan: Wm. B. Eerdmans Publishing Co., 1994), p. 405.

[4]John Joseph Owens, *Ezra–Song of Solomon,* Analytical Key to the Old Testament, vol. 3 (Grand Rapids, Michigan: Baker Book House, 1991).

[5]Derek Kidner, *Proverbs: An Introduction and Commentary,* Tyndale Old Testament Commentaries, ed. D. J. Wiseman (Downers Grove, Illinois: InterVarsity Press, 1964), p. 173.

[6]Matthew 5:9a (NIV).

[7]Whybray, pp. 400–1.

[8]F. Delitzsch, *Proverbs, Ecclesiastes, Song of Solomon,* Commentary on the Old Testament, by C. F. Keil and F. Delitzsch, vol. 10 (Grand Rapids, Michigan: Wm. B. Eerdmans Publishing Co., 1978 [1872]).

[9]Delitzsch; Rashi (the medieval Jewish rabbi); Owens.

[10]Whybray (p. 401) sees the connection in slightly different terms.

[11]See endnote 2.

[12]Crawford H. Toy, *Proverbs,* The International Critical Commentary (New York: Charles Scribner's Sons, 1899).

[13]Whybray, pp. 402–3.

[14]See endnote 1.

[15]NJB; Owens.

[16]See endnote 2.

[17]Ibid.

30

PROVERBS 30

30:1-33

At first glance, one might be tempted to treat Proverbs 30 as a mere appendix, an additional word of advice from another sage tacked onto Solomon's wisdom. It represents much more than this, however, for without it Proverbs would present a different message. Much of the wisdom of this book, though certainly not all, arises from common sense. Look around and you will learn that hard work brings prosperity, that foolish speech lands you in trouble, and that pride goes before a fall.

There exists, therefore, the temptation to arrogantly assume I can make myself wise. This chapter squelches that temptation in two ways. First, it takes humility as its theme, encouraging reverence (30:1-9), restraint (30:10-17), wonder (30:18-31) and peaceful behavior (30:32-33).[1] Second, the opening section (30:1-9) takes great pains to remind us that there is more to wisdom than what we can acquire on our own.

1. AN OLD MAN SPEAKS (30:1-9)

Proverbs 30:1-9 represent the pious last words of an elderly man, **Agur son of Jakeh** (30:1). In them he offers wise counsel like that found in the preceding chapters, but with the sobering realization that, ultimately, **wisdom** requires a revelation from God (30:3). That he speaks as one near death is implied in 30:7: **before I die.** If this is true, Proverbs begins with words of advice for a young man and nears its conclusion with the deathbed advice of an old man.[2] After a brief introduction (30:1), **Agur** confesses his ignorance (30:2-3) and elaborates with two quotations (30:4; 30:5-6) before his closing prayer (30:7-9).

One of the difficulties in understanding this passage is knowing whether to translate several words in 30:1 as proper names or as nouns. **Agur,** whose name may be derived from the Hebrew word for "sojourn,"

313

is unknown to us, except as the **son of Jakeh.** The meaning of his name suggests it may be a pseudonym. If the Hebrew behind **an oracle** is actually a proper noun (see NIV margin note), we learn that **Agur** (or "Sojourner") is from Massa (as indicated by the margin note in the NIV), a tribe in North Arabia descended from Ishmael. **Oracle** may be the best translation, however, since Agur's speech resembles prophetic speeches which are commonly introduced as "oracles," and since only prophetic speech in the Old Testament is **declared** to others (see Numbers 24:3, 15; 2 Samuel 23:1). Because prophecy does not originate in observation but in revelation, **Agur** reminds the reader that becoming wise takes more than common sense. It is possible, with only a slight change in the Hebrew, to translate **to Ithiel, to Ithiel and to Ucal** as "I am weary, O God; I am weary, O God, and faint" (see NIV margin note), a meaning which makes more sense to the passage (Prov. 30:1).

Agur's opening confession (see 30:2-3) provides a more explicit caution against gaining **wisdom** only through observation. Although the rest of chapter 30 (assuming it comes from **Agur**) betrays his skills of observation, he must confess ignorance of God. This is true however you translate 30:3. Since a very literal rendering[3] seems to contradict other passages of Proverbs which make knowledge of God synonymous with wisdom, the New International Version has inserted the word **nor** at the beginning of the second line. A better alternative, since it involves no change in the Hebrew, might be,

> I do not have wisdom,
> that I should have knowledge of the Holy One.[4]

A response to Agur's confession follows in 30:4, which sounds very much like passages in Job. These rhetorical questions show that God has revealed himself so clearly in nature that not only He, but others in His family (His **son**) should be well known. But observation alone cannot satisfy the ignorance of God's true nature which Agur confessed in 30:3. The Hebrew verb included in the challenge which concludes 30:4 (translated **if you know**) is the same verb which concludes 30:3 (translated **have I knowledge**).[5] Verses 5 and 6 provide the solution to Agur's search for true knowledge: It is found in God's revelation of himself in His **word.** This **word . . . is flawless**—that is, it comes without any dross or impurities, like refined gold or silver (see very similar language in 2 Samuel 22:31; Psalm 18:30). Those who trust completely in this **word** find protection and demonstrate that God's revelation is meant to be believed, not merely learned (Prov. 30:5). Verse 6 warns that God deals harshly with liars who arrogantly add to His pure Word (see Deuteronomy 4:2). If God can only be known by His words, then adding to them is a serious matter.

The closing prayer in Agur's introduction (see 30:7-9) is unique in Proverbs; prayer of any kind is uncommon in this book, and this particular example serves an instructional purpose (similar to the Lord's Prayer in the Gospels[6]),[7] as well as a devotional one. It teaches the importance of moderation in all things, but most importantly, it asks for integrity. After the introduction in 30:7 (where we see the first of several numerical categorizations in this chapter), comes the petition (30:8), which is followed by his motive for the petition (30:9). The **two things** Agur seeks—honesty and the meeting of his basic needs—both lead to the same goal: integrity. What he fears, according to 30:9, is a relationship with God broken either through neglect (where one no longer seeks for what was missing in 30:3) or through dishonor (the loss of the relationship so hard to come by). With integrity he can endure **riches** and **poverty** and still emerge knowing God. This is a knowledge which cannot be gained from observation alone, but must be found in God's revelation of himself through His Word. It is preserved by a humility which makes integrity its highest goal.

That God can ultimately be known only through His Word does not negate what can be learned through observation and common sense. As if to reinforce this point, some very insightful observations follow in 30:10-33. Characteristic of these verses is the use of numerical devices, either by listing a certain number of objects (for example, "four things" in verse 24) or by speaking of x, then x + 1 (for instance, in verse 15b, "There are three things . . . four . . . that are never satisfied"; see also verses 18, 21, 29).

2. THE SLANDEROUS SON (30:10-14)

Proverbs 30:10 could be understood apart from 30:11-14, but makes more sense when all five verses are read together as a warning against cursing one's parents. The argument moves from a minor case to a major one. If cursing a slave to his master is bad and brings problems (see 30:10), how much more serious is it to **curse** your parent (30:11) before God, who hears all curses whether we realize it or not. The seriousness of such behavior can be seen in the description found in 30:12-14. Such children think of themselves as righteous when, in fact, they are filthy (see 30:12; a very strong word in the Hebrew). They are proud of themselves (in verse 13 **glances** is, literally, "eyelids") although they are oppressive and greedy, like wild animals. Each of these characteristics is condemned elsewhere in Proverbs.[8] Commentator Derek Kidner notes the movement of these verses from disrespect for superiors (30:11), to oneself (30:12), to the world at large (30:13), and to supposed inferiors (30:14).[9]

3. NEVER ENOUGH (30:15-16)

The humble person knows how to be satisfied, when to **say "Enough!"** (30:15). This point is made indirectly by offering several examples of the insatiable from the world of nature. The **leech** is never satisfied, for it drinks the blood of its host until it cannot physically hold any more, nor are its **two daughters,** probably a reference to the two suckers found on many types of leeches. Since the Hebrew does not contain the words **they cry,** the repeated imperatives, **Give! Give!** could be the names of the daughters. Four more insatiable things are now mentioned (note the numerical progression: one **leech, two daughters, three . . . four**). **The grave** (Sheol) is never satisfied, for it never stops demanding new victims (30:16; see 27:20). A childless **womb** continually longs to be filled, especially in the culture of ancient Israel (see Rachel's demand of her husband in Genesis 30:1). Pour **water** onto dry ground, and watch how quickly it is absorbed, virtually without a trace. The agricultural economy of Israel and the absence of a dependable **water** supply for most of the country made this example of more than passing interest. **Fire** never burns itself out for lack of interest; as long as there is fuel and oxygen, it will keep going. Like these other examples, it **never says "Enough!"** Since **"Enough!"** translates the same Hebrew word elsewhere rendered "wealth" and "possessions," we are again warned against greed.

4. THE MOCKING EYE (30:17)

This graphic picture of **the eye that mocks** parents being **pecked out** of a dead carcass by **vultures** (30:17) is meant to encourage the keeping of the fifth commandment to honor one's parents (see Exodus 20:12). It picks up the theme of Proverbs 30:11-14 (especially verse 13), but also the arrogant greediness of 30:15-16. Because the Hebrew for **obedience** is obscure, some suggest that **scorns obedience to a mother** should be "scorns his aged mother."[10] At least two connections exist between this verse and 30:18-19: "eagle" (30:19) translates the same Hebrew word here rendered **vulture,** and both passages speak of humility.

5. FOUR WONDERS (30:18-19)

Humility, sadly lacking in 30:10-17 with disastrous consequences, appears here dressed as wonder, mouth agape, eyes staring in awe at sights which mystify. The four examples in Proverbs 30:19, each of which begins with the same phrase, **the way of,** describe inexplicable movement. How does the **eagle** fly without flapping its wings? How does the **snake** move without legs? How does **a ship** move forward without visible means of propulsion? Several explanations have been offered for the fourth example which is deliberately ambiguous. Some suggest it refers to the marvelous mystery of childbearing. Others propose it refers to sexual relations or, more generally, to the wordless intimacy between a man and a woman which includes but surpasses the merely sexual.

6. INCREDIBLE IMPUDENCE (30:20)

Proverbs 30:20 most definitely does not belong with the four wonders in 30:18-19, but its placement immediately following is anything but accidental. We are meant to see the **adulteress** as a marvel in her own right, a marvel of impudence. The same phrase is used here which appeared four times in 30:18-19 (**the way of**), and the verse begins with a Hebrew word which usually connects two thoughts. Both the fourth example of 30:19—"the way of a man with a maiden"—and the **adulteress** (30:20) have sexual connotations (for a similar contrast between proper sexual relations and illicit ones, see 5:3-20). Derek Kidner titles the combination of verses 18 through 20 as "Four marvels and a jarring fifth."[11] It is incredible that she would sin with such a disregard for God; illicit sex means no more to her than a satisfying meal for which no repentance is required. She is more concerned about sauce on her chin than sin in her heart.

7. FOUR THINGS TOO HEAVY TO BEAR (30:21-23)

Arrogance, repeatedly warned against in Proverbs 30, is a constant threat to those who move from being denigrated in society to occupying positions of respect. **The earth trembles** under the weight of their pride (30:21). A **king** who had been a slave will likely rule poorly either because of poor training or to indemnify his earlier ill treatment (30:22; see 19:10). This satisfied **fool** (a serious term is used here), already undeserving of what he has just eaten and too lazy to provide it, proudly applauds himself for his diligence and prosperity. Our hearts go out to the married, but **unloved woman** (30:23; see Genesis 29:31), although it is hard to see how this fits with the theme of pride or how it makes the earth tremble. If we translate instead, the "hateful woman wed at last" (Prov. 30:23 NJB), then our hearts go out to her husband and to all the old maids she knows on whom she will look down with scorn. Like the slave **king** (30:22), the maid manager rules poorly, and the whole household trembles under her tyrannical step.

8. SMALL, BUT MIGHTY (30:24-28)

Neither strength nor size makes someone **wise** (30:24). To prove it, Agur offers four examples. Each contrasts sharply to the ridiculous figures in Proverbs 30:21-23. **Ants** feed themselves through their diligence and forethought, and **coneys** (or, as the NIV margin note says, a badger) are kept safe, although they have little power to defend themselves (30:25-26). **Locusts** maintain strict discipline without any commander, and **lizards,** although seen everywhere, audaciously secure an audience with the king (30:27-28). If God can make these little creatures **wise** (30:24), how much more can He do so with us?

9. STATELY IN THEIR STRIDE (30:29-31)

As the three animals in Proverbs 30:29-31 are regal in their own realm, the **king** is majestic in his. The **lion,** king of the beasts, backs down for no animal (30:30). **Strutting rooster** is, literally, "the girt-of-loins," probably the name of some animal (30:31). The readers of Proverbs knew which one, but that information has been lost to us. Several possibilities have been proposed (for example, a starling, a type of dog, or a horse), but the New International Version preserves the choice of nearly all early translations and most modern ones. The proudly stepping **rooster,** king of the barnyard, and the **he-goat**—king of the pasture (the Hebrew for **he-goat** rhymes with that for **lion**)— complete the animal examples (30:31). Although many translations side with the NIV margin note, the last line probably refers to **a king** surrounded by his people (though not necessarily **his army**). By thus portraying the king's majesty, Agur accomplishes at least three things.

First, he provides a model for the king to follow (unlike the poor example in 30:22). Second, he gives the king's subjects reason to rejoice for they not only have a great king, but they share in his greatness. Note how the picture in 30:31 includes them: "in front of their people" (TEV). Third, this comparison points beyond the human monarch to the Divine King, whose greatness is unsurpassable. For both king and people, here are reasons for legitimate pride.

10. CHURNING UP ANGER (30:32-33)

The last word in Proverbs 30 on humility is what happens when humility is absent. Verse 32 counsels the one who has **played the fool** (the more serious type of **fool;** see 30:22b) by proudly planning something **evil. When you clap your hand over your mouth,** you remove the possibility of saying anything more and admit your mistake in saying anything at all. Verse 33 contains three examples of what happens when the foolish behavior continues, each using the same verb (translated three different ways by the NIV). Just as **butter** was produced by "pressing" **the milk** inside a goatskin or cloth container, and just as **blood** was produced by "pressing" **the nose,** so the angry "pressing" home of one's point **produces strife.** The point is made more emphatically by the word play between **nose** *(aph)* and **anger** *(aphim).*

ENDNOTES

[1]Derek Kidner (*Proverbs: An Introduction and Commentary,* Tyndale Old Testament Commentaries, ed. D. J. Wiseman [Downers Grove, Illinois: InterVarsity Press, 1964], p. 182) makes this point and provides these summaries.

[2]Rick D. Moore, "A Home for the Alien: Worldly Wisdom and Covenantal Confession in Proverbs 30, 1–9," *Zeitschrift fur die Alttestamentlich Wissenschaft,* vol. 106, no. 1 (1994), pp. 96–107.

[3]"I do not have wisdom,/but I have knowledge of the Holy One."

[4]Suggested by R. N. Whybray, *Proverbs,* The New Century Bible Commentary (Grand Rapids, Michigan: Wm. B. Eerdmans Publishing Co., 1994), p. 408.

[5]Whybray (p. 410) takes **tell me if you know** in a positive sense: "Surely you do know something of God."

[6]The Gospels include the New Testament books of Matthew, Mark, Luke, and John.

[7]Whybray (p. 411) makes this observation and comparison.

Proverbs 30

[8]Unfilial (see 19:26; 20:20; 28:24); self-righteous (see 16:2; 20:9); arrogant (see 6:17a; 21:4); and rapacious (see 1:10-19; 6:17b; 12:6 [Whybray, p. 413]).
[9]Kidner, p. 180.
[10]Whybray, p. 415.
[11]Kidner, p. 180.

PROVERBS 31

31:1-31

Placed strategically at the end of Proverbs are two more pieces of advice: one from a faithful mother (see Proverbs 31:1-9), the other concerning a faithful wife (see Proverbs 31:10-31). Lady Wisdom, who has been our guide throughout this book of the Bible, speaks through Lemuel's mother; 31:10-31 portray what it would be like to have her for a wife.

1. MATERNAL ADVICE (31:1-9)

The same questions asked about Proverbs 30:1 can be raised with 31:1. Since no king of Israel or Judah is known by the name **Lemuel,** it may be a pseudonym, perhaps meaning "belonging to God" or "God is a refuge"[1]; that it is being used as a proper name is suggested by its appearance in 31:4. If so, it probably refers to a king ruling in another country, possibly Massa (see NIV margin note), a north Arabian tribe. There are fewer compelling reasons to insist on **oracle** in this verse than there were in 30:1 (although it is awkward to treat *massa* as a noun there and a place name here).

The vocabulary and grammar of Proverbs 31:1-9 differ from the rest of the book, for it contains Aramaic words (a language related to Hebrew). **Son,** used three times in 31:2, translates the Aramaic word *bar*—from which we get the term "Bar Mitzveh" ("son of the commandment"), the ritual which ushers Jewish boys into manhood, and proper names like Barnabas ("son of encouragement"; see Acts 4:36). The use of "Aramaisms" may support a late date for the origin of this passage, or an origin outside Israel.

Lemuel, whoever he may be, is only the recipient of this counsel which comes from **his mother.** The queen mother played a very important role in many civilizations of the ancient Near East, including Israel and Judah (see 1 Kings 1:11-13; 2:19; 15:2, 13). Lemuel's mother's advice is simple and agrees with advice given to the king elsewhere in Proverbs: Rule justly. After her introduction (see 31:1-2), she warns against two potential problems for any king: **women** and **wine** (31:3-4; see 31:3-7; no mention is made of song). These obstacles removed, her **son** can do what a king must do—guarantee justice (31:2; see 31:8-9).

"Watch out for the wrong kind of **women**," Lemuel's mother warns him in 31:3. They will sap your physical and emotional strength. She could have used Samson as an example (see Judges 16). "Beware of **wine** and **beer**," she continues (Prov. 31:4), for these hinder one's ability to think clearly. According to the queen mother, drink has its place among those **perishing** or **in anguish,** those for whom the ability to shake off reality would be a blessing (see 31:6). She deliberately repeats the verbs for **drink** and **forget** (31:5, 7) to strengthen the connection between verses 4 and 5 and verses 6 and 7. "Let those forget who have something to forget," she reasons. "You, my son, have something important to remember."

Perhaps the most significant duty of the king was to maintain justice. Both verses 8 and 9 begin with the same phrase: "Open your mouth." Do not open it to pour in alcohol, but to **speak up for those who cannot speak for themselves** (literally, "who is dumb"), those whose voices have been stolen by oppression. The **destitute** are, literally, the ones "passing away." Someone must stand up for them before they are swept away by more powerful forces. In verse 9, Lemuel's mother builds on this summons as she calls her son to **judge fairly** and **defend the rights of the poor and needy.** The same root word is used for **rights** in verse 8 (as a noun) and verse 9 (as a verb).

2. IN PRAISE OF A VIRTUOUS WOMAN (31:10-31)

How to choose the right **wife** (31:10) was a subject commonly addressed in wisdom literature from the ancient Near East,[2] so it is not surprising to find this topic addressed in Proverbs. Even its placement as the last word in the book is not unexpected. This picture of the ideal **wife** caps off a book in which marriage has been encouraged, celebrated, and protected. Lady Wisdom appears prominently throughout Proverbs, especially in the first nine chapters. These closing words reveal not Lady Wisdom herself, but an example of what she would be like as a wife. After the queen mother's warning against the wrong kind of women (see 31:3), a description of "Mrs. Right" fits well.

Verses 10 through 31 comprise a poem, an alphabet acrostic—the first letter of each line (in the original) begins with the succeeding letters of the Hebrew alphabet. This type of poetry is found in the Psalms (see chapters 9–10, 25, 34, 37, 111, 112, 119, 145) and elsewhere (see Lamentations). One of the reasons for writing a poem as an acrostic was to make it easier to remember and apply. Acrostics also emphasize orderliness and completion; this woman took care of the needs of her household from A to Z. Because these poems are more difficult to write, themes are less well-developed, which is the case with Proverbs 31:10-31. Emphasized in these verses is the woman's self-sacrifice (31:11-12, 15, 20-21, 26-27), self-discipline (31:13, 15, 17-18, 25, 27), and wisdom (31:16, 18-19, 24, 26, 30). These qualities result in her being of great value (31:10), trusted (31:11), **of noble character** (31:10; see 31:25, 30), confident (31:21, 25), and the source of honor for her husband (31:11-12, 23) and rewards for herself (31:22, 28-31).

The **wife of noble character** (31:10; see 12:4) is introduced with the question, **"Who can find** such a one?" This indicates that the audience included those looking for such **a wife,** that such a search was highly recommended (they are **worth . . . more** than precious gems), and that finding one would not be easy. The description begins, appropriately, not by describing what this woman does, but who she is in her most important social role, that of **wife** (see 31:11-12). **Her husband** trusts her completely, a wonderful compliment for any wife (31:11). His trust is amply rewarded; he **lacks nothing of value** and only receives good things from his wife.

The next six verses describe various aspects of her diligent labors. She chooses raw materials, works eagerly (see 31:13), and brings food to her household like a merchant ship (31:14-15). Her ship always arrives in port fully stocked because it begins its journey early. **Portions** suggests that she supplies food for her household, including her servants (see 31:15). That word might better be rendered "giving orders" (31:15 NJB); she arises early to make sure that all her household operates at the highest level of efficiency. Her diligence extends to the marketplace (**she considers a field and buys it**) and field (**she plants a vineyard** [31:16]).

Her effort is as vigorous and strong as any man's (see 31:17); her schedule is rigorous, but her profit margin is healthy (see 31:18). Although her profit comes from the work of her hands (see 31:19), she willingly **opens** those **hands** to **the poor** and **needy** (31:20; the same two groups whose cause the king must champion according to 31:8-9). These verses are linked by the repetition in verses 19 and 20 of the same

Hebrew words for **hand[s]** and **arms.** That she maintains high standards of work and wealth while still helping those unable or unwilling to do the same speaks to her spirit of charity.

Her more than adequate preparations remove any need to fear the cold or snow, although **scarlet** is not an especially warm garment (31:21). For this reason, some have changed the Hebrew vowels and rendered this word as "two"—that is, double garments.[3] She is able to bring herself comfort and beauty (31:22) while also boosting her husband's reputation (31:23) and conducting a profitable garment business (31:24). She not only clothes herself in rich apparel but, more importantly, in the noble qualities of **strength, dignity,** and confidence (31:25). **She speaks with wisdom, and faithful instruction** (31:26). The latter term (literally, "teachings of kindness") could refer to her method of teaching (see RSV; NIV) or to its content ("reliable").[4] Once again, she is commended for her careful supervision and diligent labor (see 31:27).

The poem concludes with the singing of this woman's praises (see 31:28-31). This praise comes from her **children** (the first specific mention of **children**) and **husband** who **arise** ("a preliminary to making an important declaration"[5]) to announce their adulation (31:28). Verse 29 contains the content of their praises: She is outstanding among **women** who are **noble.** More than all she does, however, this woman deserves praise because she **fears the LORD** (31:30).[6] So the book comes full circle, beginning and ending with the fear of **the LORD.** Not only her family, but her works will praise her **at the city gate,** where a large crowd would be found and where Wisdom has often traveled to find an audience (31:31; see 1:21; 8:3).

ENDNOTES

[1]Derek Kidner, *Proverbs: An Introduction and Commentary,* Tyndale Old Testament Commentaries, ed. D. J. Wiseman (Downers Grove, Illinois: InterVarsity Press, 1964); F. Delitzsch, *Proverbs, Ecclesiastes, Song of Solomon,* Commentary on the Old Testament, by C. F. Keil and F. Delitzsch, vol. 10 (Grand Rapids, Michigan: Wm. B. Eerdmans Publishing Co., 1978 [1872]).

[2]R. N. Whybray, *Proverbs,* The New Century Bible Commentary (Grand Rapids, Michigan: Wm. B. Eerdmans Publishing Co., 1994), p. 425.

[3]Ibid., p. 428.

[4]Ibid., p. 430.

[5]Ibid.

[6]The New International Version and other translations use LORD in small capitals following an initial capital *L* to denote "Yahweh" in the original Hebrew.

SELECT BIBLIOGRAPHY

Berry, Donald K. *An Introduction to Wisdom and Poetry of the Old Testament.* Nashville: Broadman and Holman, 1995.

Bullock, C. Hassell. *An Introduction to the Old Testament Poetic Books,* revised and expanded edition. Chicago: Moody Press, 1988.

Carasik, Michael. "Who Were the 'Men of Hezekiah' (Proverbs XXV 1)?" *Vetus Testamentum.* Vol. 44. No. 3 (1994).

Cohen, A. *The Psalms.* Soncino Books of the Bible. A. Cohen, ed. London: Soncino, 1950.

Crawford, Patricia L. "Fig." *Harper's Bible Dictionary.* Paul J. Achtemeier, gen. ed. San Francisco: Harper Collins—Society of Biblical Literature, 1985.

Delitzsch, F. *Proverbs, Ecclesiastes, Song of Solomon.* Commentary on the Old Testament, by C. F. Keil and F. Delitzsch. Vol. 10. Grand Rapids, Michigan: Wm. B. Eerdmans Publishing Co., 1978 [1872].

Fox, Michael V. "Ideas of Wisdom in Proverbs 1–9." *Journal of Biblical Literature.* Vol. 116. No. 4.

Goldingay, John. "The Arrangement of Sayings in Proverbs 10–15." *Journal for the Study of the Old Testament.* Vol. 61 (1994).

Grossberg, Daniel. "Two Kinds of Sexual Relationships in the Hebrew Bible." *Hebrew Studies.* Vol. 35 (1994).

Kidner, Derek. *Proverbs: An Introduction and Commentary.* Tyndale Old Testament Commentaries. D. J. Wiseman, ed. Downers Grove, Illinois: InterVarsity Press, 1964.

Kugel, James. "Wisdom and the Anthological Temper." *Prooftexts.* Vol. 17. No. 1 (1997).

Maire, Thierry. "Proverbs XXII 17ss.: Enseignment a Shalishom?" *Vetus Testamentum.* Vol. 45. No. 2 (1995).

McKane, William. *Proverbs* in The Old Testament Library. Philadelphia: Westminster Press, 1970.

Moore, Rick D. "A Home for the Alien: Worldly Wisdom and Covenantal Confession in Proverbs 30, 1–9." *Zeitschrift fur die Alttestamentlich Wissenschaft.* Vol. 106. No. 1 (1994).

Murphy, Roland E. "Wisdom and Creation." *Journal of Biblical Literature.* Vol. 104. No. 1 (1985).

Nel, Philip. "The Voice of Ms. Wisdom: Wisdom as Intertext." *Old Testament Essays.* Vol. 9. No. 3 (1996).

Owens, John Joseph. *Ezra–Song of Solomon.* Analytical Key to the Old Testament. Vol. 3. Grand Rapids, Michigan: Baker Book House, 1991.

Pritchard, James B., ed. *Ancient Near Eastern Texts Relating to the Old Testament.* 3rd ed. Princeton: Princeton University Press, 1969.

Scott, R. B.Y. *Proverbs, Ecclesiastes.* The Anchor Bible. Vol. 18. William F. Albright and David Noel Freedman, eds. New York: Doubleday, 1965.

Toy, Crawford H. *Proverbs.* The International Critical Commentary. New York: Charles Scribner's Sons, 1899.

Whybray, R. N. *Proverbs.* The New Century Bible Commentary. Grand Rapids, Michigan: Wm. B. Eerdmans Publishing Co., 1994.

Wilson, Lindsay. "The Book of Job and the Fear of God." *Tyndale Bulletin.* Vol. 46. No. 1 (1995).

Witherington, Ben. "Three Modern Faces of Wisdom." *Ashland Theological Journal.* Vol. 25 (1993).

Wyse, R. R. and W. S. Prinsloo. "Faith Development and Proverbial Wisdom." *Old Testament Essays.* Vol. 9. No. 1 (1996).